D1220413

FAITH
ACROSS THE
MULTIVERSE

FAITH

ACROSS THE

MULTIVERSE

Parables from Modern Science

ANDY WALSH

Faith across the Multiverse: Parables from Modern Science

© 2018 by Andrew S. Walsh
Hendrickson Publishers Marketing, LLC
P. O. Box 3473
Peabody, Massachusetts 01961-3473
www.hendrickson.com

ISBN 978-1-68307-076-4

All rights reserved. No part of this book may be reproduced or transmitted in any form or by any means, electronic or mechanical, including photocopying, recording, or by any information storage and retrieval system, without permission in writing from the publisher.

Printed in the United States of America

First Printing— July 2018

Scripture quoted by permission. All scripture quotations, unless otherwise indicated, are taken from the NET Bible® copyright © 1996–2017 by Biblical Studies Press, LLC. All rights reserved.

Library of Congress Cataloging-in-Publication Data

A catalog record for this title is available from the Library of Congress
Hendrickson Publishers Marketing, LLC ISBN 978-1-68307-076-4

To Ronnie Simon,

Who introduced me to X-Men comics in the 7th grade
and changed my life

Contents

Taste and see that the Lord is good!

— Psalm 34:8

If you knew the science,
maybe I'd listen to a word you're saying.

— *Todd Ingram,* Scott Pilgrim vs. The World

CHAPTER 0

The Power of Babel Fish

I don't know if you've heard, but it's going to be the future soon. Who wants to wait that long to see how it turns out, though? We can find spoilers for our favorite movies, TV shows and books; we should be able to do the same for reality. If we want to peek ahead, may I propose examining the Bible.

"How did the Bible get into it?" I hear you cry. What could it possibly have to do with the future, a land flowing with math and science? True, the Bible was written in an ancient context and contains ancient history, yet its teachings can supposedly be implemented in a variety of contexts. So let's run the experiment.

Can we define abstract ideas like faith and sin and grace in terms that make sense to nerdy, funny scientists? Can a life lived two thousand years ago shed light on our modern situation? Can we develop a community that incorporates a diverse assemblage of people? Can simple principles from the past encompass the complexity of the present? Our task here is to find out.

Let's begin at the end, as in the end of the world. As it happens, there's this great place to eat. Everyone wants to get in, only it's prohibitively expensive. That's the bad news. The good news is that if you make an investment now, you can afford the price when you get there.

If you have studied your Douglas Adams (which I have), you may recognize the Restaurant at the End of the Universe from his sci-fi comedy novel of the same name. In his cosmology, the universe collapses back in on itself at the end of time. A space restaurant opens up shortly beforehand, so the primarily time-traveling patrons can have a meal while they enjoy the view. The only way to afford the prices is to invest in the present—even a penny will do—and let the power of compound interest do the rest.

Yet I was thinking of the Bible, which has a similar story arc. The very last chapters of the Bible describe a great wedding feast at the end of the world. People from all over the world and all throughout time celebrate together; it is *the* place to be. Money isn't an issue; no one could afford the price if it were. A strict dress code is enforced, however. The good news is that if you choose to attend, arrangements have been graciously made to provide the necessary clothes for you.

That wedding gives the Bible the structure of a comedy, not in the humorous sense of Adams' books but the classical sense of resolving with a community reconciled to itself via symbolic or literal marriage. The people who appear in the Bible grapple with questions about purpose and seek to understand where they came from and where they are going as they confront the possibility that the world within their immediate experience may not be all there is. Adams' protagonist Arthur Dent shares those concerns as he discovers humans are not alone in the universe and that the Earth may factor into a plan on a scale he cannot imagine when the story begins. Of course, there are plenty of points of departure between the two texts, and I'm not remotely suggesting that Adams was just cribbing the Bible. Yet the thematic overlap suggests the possibility that the Bible may not be as irrelevant to today as its age might imply.

Imagine chatting with someone from the Bible. For allegedly primitive texts, the Bible contains some remarkably modern individuals with whom we might find common ground. Consider Gideon, whom we meet in the book of Judges chapter 6. He believes he heard a message from God, but he has doubts, so he devises a remarkably rigorous confirmation process. He asks God to make a fleece wet with dew overnight. He further asks for God to leave the ground dry, which we would call a negative control in modern scientific research. The next day, just to make sure it wasn't a fluke or some unappreciated property of fleece, he repeats the experiment in reverse. Even if you don't believe the account is historical or you can think of an alternate explanation for the data, you can still appreciate the sophistication of Gideon's methodology.

Then there's Elijah. In 1 Kings 18, Elijah confronts prophets of the deity Baal. Elijah suggests an empirical test: both parties will prepare a burnt offering but let the deities provide the flame in order to make their existence known. Elijah even douses his meat and altar with water, just to rule out the possibility of an errant spark lighting it. Then, while the prophets of Baal make their entreaties, Elijah heckles them sarcastically. His biting and even at times scatological material would play at a roast. (Actually, I suppose it did.)

One last example—the writer of Ecclesiastes. Identified only as a teacher in the text, he is traditionally thought to be the famously wise Israelite king Solomon. This teacher has a crisis of faith; he looks at the world around him and thinks it is all pointless, meaningless, futile. He seeks purpose in education, in material pleasures, in prestige and accomplishment, and he finds them all wanting. He wonders why there is so much evil in the world and questions the value of working when everything one does can be undone. In the end, he concludes it is still better to be alive than dead, to do something rather than nothing, to build rather than tear down. He affirms the value of creating meaning collectively.

Those questions sound awfully relevant to the present. And the conclusions seem pretty modern as well. Is it so unreasonable to think someone like this teacher might have something to say to us today?

Of course, the language barrier would still be a concern for these cross-time conversations. Whatever common human nature we might share with Elijah or Gideon would be challenging to discover conversationally. In Douglas Adams' fictional world, we could solve this problem with the Babel fish. Babel fish are alien organisms that have developed the ability to translate language. Just stick one in your ear (yep) and you will instantly be able to understand everything anyone says, no matter what language they speak.

I have a particular affinity for Babel fish because I've spent much of my career filling a similar role within the sciences. I wound up learning a lot of math for a graduate student in microbiology, so I spent a lot of time teaching statistics to my fellow biologists. That helped me get a postdoctoral fellowship facilitating collaboration between computer scientists and biologists by pointing out where their ideas overlapped and, just as importantly, where they thought they were talking about the same thing because they were using the same word, but they actually had very different concepts in mind. And now I work for a public health software company, translating between public health users and software engineers and teaching everyone a little math and basic biology along the way.

My favorite word from those cross-discipline conversations is "vector." To someone with a math or physics background, a vector is a quantity associated with a direction, such as wind velocity. To a computer scientist, a vector is a collection of data elements that may or may not be numeric. To a molecular biologist, a vector is a circular DNA molecule used to add external gene functionality to a cell. And to an infectious disease specialist, a vector is an animal that carries a disease, like a mosquito or a rat. Many folks are aware of the different, domain-specific meanings, but even experienced interdisciplinary researchers can get caught thinking about numbers while their colleagues mean ticks. And so having a "multilingual" Babel-human like me around helps keep conversations on track.

Language barriers are also a common problem in science fiction. Aliens should speak a variety of languages. Making every character a polyglot is unrealistic, and constant fumbling over language barriers would get in the way of good storytelling. Conjuring Babel fish or Universal Translators or literal magical spells simultaneously acknowledges and shelves the issue.

Translation is not science fiction. Making it instantaneous and perfectly accurate is the unrealistic part; sometimes we have to wait for the translation. Translating is not just a matter of swapping one word at a time for its equivalent, which is how something like the Babel fish apparently works. Anyone who has studied a foreign language has encountered idiomatic phrases whose meaning is not captured by a word-for-word translation. For example, I made my German teacher giggle while practicing pet-related vocabulary because my grammatically correct and word-by-word accurate *Ich habe einen Vogel* ("I have a bird") was simultaneously an admission to having bats in my belfry, so to speak.

Unlike most science fiction, the film *Arrival* digs deep into matters of translation. Aliens arrive on Earth for the first time and linguist Louise Banks leads a team to establish communication with them. Learning individual vocabulary words and idioms is challenging enough without a dictionary, but Louise recognizes the possibility of even deeper problems. The aliens' experience may be so different from ours that they think about different concepts. Do they have a notion of war? Do they distinguish between tools and weapons? These are the immediate concerns of world leaders wondering if these aliens come in peace, but Louise eventually discovers that the conceptual gulf runs deeper still.

Even human languages don't overlap fully in terms of the concepts they can represent. If we give it any reflection at all, we probably think of our languages as complete. Sure, maybe we need to invent new words when we invent new technologies, like the telephone or

Facebook. But for regular ideas, surely we must have the words to say what needs to be said. Only, how would we talk about the things our language lacks the vocabulary to describe?

The Germans have a very useful word: *Weltschmerz*. Translating the parts of this compound noun into English yields "world pain" but a more faithful translation might be the feeling one experiences upon recognizing the divergence between reality and an ideal vision of the world. English lacks an equivalent word; the closest match might be Charlie Brown's exasperated "Good grief!" But even that is more of a groan, signifying Charlie Brown is experiencing *Weltschmerz* without actually naming it. All languages differ in which concepts they can readily express with a single word or common idiom; even fundamental features like the number and kind of verb tenses can vary. What is easy or hard to express in a given language influences how speakers of that language talk and possibly think.

Another example that might be more familiar to Bible readers is love. We can say a lot about love in English; poems, songs, and tales of love abound. Love is such a fundamental part of the human experience that we might think it would be a foundational part of any human language. In fact, the ancient Greeks had several words to differentiate experiences we lump together as love. These include the familial bond between siblings, parents, and relatives; the brotherly affection shared by comrades-in-arms; and the romantic or physical connection that we generally mean when we say one is "in love."

Most of the time English speakers don't consciously experience a deficiency or limitation in their language regarding love. We blithely say "I love you, my dear" and "I love you, dad" and "I love you, man" and "I love you, delicious chimichanga" and generally everyone knows what we mean. But sometimes we *don't* say "I love you" when maybe we should. Perhaps we sense our feelings for our spouse are not the same as our feelings for our children but we lack the language tools to express that nuance succinctly.

In *Arrival*, Louise Banks addresses this conceptual gap between her language and the aliens' by combining written language with demonstrations. She and her team act out the words and sentences as they speak and write them. In this way, they build shared experiences with the aliens so that their communication has something to reference. Without that experience, the two parties might wind up using the same words but internally connecting them to very different concepts. As an example, she brings up the Sanskrit word गवष्टिट्ि, which some linguists translate as "an argument" while she prefers "a desire for more cows."

0.1 The Revealed Word

Louise needs to learn why the aliens have come to Earth. Thinking back to the biblical banquet at the end of the universe, we might ask a similar question: why do people want to attend? The primary attraction, as with many banquets, is to be in the presence of the guest of honor. In this case, that guest is God.

If we are to make an informed decision about whether we want to attend this banquet, we need to know what we are committing to. Who is God? What is he like? Is he the sort of God with whom we would wish to spend a possibly infinite amount of time? Even brief social occasions can drag insufferably when we are with the wrong people; that goes double for eternity.

The Bible provides information to guide such a decision. Through it, we may know God. God revealed himself in particular ways to specific people at specific times, in order that the whole of the human race could come to know him. In the Christian tradition, this is called special revelation. We can also think of special revelation as equivalent to the written and spoken language lessons in *Arrival*. Both serve the purpose of providing specific details that are not readily inferred by generalizing.

There is also a tradition of general revelation, God revealing himself through creation to all people. We all experience the physical world and so build up a repertoire of concepts and ideas to connect with our language and the special revelation communicated via that language. In this way, we can construct an understanding of God, whom we can't experience directly via our senses, through a series of analogies to the world that we can experience. Toward this end, the Bible invites readers to study the physical world and reflect on what they find. For example, the aforementioned Solomon recommends that we "go to the ant . . . observe its ways and be wise!" (Proverbs 6:6) while Paul encourages pragmatic curiosity as we "examine all things; hold fast to what is good" (1 Thessalonians 5:21).

Actually constructing these analogies is not simply left as an exercise to the reader. The Bible models this approach extensively, with the most explicit examples being Jesus' parables. The word *parable* comes from the Greek word for analogy; parables are illustrations used to explain a concept metaphorically. In one parable, Jesus illustrates the importance of context using the practice of sowing seeds. The sower spreads seed everywhere, but only some soils are prepared to receive it and allow the seeds to take root and flourish into plants. Likewise, not all minds are receptive to all ideas. But just as soil can be prepared by tilling and adding nutrients to create the right context, minds can be transformed using metaphors to introduce needed concepts and building connections to existing ones.

The sower parable is not the only instance where Jesus used familiar, concrete experiences to introduce abstract ideas. He draws other illustrations from botany ("The kingdom of God . . . is like a mustard seed" [Mark 4:30–31]), from animal husbandry ("I am the good shepherd. The good shepherd lays down his life for the sheep." [John 10:11]), and from microbiology ("The kingdom of heaven is like yeast that a woman took and mixed with three measures of flour until all the dough had risen." [Matthew 13:33]). Other biblical illustrations explore entomology (Joel compares an invading army to a swarm of locust), metallurgy ("Such trials show the proven character of your faith, which is much more valuable than gold—gold that is tested by fire, even though it is passing away" [1 Peter 1:7]), and astronomy ("I will make the children who follow one another in the line of my servant David very numerous. I will also make the Levites who minister before me very numerous. I will make them all as numerous as the stars in the sky and as the sands which are on the seashore" [Jeremiah 33:22]).

Going a layer deeper, we see that Jesus himself is the ultimate expression of both general and special revelation. He was part of the physical world and lived his life to illustrate concepts that would otherwise have been inconceivable, such as a king who washes the feet of his subjects, a prophet who teaches on his own authority, and a priest who sacrifices himself. He also came with specific teachings from God to share with his disciples, to explain those ideas he was illustrating with his life. For this reason, he is described as the Word of God; he was the word we needed to add to our language to be able to talk about all these principles.

0.2 You Got Your Science in My Theology

Once you start looking for them, these metaphors from the physical world are all throughout the Bible. Christians have taken to heart the encouragement to study that world, creating an extensive shared heritage between theology, the study of God, and the branch of philosophy concerned with studying the physical world that would ultimately become science. The Greeks, including Plato and Aristotle (who had nothing else going on), articulated the foundations of this natural philosophy, and as the Christian church developed it fostered scholastic institutions where those classical texts as well as the Bible were studied. Muslim scholars also preserved and expanded on those classical ideas, demonstrating a broader affinity beyond Christianity between religious traditions and study of the physical world.

Christian scholars also played a role in transforming that study from natural philosophy, focused on knowledge from antiquity, to empirical science, focused on observation and experiments. From Francis Bacon, who began formalizing that transformation, through notables such as Robert Boyle, Isaac Newton, and James Clerk Maxwell and up to the present day, Christians and believers of many faiths have added to our growing body of scientific knowledge. Along the way, there were also pioneers like Maria Agnesi, the first woman appointed as a mathematics professor, Mary Anning, a citizen paleontologist who found significant fossils at a time when only men were admitted to the relevant scientific societies, and Sister Mary Kenneth Keller, the first woman and one of the first people, period, to earn a PhD in computer science. Their belief that God created the world in an orderly and comprehensible fashion provided a foundation for their scientific exploration, and a desire to learn more about God and to marvel at his creation provided motivating energy.

Sometimes the religious inspiration is even more specific. For example, the Deborah number is used to characterize the fluidity of materials; liquids or fluids will have low Deborah numbers, while solids will have high ones. The name is a reference to Judges 5:5, where the prophet Deborah talks about mountains flowing before God, at least in some translations. Deborah was likely trying to express how even mountains are subject to God's power, but we have since learned that mountains can indeed flow on long enough time scales. Incidentally, I learned about Deborah numbers from the Ig Nobel-winning research on whether cats are fluids (because of their tendency to assume the shape of their container), a testament to the Ig Nobel mission that science can be educational even when not taking itself too seriously, and a reminder that not every scientist is a Newton or Maxwell.

Complementing these scientific pursuits inspired by religious belief is natural theology, a primarily religious pursuit inspired by science with roots going back to Augustine of Hippo and Thomas Aquinas. Natural theology covers a variety of concerns. Some natural theologians are interested in a theology of our relationship to God's creation, as demonstrated in Pope Francis's encyclical on ecology, which lays out a biblical and theological case for responsible stewardship of shared environmental resources. Physicist-theologian John Polkinghorne has an interest in how the process of science resembles the process of theology and how the two can mutually benefit from shared methodological insights.

Mainly, though, natural theologians focus on what we can learn about God himself from his creation. We might infer certain attributes of God from attributes of the physical world; for example, the reliability of sunrises and sunsets suggests that God is reliable. (At least on Earth; on Pluto, sunrise and sunset are literally unpredictable, which makes me wonder how we'd think about God if we lived there instead.) This then feeds forward into an expectation of further predictability in creation, which as we noted can encourage scientific study. One attribute of God we might infer is his very existence. That specific inference seems to be where much of natural theology is presently focused, at least in the popular consciousness.

Attempting to argue for or prove the existence of God to varying degrees of rigor from the facts of the physical world is a long-standing tradition. Thomas Aquinas offered several versions, William Paley's approach is widely known, and the contemporary Intelligent Design movement represents yet another take. Such arguments are not limited to Christianity; Islamic theology has examples as well, such as the work of al-Ghazali, which was studied by Thomas Aquinas. Many rely strongly on philosophy and logic as well, but all draw on observations of the world to some degree. There are even tongue-in-cheek versions, basically variations on "chocolate is delicious, therefore God exists."

The appeal of such proofs to believers is clear: they bring apparent scientific rigor to religious belief and take as their starting point common knowledge from science rather than religious texts like the Bible that are not universally accepted as authoritative. Still, they have their downsides. Many boil down to identifying the limitations of known causal mechanisms and noting that an all-powerful, all-knowing entity could satisfy the requirements, but that still leaves us far from the specific God of the Bible, leading to the invention of pasta-based deities and the like as explanatory equivalents. And the emphasis on what can be proved from the facts of science can be stretched thin by expecting the ancient writers of the Bible to have expressed modern science facts in ancient language.

Maybe it's my introverted nature, but when I see a topic getting a lot of attention, I tend to wonder if there's someplace quieter to work. Since proving the existence of God from the facts of science is well-trod territory in the present day, I am interested in exploring another avenue of natural theology. Drawing inspiration from the parables and other passages I mentioned, I am curious about what other attributes of God and our relationship with him can be articulated in modern scientific terms. I see this as an act of translation more than an exercise in inference. Where science and theology do share common concepts, the language around them can be so different that work is needed to make the connections.

How did science become unfamiliar when it used to be a common point of reference? In the eras when the Bible was lived and written, everyone had comparable experiences of the physical world. Maybe not everyone herded sheep or smelted gold (many of them had probably smelted sheep), but those experiences were accessible on a human scale. If you wanted to know more about sowing seeds you likely knew whom to ask and you could readily understand the answers. And some experiences, like the view of the night sky, were common to all.

Right up until they weren't. Once the telescope was invented, suddenly some people had a different way to experience the world around them than everyone else. The resulting shift from a geocentric model of the solar system to a heliocentric one is regularly cited as a milestone in how we understand the Bible's relationship to science, and rightly so. The telescope also inaugurated an era, still ongoing, where direct experience with the observations that shaped our scientific understanding is available only to a select few. We have an ever-widening metaphor gap, so that even when we speak the same language, we aren't able to understand each other.

Just think about where science has gone in the past few centuries. Telescopes made it possible to explore the profoundly big: planets and solar systems and galactic clusters in every direction. Microscopes opened up the world of the infinitesimally small, microbes and viruses, atoms and quarks. We may not know what God-scale is (or if "scale" is even relevant), but surely pushing our minds beyond the human scale can help us begin to comprehend it. That is why I think science has the possibility to offer a rich world of metaphors for those of us who want to know God better, deeper, more.

0.3 Have You Heard? Nerd is the Word

One facet of God's nature he desires us to know is his sense of *Weltschmerz*. The Bible opens with a vision of how the world could have been. Whether the Garden of Eden ever existed as a physical place on Earth is a question covered extensively elsewhere. For our purposes, it is sufficient for it to be a model of how God could relate to humans, how humans could relate to each other, and how humans could relate to the rest of the world. We already noted that the Bible closes with a picture of what the world could be like, and indeed if it is telling the truth, what it will be like. In between, we are regularly reminded that the world-as-it-is fails to live up to either model and that intentional action is necessary to transform the world-as-it-is to the world-it-could-be. We are invited to be a part of that work so that we can share in the resulting world.

Telling stories about how the future could look, being acutely aware of how the present world falls short and working out how to bridge the gap—all that makes me think God could be a nerd. I'm sure you're shocked, given that I've already demonstrated a fondness for science, Douglas Adams, and movies about contact with aliens. Of course I'm going to picture God in my image. But I don't mean God is the ultimate dungeon master or that we're his fully articulated action figure collection or anything like that. Rather, I believe a sense of *Weltschmerz* such as God's is at the essence of nerdiness.

Do you ever wonder what science fiction and fantasy stories, board and video games, and science and technology have in common that makes them nerdy? The usual circular definition—those are the things nerds like—isn't very informative. What they share is potential for exploring the world, not just as it is, but how it might be, could be, perhaps should be. We tell stories about other kinds of worlds because we don't have the luxury of trying every idea in reality; we need to experiment with models. Games go a step further and allow us to experience those alternatives interactively. Even games that model worlds we don't actually wish to live in (*Grand Theft Auto* comes to mind) provide an opportunity to try different experiences while keeping the consequences simulated.

Thus to be a nerd is to be in touch with reality, yet not beholden to it. This definition also explains why sports, or "jock," culture and nerd culture don't readily mix. While sports are games, sports culture diverges from nerd culture when it takes all of the potential outcomes and possibility for exploration and ignores them in order to say that the only possibility that matters is the outcome that happens to occur. From that perspective, the world could only be as it happens to be and thus everything leading up to a particular outcome was a necessary element, including the socks worn by the guy watching at home on his couch. Individuals may employ different mixtures of nerd and jock approaches to different topics and at different times, but the two cultures are distinct enough to warrant articulating the differences.

At first glance, science might also seem rooted in the world as it is, and thus anti-nerdy. While the goal of science is to describe the actual world, the practice of science requires a robust ability to imagine different possible worlds. A scientific hypothesis basically says "If reality is like so, then *A* will happen, but if reality is some other way, then *B* will happen." And even when experimental results reveal how the world happens to be, the process may illustrate how to transform the world from the way it is to the way we think it should be. Then we can develop technology to bring the best of those alternatives to reality.

This helps us achieve our ultimate goal of improving the actual world for the inevitable future. Sometimes that desire will be focused on improving one's own future. For most, that desire eventually expands to include the future of others. The nerd ur-myth, the story of Peter Parker, better known as Spider-Man, is a great example. Peter is bullied for his nerdiness, so when his spider powers afford him new possibilities, his first priority, understandably, is improving his own lot in life. Then he famously learns that with great power comes great responsibility. Or, as Jesus said, "from everyone who has been given much, much will be required" (Luke 12:48).

New words are themselves a technology that science provides for transforming the world from what it is into what it could be. As we encounter new objects, or new phenomena, we need to name them in order to be able to talk about them. Once those names and the entities they reference enter our vocabulary and our experience, they become available as metaphors as well. When we stay at a job because it's comfortable, we blame it on inertia. When our favorite sports squad comes from behind to take a lead, we cheer a shift in momentum. Oh, and the paths those sports balls follow due to actual inertia or momentum? The Greeks used geometric curves called parabolas as the metaphor to represent them, which is why a metaphorical narrative used as an illustration is called a parable.

See? Scientific metaphors are already more a part of our language than we generally appreciate. Unfortunately, our everyday language hasn't kept up while the leading edge of science moved further away from common experience. The metaphors we use to talk and think about the world aren't always up to date.

Think about the upper respiratory illnesses we all get—the runny noses and sore throats. They come around more often in the winter, when it is cold outside (at least in temperate zones). The association is strong enough that it seems causal, to the point where "cold" became the name of the disease as well as the cause. Now we know that a variety of viruses, such as rhinovirus, are the proximal cause of these colds. There is still a connection to cold weather, possibly because we stay inside more when it is cold outside, possibly because the air is drier, but just going out into cold air with wet hair or no coat is not sufficient to make one sick. Try telling that to your mom, though. It's a hard idea to shake, because it's right there in the name! But our understanding of the world, or of God, needn't be held back just because the science baked into our language is from an earlier era.

Updating our individual scientific awareness might allow us to become familiar with useful concepts that are otherwise absent from our language and our thinking. Along the way, we might hope to broaden our understanding of God. This practice of expanding our language with names and descriptions for the things we encounter in the physical world, in order to relate to God, has a long tradition. In the Bible, it goes all the way back to Adam.

In the first two chapters of Genesis, God gives Adam two jobs. The first is a long-term, open-ended project given to all living things, to be fruitful and multiply (we'll explore the significance of that command later in the book). The second is a task specific to Adam: to name all of the animals. In one sense, the job is done when Adam names them all. In another, Adam has merely initiated the ongoing work of science to name everything in the physical world. And by giving Adam this job, God gave Adam, and by implication all of humankind, a powerful tool for knowing God.

Since we will be expanding our language by exploring science, that means we're going to be talking about some unfamiliar topics; if they were familiar, we'd already have the conceptual tools we are trying to acquire. I suspect these discussions will sound like speaking in tongues to some. But fear not! There will be interpretation. And we'll discuss observations of the physical world that inform those concepts, compared and contrasted with familiar experiences as appropriate.

0.4 The Waiting Time from This Point Is 2,000 Years

Let's try an example. This one is about the future. Some of us are anticipating the arrival of a Messiah, either for the first or second time. Some of us don't go in for that sort of thing; surely he should have been here by now. Either way, we all might wonder—just how long does one wait for a Messiah?

Several sections of the Bible tell the reader to expect Jesus of Nazareth, having died and returned to life, to come back to Earth in the flesh. When those texts were written, his return was expected at any moment. Jesus himself implied he could come back at any time. "Therefore you also must be ready, because the Son of Man will come at an hour when you do not expect him" (Matthew 24:44). Yet here we are, two thousand years later, still waiting.

We all have ample experience waiting for other people. Our intuition tells us that the longer we wait, the less likely the person we are waiting for is actually coming. On average, people arrive on time. It is very common for someone to arrive one minute early or late; five minutes one way or another isn't surprising.

Eventually, we all reach a point where too much deviation becomes unexpected and uncomfortable. Being extra early can be awkward, and being extra late starts to require an apology or an explanation. We want to be on time, and so we make arrangements to arrive accordingly. Thus our experience tells us it's more likely the late person isn't coming rather than just really late. Jesus didn't actually give us an exact time, so technically he can't be late. But at the very least, maybe we don't have to wait quite so expectantly.

Trying to understand the likelihood of Jesus' return from this perspective is a challenge. Some who study the Bible arrive at similar sentiments—if Jesus hasn't returned in two millennia, he's probably not returning tomorrow. It was in the midst of a conversation on this topic with a group of friends that I suddenly remembered my probability theory. I had recently encountered something called the exponential probability distribution. Perhaps this mathematical idea could enlighten our discussion.

First, let's unpack the idea of a probability distribution. You are perhaps familiar with the Gaussian probability distribution, sometimes called the normal distribution or the bell curve. It is a mathematical model that describes how likely certain observations are. Because it is high in the middle and flat on the edges, it represents systems where most observations are close to the average, or "normal," and the further you get from the average, the less likely an observation is.

The idea that most everything is average is pretty intuitive, to the point that we kind of expect the whole world to work that way. We saw already that it is a good description of arrival times; most people arrive close to the average of on time, and the further you get from on time, the less likely someone is to arrive that early or late. Other commonplace experiences confirm this intuition. People are likely to be near average height; it is relatively rare to see someone very short or very tall. No one is surprised when the temperature is near average for the given time of year; we only notice when it is unusually cold or warm. We are so comfortable talking about extremes as unlikely, and the unlikely as extreme, we may not even realize those are different concepts.

Nevertheless, the Gaussian distribution doesn't actually describe everything, which is one reason why mathematicians and statisticians are careful to call it the Gaussian distribution rather than the normal distribution. There are plenty of normal phenomena that deviate from the Gaussian distribution. Word frequency within a text—say, this book—is a convenient example. Under a Gaussian model, most words

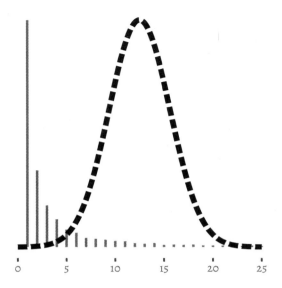

Figure 0.1: The Gaussian distribution (dotted line) does not describe how many words will appear once, how many appear twice, etc. in a text (gray bars).

would be used close to the average number of times while a relative few would appear very often and a similar amount would appear one or two times. In reality, many words appear only once in a given work or body of text and a few are used repeatedly, as demonstrated by the word frequency plot for this book (Figure 0.1). People are more likely to use familiar words, which only makes them more familiar and more frequently used; this is one possible explanation for the observed distribution of word frequency.

Failure times of electronics also follow a distribution other than the Gaussian. After you eliminate the electronics that fail quickly because something went wrong in manufacturing, how long a device has been running tells you very little about how likely it is to fail. This is because electronics don't wear out the way that mechanical parts do. Mechanical parts grow more likely to fail the longer they are used because they are being worn out; they lose material from a finite supply that is eventually exhausted. Electronics don't work that way. Some electronic components work just fine, right up until they don't; there is rarely a measurable indication that failure is getting closer.

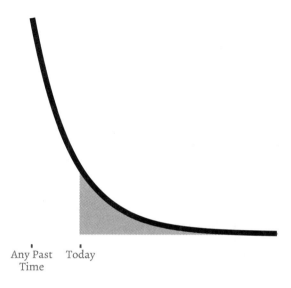

Any Past Time   Today

Figure 0.2: The shaded area is proportional to the area under the entire curve, implying that the probability of the event happening after today given that you've waited until today is equal to the probability of the event happening after any point in the past.

Unexpected, unscheduled arrivals work the same way; the person isn't there right up until the moment they are, with no signal of their approach.

The exponential distribution can model wait times for these scenarios well. One reason is the fact that the model is memoryless. Memoryless means the probability of our friend showing up after now, given that we've been waiting ten minutes, is the same as if we'd been waiting for ten years or ten seconds or ten centuries. One way to understand why this is the case is to look at a plot of the distribution, which shows that any later portion of the distribution is proportional to the whole (illustrated in Figure 0.2).

This memoryless property of the exponential distribution turns out to be exactly what my group of friends was looking for. Even though it is counterintuitive, it is perfectly reasonable from a mathematical perspective to say that the return of Jesus is just as likely now that we've been waiting for two thousand years as it was when his disciples had only been waiting for ten hours or ten weeks. When I mentioned this observation to the group, we found the connection very exciting.

The discovery that a math concept could illuminate my reading of the Bible was my first real experience of knowing God through science, rather than just knowing of him. I didn't recognize it as such at the time, but it was still an invigorating discovery. And it would prove to be the first of many, until they accumulated in such great quantity that this book precipitated out. Soon, everywhere I looked within the domain of science, I saw common themes and motifs, both between scientific disciplines and between science and the Bible.

0.5 Author! Author!

Common motifs suggest a common author. Still, authorship of creation and of the Bible are thorny subjects. We are most likely to think of an author as a solitary writer toiling with a quill pen or a typewriter, carefully choosing each word, then transmitting the unmediated end result as directly as possible to an audience. In other words, the author is the most proximal cause, indeed the sole cause, of every detail of the final product. This is a rather romanticized notion of writing and authorship, at least partially perpetrated on us by writers themselves. In reality, even the most hermetic writer is not quite so independent, and there are plenty of other authorship models.

I am a fan of comic books, movies, and symphonic music; all of these are much more collaborative creative endeavors. Comic books are generally partnerships between writers and artists, with all parties contributing to the storytelling. Movies are usually said to be authored by the screenwriters or the directors (or, less often in the present day, producers), but neither directly realizes their vision for the complete film; instead, scores of other contributors are involved in creating the final product. Similarly, a composer may author a symphonic composition, but some employ orchestrators to adapt melodies and harmonies to the capabilities of each instrument and many instrumentalists are required to actually realize the piece for an audience. Professionally, I read publications in the natural sciences, which also have multiple authors providing research effort and expertise and jointly composing the manuscript.

None of these models preclude the possibility of recognizing the participation of the different authors. I've met symphonic music connoisseurs who can recognize the signature sound of particular orchestras, conductors, and soloists. I myself am not that proficient, but I have some fluency in recognizing the signature style of various composers. *Scott Pilgrim vs. the World* is undeniably an Edgar Wright film, but it is tonally and thematically distinct from Wright's collaborations with writer and actor Simon Pegg. A Grant Morrison comic will always be recognizable from its heady metafictional elements, even when not illustrated by frequent artistic co-storyteller Frank Quitely.

Why is it possible to identify the common author of these diverse works? Authors create in order to be known. "Write what you know" is a popular writers' maxim, which means stories often exhibit autobiographical elements. If an author is any good at his craft, some part of himself will be evident in what he produces, even when other authors are also making themselves known.

With these sorts of authorship models in mind, I think it is plausible to consider God as the author of general and special revelation. This is already a traditional understanding of how the Bible was written. Since it was a collaboration between God and human writers, individual authorial voices of, for example, Solomon or Paul, are distinguishable between books. If God had dictated or otherwise directly contrived the exact wording of every verse, we would not expect such distinctions to be possible. Nevertheless, core themes tie the entire Bible together and shed light on God's perspective.

Why shouldn't it be the same with the physical world? When I say God is its author, I do not mean God has scripted every last vibration of every last quark. What I mean is that God collaborates with creation itself to realize the ultimate form of that creation. If this is true, then a close reading of the physical world should also shed light on God's perspective. And if God is any good at his craft, then some consistent sense of his personality should be evident in both of his major works, motivating the work of natural theology.

Furthermore, we would expect that the more we learn and understand, the more these commonalities would be evident. The language, the metaphors, the mental tools we acquire from learning to talk about the physical world should be relevant to topics from scripture, perhaps even clarifying concepts whose nuances are challenging to describe because we don't have the words. If, on the other hand, there is no common author, then modern scientific ideas should find no analogue in the Bible. As the products solely of human thought at the time, the books of the Bible could scarcely contain notions for which their human authors lacked the mental framework to even contemplate.

What follows, then, is an attempt to demonstrate that the first scenario is the one that best describes our world. We will visit several domains of science and see how each one has illuminated my reading of the Bible, using science fiction to help us wrap our minds around the new ideas. I'll point out what I see as the common themes and motifs; you can judge for yourself if my reading is valid. I'll share how the metaphors that I've discovered by learning what modern science has been up to for the past few centuries have helped me make sense of words written several millennia ago.

Our first stop will be the realm of mathematics. Math is a powerful tool for describing the abstract with precision. We will see how it can help us understand the abstract ideas of the Bible, concepts like faith, sin, and grace that often seem so fundamental we have a hard time articulating what they mean because we define everything else by them. Perhaps we might even get a better handle on what it is we mean by God, anyway.

Next up is physics, where the abstractions of mathematics meet concrete reality. Fittingly, we will use physics to discuss the person of Jesus, who, according to the Bible, is the person in whom the rather abstract idea of God became a concrete reality. In particular, we will look at several dimensions of the physics of light, since Jesus described himself as the light of the world. As predicted, the deeper we look into that metaphor, the more apt it will seem to be.

If Jesus is the idealized, frictionless sphere of humanity, appropriate for the kind of analysis physicists prefer, then the rest of us are the messy, complicated specimens around which biology was built. Here again we will expand on a scientific metaphor from the Bible, in this case the idea that the human body is a microcosm for how humans should relate. This sort of self-similarity is actually a fairly central idea in modern biology. It is therefore intriguing to see it anticipated many centuries prior in fairly explicit terms, well before cells or genes were imagined.

Finally, we will take a look at computer science. In some ways, this is a return to the beginning, since computer science has deep roots in mathematics. Personally, I find it to be math at its most biological because it is algorithmic rather than analytic, so this seems like a natural progression. Computer science is concerned with finding the best methods for getting a job done, so it can give us some language for discussing practical questions about how we should then live.

The end result should be a trajectory from abstract questions about the nature of God to concrete questions about how to live our day-to-day lives. This trajectory also takes us from more general concerns to the specifics of the Christian tradition. There is little point in describing how to live as part of a Christian community if we haven't first addressed why one might want to a part of that community. The topics from science will also build on each other as we move to higher levels of organization whose behavior is informed by what happens at the lower levels.

As we go, I desire to introduce you to the God I've come to know, and to the science that helps me think more clearly about him. It is my hope that, when all is said and done, you'll want to know him more for yourself. However, I also acknowledge your right to decide that he is not someone you want to have anything to do with; after all, I believe God also strongly affirms that right. The important thing is that you are able to make an informed decision about whether you want to attend that banquet in his honor at the end of the universe.

The Bible tells us to expect multitudes at that banquet, so the invitation is not only to be with God but also with the other guests, which is why we will be talking about how to function as a community. As practice, consider reading and discussing this book with current or future friends. Maybe they can help you with some unfamiliar science or share their enthusiasm for God. You'll have a head start on getting to know your fellow banquet guests if that is indeed where we are headed. And even if we're not, you'll build some relationships for the here and now.

PART I

The Language of Mathematics

CHAPTER 1

This Chapter Has No Title

This book does not exist.

I'm not making a philosophical assertion about the ephemeral nature of ideas or the meaninglessness of words, or a declaration that reality is an illusion. Books exist; I just don't see how this one can. I know you don't want to hear that you just spent money on something that doesn't exist. And yet, how else would you describe a book written by no one?

I'm not trying to be self-deprecating. I don't mean that I'm not important or famous. Quite the contrary, actually; people talk about me all the time. "No one will need more than 637 kB of memory for a personal computer." Very prophetic; I needed a lot more than that just to run Emacs and type this book. "No one gets tuberculosis in America anymore." Indeed, I did, and I was very disappointed when I didn't get to convalesce at a sanatorium in some exotic locale like consumption patients before me. "No one likes the sequels to *The Matrix*." Yup, I'm a fan. Sure, they have their flaws, but I admire their ambition and enjoy the things they do well. "No one is going to marry me." That's what my then-future wife told me, and I knew it was true the moment she said it.

I haven't always known I was no one. I appear in photographs, I cast a shadow, and I have a Facebook page; I clearly exist. But over time, listening to one description of no one after another and finding them applicable to me, I eventually reached a point where I had to accept that I was, in fact, this no one everyone was talking about. I mean, what are the odds there's another person out there just like me? So if you told me no one would read science books—written in many cases by atheists, sometimes for the express purpose of proving that God does not or need not exist—in order to get to know God better, well, I'd hear a personal calling rather than a statement of the impossible.

What we accomplish with math sometimes seems impossible too. We take the products of our imagination, scrawl them on napkins and chalkboards and notepads, apply a few rules, and watch results we've never dreamt of pour forth. Even more astonishing, a stranger halfway around the world who thinks and speaks in an entirely different language can apply the same rules and get the same results, even if she represents them differently. The key to this magic is expressing our ideas precisely enough that we can work with them systematically, and so that we can recognize when the same ideas appear in different contexts. Math helps us communicate precisely about abstract ideas, which is why I think it can help us wrap our minds around abstract qualities of God and our relationship with him. And if that sounds like attempting the impossible, well, I like to think in that regard I'm following in the footsteps of noted public intellectual Professor Henry Jones, Jr.

1.1 When Four Camels Are Too Many, and Other Fictional Paradoxes

Indiana Jones doesn't know the meaning of the word *can't*. Forget hard to find—he chases after relics most of his peers believe do not exist. He goes up against entire militaries armed only with a bullwhip and his charm. And perhaps most impossible of all, he thinks these activities will merit tenure.

A rarity himself, Indy credibly manages to be both an intellectual and a believer in the spiritual. Archeology may not be considered a hard science, but it is empirical and observational at its core. Yet for him it also involves pursuing relics from specific religious traditions, not just as artifacts of the past, but also foci of power for the present. He may not confess all the doctrines of a particular religion, but he believes in the reality of higher authorities and acts accordingly.

One interpretation of *Raiders of the Lost Ark*, most famously presented on *The Big Bang Theory*, argues that Indy doesn't actually do anything to change the course of events in the film. I wonder if we read it that way because we can no longer accept believing as a worthwhile activity for a hero. After all, Indy's belief and his willingness to act on that belief makes a difference in the end. He averts his eyes out of his respect for the power the ark represents. By doing so, he saves not only his own life but also that of Marion. If nothing else, his presence in the story means that she lives; to my mind, that qualifies him as a hero.

As far as I can tell, he is also one of the last heroes who combine both traits. More recent stories are populated with polar archetypes, characters who either believe in the possibility of a deity *or* are rational intellectuals. Matthew McConaughey's preacher and Jodie Foster's radio astronomer from *Contact* come to mind. Dr. Gregory House of the eponymous medical drama is a consummate rationalist skeptic. *Lost* was perhaps most on the nose, with its central conflict between "man of science" Jack and "man of faith" Locke. Even the most recent adventure of Dr. Jones reveals a science fiction explanation for a seemingly religious phenomenon, rather than leaving a spiritual explanation as a possibility; is that why it doesn't feel like it belongs with the other films?

Of all these dichotomous characters, I'm especially fond of Dr. Henry McCoy, also known as Beast of the X-Men. Beast is their preeminent scientist, nominally a biologist but frequently depicted as an expert in anything mathematical, scientific or in the leastwise technical (as most fictional scientists are). Because of our perceptions of real scientists, he is written as a typical skeptical rationalist, unwilling or unable to believe anything traditional religions teach. The catch is that he and his teammates have died, visited various afterlife destinations, and come back to life; met demons and rulers of various hellish underworlds; and fought alongside deities from assorted pantheons. By his own observations and experience, he has confirmed the truth of the claims made by a variety of world faith traditions. Rather than acknowledge this, he maintains his skepticism. Or, he reappropriates those truths; if he as a scientist proves something true, then by definition it becomes a matter of science and not one of faith or religion. Therefore, religious matters can only ever be false or indeterminate.

So who is the paradox? Is it Beast, whose skepticism has verisimilitude but borders on the absurd within the fantastical world of superhero comics? Is it Dr. Jones, whose spiritual beliefs and academic rigor can be described in fiction but perhaps not realized in reality? Is it me, for thinking faith in God is acceptable for a scientist?

1.2 No One Likes a Paradox

Some find paradoxes off-putting, aesthetically irksome, possibly to the point of repulsion. I find that they can be illuminating; they invite us to closely examine what it is that we really mean by a statement and each of its parts. Are we making assumptions that we don't even realize? Perhaps what we think is a paradox is really a failure to understand reality from the right perspective.

When faith is set at odds with science, it is defined as unquestioning acceptance of dogma or belief in the face of contrary evidence. Given that definition, the contrast is hard to deny, and at least the potential for incompatible priorities is evident. Yet I don't recognize my own faith in that definition. Instead what I see is a Dr. McCoy situation where boundaries are drawn so that faith can only ever be false because anything true would belong to science.

Dogma is a product of religion, but I don't have faith in a religion. I practice a religion because I have faith in God. Dogma is certainly up for questioning; no less a champion of faith than Jesus challenged the dogma of his day. And Jesus did not ask us to have faith in God regardless of evidence; he presented himself as evidence of God and his nature. So I think we can come up with a better definition of faith that more closely matches my experience.

That's where math comes in. Math encourages precise definitions of abstract concepts in order to clearly reason about them and their properties. Sure, math often involves numbers and calculations with numbers—arithmetic and algebra and maybe calculus if we're feeling adventurous. And yes, these calculations are challenging for many, which is totally understandable because our minds don't automatically come equipped with the tools to do sums or long division precisely. Rest assured, you won't have to actually do any calculating. Numbers happen to be one very useful tool for communicating clearly and concisely, but we are ultimately seeking concepts we can use to make analogies to God and his properties.

In fact, math is so good at clarity and precision of communication that we might expect it to eliminate our paradox problems altogether. The languages we use to speak and write are full of ambiguity, both intentional and unintentional. Many comedies build their plots around misunderstandings; many jokes are constructed around double meanings, the setup steering you toward one while the punchline reminds you of the other. I've certainly gotten a lot of mileage out of those ambiguities for comedic purposes. That "No one" bit wasn't just a contrivance for this book; in high school I actually went by that name. My best friend Ronnie was "Who" and we lived an Abbott & Costello routine for two years.

Ambiguity might be tolerable when you want to have a little pun, but there is seemingly no place for it when you want to get something done. That's when we bring in the numbers. A 1 is a 1 is a 1 is a 1; 1+1 is always 2. Math problems always have one right answer. How could math ever betray us with ambiguity?

I'm afraid we're going to have to do some actual math now. But fear not, we will ease into it. To start, we'll just be talking about numbers. We won't be doing calculations, nor will there be equations; you can do plenty of math without either. We'll consider some topics in a discipline of mathematics called number theory.

One of the primary activities of number theory is to take the counting numbers, or positive integers—1, 2, 3, 4, 5, etc.—and put them into different groups. There are even integers and odd integers, prime integers, the integers of the Fibonacci sequence (1, 1, 2, 3, 5, 8, 13, etc.), and so on. Number theorists like to define a group and then study the properties of the group. For example, is there a biggest prime number (no), or will there always be another prime if you keep counting (yes)? Do prime numbers get further and further apart as they get bigger (no)? And so on.

As we study numbers, some of them emerge as interesting. The number 2, for example, is the only integer that is both even and prime. Then 3 becomes interesting as the smallest odd prime integer. 4 is both 2+2 and 2×2 and even 2^2; 5 is the number of Platonic solids (basically the shapes role-playing game dice come in).

Now let's assume there are uninteresting integers. We keep counting up until we find a number about which we have nothing to say: the smallest of all the uninteresting integers, unlike every number that came before it was interesting. What an interesti . . . oh dear. Have we stumbled upon some kind of paradox, or is interestingness too slippery a property? After all, the ten digit integer which reaches that delightfully charming young woman whom no one would want to marry (and did) might be of interest to me, but not to you. You might be able to recognize which integer represents Magic Johnson's career assist total or the North American box office receipts of *Searching for Bobby Fischer* whereas I wouldn't notice either one as such. Beyond these personal differences, what makes a number interesting changed even as we discussed them.

So let's try the group of integers that can be defined, in English, using eleven words or fewer; now we have a precise, objective definition to work with. The number 1 is in this group because we can define it as "the smallest nonzero positive integer"—five words. We can then define 2 as "the sum of one and one," 3 as "the sum of one and two" and so on for a while. We can't keep that up indefinitely; eventually the names of numbers take more than six words (e.g., seven million, two hundred sixty-six thousand, three hundred eighty-three) and so don't fit into this construction. But at least we know that our eleven-words-or-fewer group isn't empty.

At the same time, we know that the group has a finite number of integers. There are only so many words in English, and so many ways to combine eleven of them. Most of those combinations would be gibberish, failing to clearly define a number. The exact size of the group may be harder to nail down, but it doesn't matter as long as we are certain that it isn't infinitely big.

Since the eleven-words-or-fewer group is not infinitely big, there has to be a biggest number in the group. And there has to be a number bigger than that, because the integers go on forever. So let's talk about "the smallest positive integer not definable in fewer than twelve words." We've convinced ourselves that this number exists, and it is not part of our group because it is bigger than all of the numbers in it. And it has to be unique because there is only one integer that is one bigger than another specific integer (proof left as an exercise to the reader).

Now, did you notice anything odd about what just happened? We just defined this number in exactly eleven words. Despite our reasoning that this number is not in our group, we've defined it in a way to make it eligible for membership. It's weird; even though we'd rather not spend one more minute with them, it would seem our mind is set on paradoxes.

We tried to make our discussion as precise as possible, but we were still using English. Maybe that's the problem; maybe the word *definable* itself isn't as well-defined as we need. Why not invent a new language specifically for math? We don't need to be able to tell jokes in it, so it needn't be subjected to the whims of wits, wags, and other linguistic ne'er-do-wells who bend and stretch meaning to its breaking point. We can invent it from the ground up without ambiguity; surely then we can avoid these kinds of paradoxes.

An initiative was put together to do exactly that: create a rigorous, formal language for mathematics that could express everything that needs to be expressed for proofs and discourse, without resorting to the ambiguity of existing languages. The language's vocabulary consisted of symbols for some basic concepts and the grammar was a set of rules for combining symbols. Any statement that is constructed according to these rules will represent a mathematical truth whose proof is the sequence of statements from which it was built. The process of proving new mathematical theorems then becomes one of figuring out how to express them in this language, and how to create those expressions from other proven expressions by combining them according to the rules.

1.3 This Section Header Is False

Of course, that theorem-proving process needs somewhere to start. The symbol-manipulating rules don't cover what to do with a blank piece of paper. We have to choose a small number of statements we assume are true rather than proving them via the rules. These assumed truths are called axioms. The intention is to choose axioms so obvious and self-evident that no one would deny them.

Unfortunately, "self-evident" has proven to be as slippery as "interesting" and "definable." Arithmetic, algebra, calculus and other widely used mathematical machinery have been developed incrementally as needed, often to solve challenges in practical fields like engineering or architecture. They were not constructed from axioms initially; doing so would be a retrofit. Thus the goal was to find the right axioms that would bring forth all the familiar math we wanted and none of the paradoxes we didn't. A set of axioms and the math constructed from them that met these criteria would be considered complete.

Remarkably, not only did the proposed basis for math fail to be proven complete, it was actually explicitly proven incomplete; some questions were demonstrably unanswerable. A simplified explanation of the proof of incompleteness is that you can create an expression whose meaning is essentially "This expression cannot be proved." And yet, since it is built up from proven expressions according to the rules of the language, it should be considered proved. In other words, what was proved was the unprovability of the statement. This essentially rendered that expression undecidable, meaning there is no way to know if it is true or false, given the axioms we chose. That doesn't mean that in some absolute sense, it is neither true nor false; it just means we cannot prove it either way. Thus this system of axioms and formal language doesn't get rid of our undecidable paradoxes.

Even worse, the proof that they were incomplete actually proved that whole classes of axiomatic systems will always have undecidable, or unprovable, theorems, even when expressed using the formal language developed in the hopes of avoiding ambiguity. Any system that allows for arithmetic will suffer the same fate. It may be possible to find a complete, consistent system of logic, but it would seem to not be very useful, in the sense of being able to express the kinds of mathematics that we want.

This was not the only time mathematicians encountered an undecidable question. Geometry provides another conundrum with no definitive answer. Geometry is the math of shapes, of points and lines and circles and squares and pyramids. Since the time of the ancient Greeks, it had the kind of axiomatic foundation that arithmetic dreamt of.

For many centuries, geometry was based on five axioms. And O, the glorious theorems you could prove from them. Moreover, applications of geometry produced all manner of architectural wonders. They were the Platonic ideal of Platonic ideals, perfect little bits of capital-T Truth.

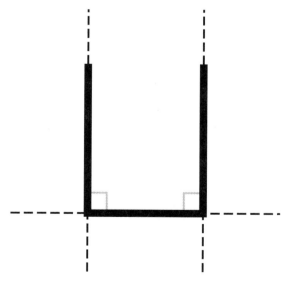

Figure 1.1: The vertical lines will never intersect, which means, among other things, that you can kick a field goal as high as you like and it will still count.

The fifth axiom deals with parallel lines. Two lines are defined as parallel if they both intersect a third line at right angles. If it helps, picture a football goal post; the two uprights intersect the crossbar at right angles and so they are parallel (see Figure 1.1). The fifth axiom says that parallel lines never intersect; if you kept extending those goal post uprights, they will never meet or cross (as it happens, the official rules of football rely on this property).

Figure 1.2: The vertical lines (longitude) are all parallel because they intersect the equator at right angles, and they also intersect each other at the poles.

Looking at a goal post, or drawing lines on paper, you would be forgiven for thinking it is obvious that such lines never intersect. And yet . . . when we draw or paint scenes with depth, we take lines that appear parallel in real life and render them as if they will meet at a vanishing point on the horizon. Worse, when we draw a globe, the lines of longitude all meet at the poles. Yet they all also intersect the equator at right angles, seemingly qualifying them as parallel (see Figure 1.2). Are these just examples where our world reveals itself to be mere shadows? Or could it be, just maybe, that parallel lines *can* intersect?

As it happens, the fifth axiom isn't strictly necessary. You can create consistent, functional treatments of geometry that assume the exact opposite of the traditional fifth axiom. The original version of geometry worked well for perfectly flat spaces, like an idealized piece of paper extending in all directions. The new version works with curved spaces, like the surface of the planet we happen to live on, and indeed like the very space that planet happens to live in. In either case, the behavior of parallel lines can't be deduced from other axioms and theorems. It is undecidable and needs to be chosen one way or the other.

Now, to be clear, incompleteness proofs and geometry theorems are rigorous results that deal with specific, well-defined mathematical constructs. But we're after new concepts to enrich our vocabulary, and I think incompleteness and the limits of formal reasoning have potential. If one cannot prove or decide all questions of interest in such a rigorously and narrowly defined field as mathematics, maybe we shouldn't expect to construct a complete and incontrovertible framework for understanding the entire world from first principles. Taking a cue from mathematics, we can switch instead to considerations of usefulness.

Incompleteness theorems are nearly a century old, but they have hardly unraveled the practice of mathematics. Mathematicians still math, even knowing there are limits on what can be proven. The axioms shown to be incomplete are still employed as a foundation for set theory and arithmetic. They are fruitful for proving theorems and doing the work of mathematics, just as both versions of geometry continue to be fruitful even though the fifth axiom turned out to be undecidable.

1.4 The Axiom of Belief

If math can function without being able to prove everything, perhaps other domains can as well. For example, what if we take belief in the God of the Bible to be axiomatic? Trying to deduce his existence from first principles has always felt a little backwards to me, since by nature he *is* first principles, the cornerstone anchoring everything else (Ephesians 2:20). Even the name he gives himself, usually translated in English as "I AM THAT I AM" (Exodus 3:14), strongly suggests a self-evident quality one looks for in an axiom.

This perspective provides us with an operational definition of faith. Instead of defining it in terms of dogma or rejection of evidence, let's say that faith is choosing a set of assumptions, or axioms, for understanding the world. And if you prefer, we can further refine this definition to state that faith is specifically choosing assumptions that either explicitly include a God or gods, or at least do not explicitly disallow the existence of such a being or beings. Many atheists and other areligious folks bristle at the idea of calling their choice of assumptions faith, and that's understandable given the general usage of the words. I don't see any need to insist on that broader definition of "faith," so long as we all understand that at some point we are all making a choice of assumptions, and that no particular set of assumptions is privileged *a priori* nor the only option for a consistent view of the world.

Assuming God rather than proving him might seem like dodging any requirement to provide evidence. Axioms can certainly be informed by evidence, and my belief in God is definitely informed by historical corroboration of the Bible. But axioms cannot themselves be deductively proven; as with pudding, the proof is in the tasting. I am primarily interested with what conclusions follow from my belief in God and how useful they are in my real life. This is comparable to the situation in geometry, where multiple geometries are logically and mathematically valid but the ones where parallel lines intersect are useful for describing a wider range of real world experiences.

This idea that God is not a provable conclusion but an axiomatic assertion, and just one possible axiom among several alternatives, may be uncomfortable for some believers, but I think this idea is consistent with the Bible. Take the refrain of Ecclesiastes: "Futile! Futile! . . . Absolutely futile! Everything is futile!" The teacher who wrote the book is looking at the world around him and finding no meaning or value intrinsic in anything he finds there. Rather than descend into nihilism, he ultimately chooses to build a framework for understanding the world and living in it based on a belief in God. He does so, not out of the logical undeniability of the premise, but because he found a life so constructed to be fruitful. Usefulness is also the criterion Paul applies to the Bible, describing scripture as "useful for teaching, for reproof, for correction, and for training in righteousness" (2 Timothy 3:16).

When Jesus talks about his parables, he observes of some people, "Although they see they do not see, and although they hear they do not hear nor do they understand" (Matthew 13:13). Jesus does not expect everyone to accept his teachings; to some they will be nonsensical. Perhaps different outcomes arise because some have chosen a way of interpreting the world that renders such teachings as nonsensical. In order for his audience to come to a particular conclusion based on a deductive argument, they would have to start from the same axioms. Jesus is acknowledging that they don't and so does not rely on deduction. Instead, Jesus describes the kingdom of God that follows from his view of the world, and invites us to be a part of that kingdom. This is an appeal to the usefulness of his assumptions, not their completeness.

We've already seen one example where mismatched assumptions produce nonsense. In most cases, we assume words like *who*, *what*, or *no one* have a single meaning. When we encounter someone assuming instead that any word can be used as a name, their statements seem nonsensical. "No he didn't, no one did" is not a sensible response to the question "Who wrote this book?" when we adopt the usual axioms of English. But to someone crazy enough to choose the alternate foundation, well, that answer is perfectly cromulent. Fortunately, no one is that obnoxious.

Mismatched assumptions play into the plot of *Raiders of the Lost Ark* as well. In order to find the ark, one needs to place a bejeweled staff in a particular place on a map at a particular time, and refracted sunlight will mark the spot. Instructions for the height of the staff are written on the ornamental headpiece containing the jewel. The Germans assume their one-sided copy of the headpiece is complete, but Marion and Indy have the original with details from both sides. The Germans construct a perfectly functional staff and are able to get a location from the process, but because their assumptions don't match reality they wind up digging in the wrong place.

Henry McCoy has a similar problem with mismatched assumptions. He assumes that natural causes which can be described with science are the opposite of anything religious or theological and that God or gods only manifest via the supernatural. Therefore, he feels compelled to reject religious concepts in spite of his own personal experience with various deities. But the dichotomy he believes in is not required by the Bible, which is comfortable associating natural causes with God. We read that "the heavens declare the glory of God" (Psalm 19:1). And elsewhere, we find the claim that "since the creation of the world [God's] invisible attributes—his eternal power and divine nature—have been clearly seen, because they are understood through what has been made" (Romans 1:20). Drawing a sharp line between what God does and what we can understand through science isn't strictly necessary.

At the same time, I don't think these verses require us to conclude that creation itself indisputably proves God's existence. If the world was such that a belief in God was the only logical conclusion, or the only logically consistent way of understanding the world, then God's work is done from the beginning and he has no need to communicate any further. But this is not the story that the Bible tells. Instead, it indicates that God repeatedly reveals himself personally, culminating in his incarnation in Jesus. Yes, there are other purposes of the incarnation, but one of them is to enable knowledge of God. As Jesus himself says, "If you have known me, you will know my Father too. And from now on you do know him and have seen him" (John 14:7).

1.5 Shining a Bit of Light from the Old North Church

As I read the verses from the Psalms and Romans, they are more about communication than proof. They reinforce the idea that God is telling us about himself, making himself known, through creation—the general revelation mentioned in chapter 0. Communication involves a message and a meaning. Messages by their nature require a certain amount of accessibility; a message that cannot be received has arguably never been sent. Meaning is another matter; meaning is relational.

The relational nature of meaning isn't just a consequence of linguistic fuzziness; it is a feature of the mathematics of information theory. Information theory has its roots in communication. In order to make telephone signals efficient, we needed to understand how much information can be sent through a channel like a wire (for those landline telephones no one has). So we needed a way to measure information and invented units called bits.

The most famous bit in American history is probably the one sent to Paul Revere to inform him the route the British soldiers would take. "One if by land, two if by sea" was the arrangement. With either configuration, Revere would receive one bit of information, an answer to a single either-or style question about two mutually exclusive options. Note, though, that the meaning was not intrinsic; the parties had to agree in advance what the message would mean. Everyone could see the lamps, but only those with the right relationship to the lamplighter could discern his intended interpretation.

This is actually a general property of information, that its meaning is extrinsic and relational. There is a Bible story that illustrates this rather nicely as well. It's in 1 Samuel 20, which provides an account about the reigning king of Israel, Saul; his son, Jonathan; and David, who was a friend of Jonathan, a courtier of Saul, and the anointed future king of Israel. Saul and David had a very tempestuous relationship; David had served Saul faithfully and was an important ally, but at the same time Saul thought of David as a rival.

In this particular story, David isn't sure which way the wind blows in his relationship with Saul. So David and Jonathan come up with a plan, wherein Jonathan will probe his father's state of mind while David remains safe elsewhere, and then Jonathan will get word to David about what he learns. They devise a plan to communicate what Jonathan learns without meeting again or sending a message anyone could interpret. At a prearranged place and time, Jonathan will take some archery practice. After shooting his arrows, he will send someone to pick them up (he *is* royalty). While the boy is looking, if Jonathan tells him "Come toward me, the arrows didn't go that far" then David will know he is safe to return to Saul's court. If Jonathan tells the boy "Keep going, the arrows are farther away" then David knows to run.

Note that despite the number of words in the message, the message only conveys a single bit of information—"stay" or "run." But also note that the bit of information is, again, meaningless by itself. Many different meanings can be encoded by the same sequences of bits; information theory just tells you how many bits it takes to convey that meaning. Jonathan is conveying a single bit of information that David will interpret as an answer to "stay" or "run," but he is also conveying that same bit of information to the boy looking for the arrows, only to the boy the bit means the answer to "come closer" or "go further." The two receivers have different relationships with the sender, and so they interpret the same message differently.

Once you understand this principle, you will see that there are actually lots of other examples elsewhere in the Bible. We already saw one in the story of Gideon, where a wet fleece meant God was with him one day, and a dry fleece meant the same thing the next day; an agreement was needed beforehand to establish the meaning of the bit in each case. The casting of lots is used throughout the Bible to discern a message from God, from the allotment of territory in Numbers to the selection of an apostle in Acts; the arbitrariness of the medium is what allows different meanings to be assigned at different times. This is also why covenants between God and his followers, like the one made with Abraham in Genesis, are so important, because both parties have to agree on the meaning of various acts.

Interpretation of dreams comes up often in the Bible; these are another example of meaning needing to be applied to the message for understanding. Joseph in Genesis and Daniel in the book of Daniel are noted interpreters of dreams that remain inscrutable to others. The explanation is that their relationship with God is what allows them to discern his intended meaning. Joseph even says as much explicitly when he asks, "Don't interpretations belong to God?" (Genesis 40:8).

This is also consistent with the tradition that the Spirit of God needs to be involved in the interpretative process in order to arrive at the meaning intended by God. For example, the letter of 1 John is concerned with helping the reader discern true interpretations from false ones that were circulating at the time. John writes that "as his anointing teaches you about all things, it is true and is not a lie" (1 John 2:27). The anointing is generally understood as God's Spirit, which is given to help teach the truth. If meaning were not relational and extrinsic, why would this arrangement be necessary?

The concept also appears in the apostle Paul's discussion of eating meat offered to idols in 1 Corinthians 8. The new followers of Jesus wondered if eating such meat amounted to a form of worship of the gods those idols represented and so should be avoided in order to remain faithful. Paul observes that since those gods don't exist in a Christian worldview, there is no relationship one can have with them to assign meaning to the sacrifice. The God with whom Paul is concerned has already approved the eating of meat, in Genesis 9:3 and again in Acts 10:13. Therefore, the only problem with eating that particular meat arises when one is in relationship with another follower of God who has attached additional meaning to the act; in that case, if one is aware of the situation, one should abstain from eating.

Thus I think the idea that meaning is extrinsic and relational is on solid ground biblically, rather than being antithetical to the teaching of the Bible. And so we should not be surprised when others look at the world around them and claim that it is meaningless. They are looking at the bits of the message, but the meaning isn't in the bits.

Nevertheless, we can credibly assert that the information, the message itself, is there for everyone to see. God is not like the Vogon highway authority of *The Hitchhiker's Guide to the Galaxy*, who claims to have notified Earth of its impending demolition when in fact the message is filed away in an office on another planet so that the Earthlings have no chance to read it. The message in his general revelation is available to all. It's just that, as with the ultimate answer to life, the universe, and everything from the same novel, without an agreement on how to interpret the meaning, the result may seem cryptic, puzzling, or nonsensical—42.

1.6 Can Anyone Have a Complete Collection of Bits?

This understanding of information and meaning connects back to our axioms and paradoxes in a couple of ways. The incompleteness results in math we discussed earlier can be seen as an unavoidable consequence of the need to assign meaning to a message, rather than finding it intrinsic to the message. As we saw with set theory, the power to do arithmetic came with the power to construct unprovable statements. If we maintained a purely mechanical view of the symbols of the language, there would be no problem; just take the axioms and operations and crank through them. You would have theorem after theorem that you could be confident were true, with no ambiguity or undecidability; you just wouldn't know what any of those theorems said. It's only when we try to make those statements mean something—e.g., 1+1=2—that it becomes possible to create a statement which proves its own unprovability.

This ambiguity in meaning needn't be all bad; it can be an important ingredient for creativity. It allows us to see new meanings, to make the inspired metaphorical leaps that are the core of innovations both artistic and scientific. And it makes it possible for us to talk about things which do not currently exist and have not existed in the past, to imagine a world different than the way it currently is. Think of how absurd the notion of a horseless carriage would have once been. Yet even though the existence of such a thing would have seemed impossible, the metaphor would nevertheless make it perfectly clear what key features a horseless carriage would have, and it could even provide the inspiration necessary to realize such a nonsensical contraption.

This extrinsic character of meaning also makes it reasonable to say that the Bible can have layered meanings, allowing God to be known to different people at different times. If meaning were static and intrinsic, the human writers would have had to write things that would have made no sense them, in order for modern readers to find meaning to which they could relate. And modern readers would encounter parts that were incomprehensible because they were meant for readers even further in the future, who will have conceptual tools undreamt of in our current philosophy. Instead, we find that the entire Bible had meaning to its original writers and readers (or hearers), and it all has meaning for us in the present. The flip side of this is that we have to actually do the work of building a relationship with the author if we wish to discover the meaning he intended.

The other connection between information and axioms is revealed in an alternate method of understanding those incompleteness results. Recall that incompleteness means that a given set of axioms will always produce statements which cannot be proven true or false, or whose veracity cannot be decided within that context. Again, that doesn't necessarily imply that those statements have no truth value; we simply cannot arrive at a decision about their truth from a given framework. Recall also from our discussion of information that the number of bits in a message isn't always about how many words or letters are in the message. Jonathan used a full sentence to communicate one bit to David; if he wanted to be more efficient, he could have used one word or even a single syllable.

Now consider all the theorems that we can prove as true from a given set of axioms. How many bits does it take to express them? We might first suppose that we would need to write them all out, then figure out some way to encode them using just two symbols, then count the symbols. That sounds tedious; is there a more efficient option?

As it happens, there is. Where did all those theorems come from? We arrived at them by starting from our axioms, then applying the operations that generate new valid statements, then applying our operations to those statements, etc. So in a sense, all of our theorems are contained in our axioms and the rules for manipulating axioms and statements. That sounds much more efficient.

If thinking in terms of axioms and theorems is uncomfortable, consider a game instead; chess will work well. In chess, we have starting positions for all the pieces (axioms) and rules for how those pieces can be moved. Different arrangements of pieces on the board are like theorems; if you can get to a given arrangement by following the rules from the starting positions, then it is valid or true. There are many, many possible board positions, enough that you could play for your whole lifetime and not see them all. And yet, they were all there in the rules, just waiting to be played out.

This leads us to our alternate method for understanding incompleteness. If all of our theorems are contained in those axioms and rules, then the axioms and rules have all the information already in them. And if we can write those axioms and rules in a finite amount of bits, in other words, in a book that has a back cover and does not go on indefinitely, then they contain a finite amount of information. This implies that they can only prove a finite number of theorems as true. But if there are infinitely many *potential* theorems we might wish to prove, or decide whether they are true or false, then there will always be some theorems that our axioms cannot decide for us.

Understanding incompleteness and axiomatic frameworks in this way sheds light on the problem of claiming to assume nothing. There is a notion, as I understand it, that the quantum vacuum, the most rudimentary element of the universe and the closest approximation to nothing presently available in physics, can be modeled mathematically such that space, time, matter, and energy can spontaneously appear where previously they had not existed. I'm comfortable with the idea that this model might actually describe the world we live in, and that it is consistent with potentially observable phenomena such as virtual particles and black hole radiation. But naming the quantum vacuum with its specific properties "nothing" doesn't make it not a thing any more than calling myself "no one" makes me not a person.

I am reminded of the scene in *Rosencrantz & Guildenstern Are Dead* when the title characters on are a boat to England. They awake on the boat, unaware of how they got there. Rosencrantz (or is it Guildenstern?) wonders if they are dead, and Guildenstern (or is it Rosencrantz?) asserts that death is the ultimate not-being, and one cannot "not-be" on a boat. Rosencrantz observes that he has frequently not been on boats, to which Guildenstern replies that no, what he has been is not on boats. Likewise, the ultimate not-a-thing cannot be described as that which has particular qualities.

Thus any system for describing the physical world and all our experiences cannot claim to have nothing as its starting point. Starting with no assumptions means there is no information in your framework, and no theorems can be decided. In order to decide the truth of any proposition, one must have some kind of axioms to start with, however obvious they may seem.

This leads me to wonder something about God. It is common to refer to God as infinite, although what this actually means is not always specified precisely. We also read in the Bible that God is Truth. Here, we have proposed that God is axiomatic. What if we suppose that the axiom system defined by God contains an infinite number of bits? We at least then have the possibility of credibly claiming God as the source of all truth, making it sensible to say he is Truth. The axiom system he defines would have sufficient information to decide all propositions as true.

That is not to say that only those who believe in God know truth, nor that they know all truth. For one, it is possible to come to the same conclusion, to prove the same theorem as true, from different axiom systems. We mentioned earlier that there are multiple formulations of set theory, and they all prove many of the same theorems that make arithmetic possible. For the other, any individual believer's understanding of God will be finite. Thus, even if God is the foundation of an axiom system in infinite bits, none of us presently can claim to know all those bits. Going further, we can even be wrong about some of them, leading us to false conclusions. We must always be careful to distinguish between what we claim about God, and what we are actually capable of knowing.

Finally, on that topic of knowing, let's go back to our chess example. When can you say you know the game of chess? Once you have learned where all the pieces start and how they move? Perhaps, but I would submit that you are not much of a chess player if that is the extent of your experience with the game. For example, it is unlikely that you could look at an arbitrary board arrangement and know whether it was valid, nor could you assess what moves from that position would be fruitful. A grandmaster could do those things; indeed research suggests it is precisely those skills that make them grandmasters, and that the only way to acquire those skills is to spend many hours playing. That is how one comes to know chess.

Translating that to our definition of faith as choosing God for an axiom, we see that the book of James says something very similar. "What good is it, my brothers and sisters, if someone claims to have faith but does not have works?" (James 2:14). In our terms, choosing the axiom of faith is not enough to know God; it is simply a prerequisite. Knowing God is the process of taking that axiom and figuring out what truths it contains. That means playing the game—living your life according to the theorems, the true statements, that follow from belief in God. This is what James means by showing faith through works, and what separates knowing God from knowing of God, which, as James notes in verse 19, even the demons know of God.

Likewise, Indiana Jones' faith in his staff for locating the ark wasn't fully realized until he took it to the map room and then dug where the staff led him. And his belief in the power of the ark would have been for naught if he hadn't acted to close his eyes; he even had enough faith to communicate his beliefs to Marion and save her also. The real test of his beliefs was not in how rigorously they were deduced from his starting assumptions or in their internal consistency. His beliefs were shown correct by his acting on them and seeing how the results compared with the world around him.

And so we have a picture of faith that is not inherently uninquisitive or unempirical. Instead, faith represents a particular set of assumptions about the world, including that God is the ultimate author of the universe and the Bible. These assumptions are not privileged *a priori* or deductively superior; they are a matter of volition. The work of faith is to discern the meaning in what we observe in the world around us in a way that is consistent with those assumptions and then act accordingly.

This process of living our faith should then be highly exploratory, requiring active engagement and not passive acceptance. For, as we noted, even if God is Truth, that doesn't guarantee that we will know God or Truth perfectly. We need to regularly check to see if the theorems we are choosing, the actions we take, the way we live our lives, are consistent with the axioms we have chosen. It is possible that they won't be, in which case we are getting into the territory of sin, the topic of the next chapter.

CHAPTER 2

The Hound of Heaven across the Multiverse

Mark Watney was lost.

In fact, no one had ever been more lost than Mark Watney. On a good day, his home is only 33.9 million miles away. Most days are not good days.

The Martian, both the novel and the film, tells the story of how astronaut Mark Watney found himself stranded all alone on Mars. Like many shipwrecked heroes, Watney must figure out how to get enough food to stay alive, survive the perils of an inhospitable environment, and make contact with someone who can rescue him. Unlike Robinson Crusoe or Tom Hanks in *Castaway*, Mark Watney knows exactly where he is. So does everyone else, for that matter. Satellites orbiting Mars track him everywhere he goes. So if everyone knows where he is, in what sense is he lost?

Mark Watney knows where he is and knows exactly where he wants to go. His problem, the thing that makes him lost, is that he doesn't know how to get there from where he is. There's the obvious problem of traveling through space, both in the general sense of moving around in three dimensions and more specifically of traversing the vacuum between planets. He also needs to travel through time, not in the science fiction sense, but simply traveling into the future one day per day. He doesn't have enough food to keep himself alive long enough for other astronauts to get to him.

Watney's solution? Science! He'll need all of his skills as a botanist, an engineer (while fictional scientists often have an unrealistic breadth of expertise, astronauts on long-term missions are expected to have multiple proficiencies), and a problem-solver to survive. But first, he needs math.

2.1 A Poem as Lovely as an Equation

In chapter 1, we talked about numbers, groups of numbers, and their properties, which in turn helped us talk about God. From there, we can talk about how we relate to God. And in math, when you want to know how two things relate to each other, you can use an equation to describe their relationship. Now, I gather that's where a lot of people part ways with math. Equations can look very intimidating, with their Greek letters and unfamiliar symbols like ∇ and $\oint$. We associate them with genius; a quick way to demonstrate that a movie or TV character is super smart is to show them filling blackboards with equations. Yet they can be very potent tools for communicating, and so I believe are worth the effort if we want to understand a relationship as potentially important as ours with God.

Here are a couple of things I have learned about equations. More often than not, the math they represent boils down to addition, multiplication, and other fairly commonplace arithmetic. Even something as seemingly esoteric as integration can be thought of as a compact, efficient way to represent a lot of addition (the $\int$ used to indicate integration is really an "S" for "sum"). That's really why equations are so challenging; they are a dense shorthand. When writing proofs or doing calculations by hand, one has to write the same thing many times, which is why mathematicians try to use as few symbols as possible in their notation.

The other thing I've learned about equations is that they can be challenging to everyone, even very intelligent mathematicians. It is a rare gift to be able to look at a brand-new equation and immediately understand what it means. Some of the notation will be standard, but least some symbols will likely represent unique quantities that have to be explained by the person who wrote the equation. Once you've figured out what the symbols represent, it can still be challenging to figure out the relationships between all the quantities. Even after a lifetime in mathematics, there can be surprises in an equation that aren't revealed until you've worked with the equation for a while (more on that in the next chapter).

That's why I like to think of equations as the poems of math. Poems are the most compact, densest forms of language and writing. They use rich symbols to convey layers of meaning in a few words. All of that can make them challenging to read and understand at first glance; one must decipher what each symbol represents.

In other words, poems and equations take a long time to read because they are information dense. Every word or symbol is meant to convey a large number of bits. As a result, ideas are expressed compactly and elegantly. But the reader senses that they are making little progress because decoding and processing all those bits takes time while only a small physical space has been traversed.

Seeing that an equation is a poem helps us appreciate the true genius behind it. It's not the ability to do complex calculations or knowing the Greek alphabet. It is seeing the relationships between two quantities (or more) in a way that no one else has seen them before and expressing that relationship clearly and precisely. Just as unpacking a novel metaphor from a poem can help you see the world in a new way, seeing a new relationship expressed in an equation can be revelatory.

Let's try a simple example: $C_T = \varepsilon d$. At first glance, that may not seem so simple. But I haven't told you what any of the symbols mean, so you have no way to comprehend it yet. I chose d to stand for days, as in the number of days Watney is living on Mars. I chose ε to represent his eating rate, in Calories per day. I chose C_T to stand for total Calories, the overall quantity of food he'll need to survive those d days.

When nutritional labels are calculated for food packages, an eating rate of 2,000 Calories per day is assumed. If Watney needs to wait 400 days to be rescued and is going to eat 2,000 Calories per day, then our equation tells us that he will need $C_T = 2000*400 = 800,000$ total Calories. Looking in his pantry tells him he doesn't have that much food, because the mission wasn't supposed to last that long. He can also take the total number of Calories he does have (let's use 100,000 for easy calculation) and work out how much he can eat every day. That gives him $\varepsilon = C_T/d = 100,000/400 = 250$ Calories per day, a fairly meager amount, especially given the manual labor needed to solve other problems.

Easy enough, right? You've probably done math like this with your car gas mileage or your monthly expenses, even if you didn't call anything a variable or assign it a Greek letter. And the relationships here are pretty straightforward. If Watney eats more each day, he needs more total food; if he needs to survive more days, he needs to stretch his food by eating less each day; and so on.

Did you notice the nerdy element to working with equations like this? Remember that we talked about nerdiness in terms of exploring alternate possibilities for the world and then applying the results to reality. Equations facilitate exactly that sort of thinking. Instead of having a bunch of actual people eat different amounts of food each day to see how long each one lasts, we can use the equation to explore different scenarios. Which is handy, because we've only got the one Mark Watney, and once he runs out of food once we've got even fewer Mark Watneys.

Another equation relevant to *The Martian* is the rocket equation $\Delta v = v_{ex} \log \frac{m_r + m_f}{m_r}$. At some point, Watney will have to accelerate, or change his velocity (Δv), into orbit around Mars in order to get home. He knows how much fuel he has (m_f), which is fixed by the size of the tanks; in general, more fuel means a greater change in velocity is possible. He knows v_{ex}, the exhaust velocity, or how fast the rocket can eject propellant to achieve acceleration; ejecting propellant faster means a greater change in velocity. He needs to get higher into orbit than originally planned for, which means a higher Δv, which means he needs to figure out how much of the rocket's mass (m_r) to discard to achieve that speed, because rocket mass slows things down.

But wait! That rocket equation assumes the only significant force acting on the rocket is the thrust of the rocket's engine. Watney is on Mars, which has gravity. Acceleration due to gravity (g) is constant for a given planet; to see how it contributes to the change in velocity we have to multiply by the amount of time t spent accelerating. For a rocket thrusting straight up like this one, gravity acts in the opposite direction, so we can simply subtract its effect, updating our equation to $\Delta v = v_{ex} \log \frac{m_r + m_f}{m} - gt$. We should also account for drag from the atmosphere, but the math starts to get tricky because it depends more strongly on the specific shape of the rocket. But you may recall that in the film, the rocket changes shape during flight, which changes the drag forces, which is why Watney doesn't end up with the expected Δv, which affects how high he can fly.

All of that drama flows from the equation, because it encapsulates the relationship of gravity and rocket fuel. The cleverness of the storytelling is to connect that relationship with Watney's relationship to his home, his future, and his fellow astronauts. The narrative establishes a new equation: lowering rocket mass equals increasing thrust equals Mark Watney catches a ride home. We intuitively understand the human elements, the need to commune with other people and to return home. By constructing the narrative equation this way, we now have a connection between something we understand well and the less familiar physics of rocket science. As we go forward here, we can build on what we have now learned about rocket science and the math involved to understand more about God.

We can also rearrange the rocket equation to understand the relationship between Watney's limited food supply and the abundance of food back home. Sending more food means a bigger rocket (m_r), which means we need more fuel. But more fuel also means more total mass ($m_r + m_f$), which complicates matters. A little algebra can show us the rocket mass in terms of the fuel mass, but also depends on the velocity change and the time. For launch, the velocity change is from zero to the escape velocity (v_{es}) of the planet, a constant that depends on the size of the Earth (or Mars, but the food is launched from Earth). Time actually also depends on the fuel because the engine consumes or burns fuel at a constant rate b in terms of grams per second, so $t = \frac{m_f}{b}$.

The relationship between the mass of fuel and the corresponding mass of nonfuel rocket parts that fuel can launch is probably easier to understand from the graph in Figure 2.1, although the curious reader can work out the equation with appropriate substitutions and rearrangements of earlier equations. Note that we reach a point where adding more fuel actually decreases the amount of food that can be launched because the thrust from that fuel is expended overcoming gravity to launch itself.

These bits of rocket science allow Watney and his collaborators to explore various alternative solutions so that when the time comes to launch for real, they can be confident that they have reduced the mass of the Mars rocket sufficiently to get Watney where he needs to be. Which is good, because again, they've only got the one Mark Watney. They also allow the mission to be planned in the first place without having to resort to costly trial and error to figure out what size rockets to build and how much food they can pack.

2.2 Two Roads Diverged in the Multiverse

Fiction operates in a similar fashion; we can explore alternative scenarios without exhausting limited real world resources. Some stories actually dramatize this feature. *Edge of Tomorrow* depicts soldiers who keep retrying a combat mission until they achieve a victory

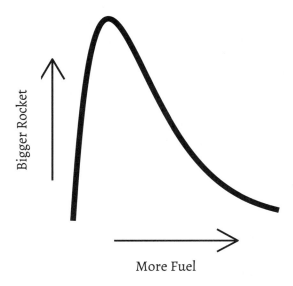

Figure 2.1: Initially, more fuel allows you to put a bigger rocket into orbit, but diminishing returns mean eventually more fuel can't even put itself into orbit.

scenario (reminiscent of repeating a video game level until you succeed). *Run, Lola, Run* shows three different ways the eponymous heroine can complete a task in order to reveal the only one that will lead to success. Even films like *Terminator 2: Judgment Day, Back to the Future 2*, and *X-Men: Days of Future Past*, while only showing one or two options, still use the conceit that events can proceed in multiple different ways. Is it any wonder such films are popular with nerds, who are united in their recognition that the world could be other than it is?

Groundhog Day is another multiple timeline story about a weatherman reliving the same day until he betters himself. The film reads as an allegory for reincarnation. As a search for a better version of oneself, reincarnation would represent a serial process, meaning one attempt after another in a series. If it turns out this life is the one and only chance we get, though, then a serial process isn't going to be terribly effective. We need something like a rocket equation so that we can try different alternatives in parallel with each other.

A parallel search for the timeline we want makes me think of multiverses. If the universe is everything observable from a fixed location in time and space, then the multiverse is the collection of all such universes defined by all the locations that exist. It's a pretty heady concept, and while a growing number of scientists believe that we live in a multiverse of one sort or another, it is still very much just a theoretical notion at this point. I'm not asking anyone to accept these multiverse hypotheses as an actual description of our world; I just think it is a useful metaphor.

Multiverses are quite popular in science fiction, especially (and amusingly) in the world of serial storytelling. When scores of writers and artists have been telling a single story for decades, as is the case for DC and Marvel Comics, inconsistencies in plot and characterization can arise. It can be convenient in those circumstances to say that the two conflicting stories took place in two different universes. Those two universes might be mostly similar, perhaps nearly identical, only in one Superman wears red briefs and in the other they are blue. As the story goes on, the universes proliferate to the point they must be catalogued; the main Marvel comics continuity is universe 616, the Marvel Studios movies take place in universe 199999, and we live in universe 1218.

A multiverse gives us another way to describe how Mark Watney was lost. He and everyone else knew exactly where he was on Mars. He was lost in the multiverse of possible Mark Watneys who eat different amounts of food each day, dismantle their rockets differently and otherwise make divergent choices. To get home, he needed to figure out which version of himself would get him there.

There are several parables in the Bible that liken people who are not followers of Jesus to items which are lost. In Luke 15, we have a lost coin, and a lost sheep; each of these items is sought once it is discovered missing, and each is ultimately found. Being found in these stories is comparable to being saved or becoming a follower of Jesus. Consequently, a lot of "lost and found" language is used when Christians talk about proselytizing. This language is comforting if you consider yourself already found, but for the proselytizee, it can be off-putting. If you know exactly where you are, and if you are right where you want to be, how can you possibly be lost?

I propose that we are lost when we are not the best possible version of ourselves. In that case, when Jesus goes looking for us—the Luke 15 parables are generally read with Jesus as the searcher—he is scouring the multiverse of possible versions of us to find the best one. He calls us to follow him from our current version of ourselves to that best version he has found.

Then again, who's to say we aren't that best version already? And why does God or Jesus get to decide what the best version is? I think it's fair to ask those questions and correct to think that there are alternatives. At the same time, according to the Bible, those alternatives may be considered sin by God's reckoning.

Yep, sin. We don't enjoy the idea of being told that we have sinned or that we are sinners. Nevertheless, the Bible does mention sin a fair bit, so if we are going to know God we need to have some idea of what it is. My primary aim is to explore the concept of sin and to establish why it is a useful idea, rather than enumerating specific sins.

2.3 Virtual Mountain Majesties

Searching through a variety of possibilities for the best option is a common problem in mathematics. Optimization is a whole discipline with multiple subspecialties. The most basic version involves an equation where the quantity you want to optimize is alone on one side and the variable(s) on the other side are what you change to find the best value. If there is only one variable you can change, you can draw a two-dimensional graph like the one in Figure 2.1 where the variable you can change runs along the horizontal axis and the quantity you are trying to optimize runs along the vertical axis. For many equations, what you get are smooth peaks and troughs, suggesting hills and valleys; if the equation has two variables you can change, the corresponding three-dimensional graph will be even more similar to a topographical map of actual geography. These similarities are strong enough that climbing hills is a useful metaphor for mathematical optimization.

Imagine that you are a surveyor exploring a region for the first time, without map or GPS. You've arrived by river, thus finding yourself at a relatively low point. From there, you might look around, find a peak, and start climbing. You'd keep ascending until you can't go up anymore, and then you'd know that you were at the top. From your vantage point on that peak, you can look around and see if there are any higher peaks and then head toward the highest. And so on and so forth, until you can't see anything that's above you. At that point, you can be reasonably certain that you have found the highest spot in the region.

Now, do it blindfolded.

For many optimization problems, drawing a graph to look for the highest point is not a feasible option. The equation of interest may have more than two variables that can change, requiring visualization in more dimensions than humans can see. While we may not be able to see all of the contours at once, we can still use the equation to get our altitude at any point. We might imagine measuring the altitude at every possible location and keeping track of where we got the highest measurement. Sometimes that actually is an option, but often there are an infinite number of points and no one has that kind of time.

If we have no additional information, we can randomly explore some of them and settle for the highest place we come across. Fortunately, we often do know something more about the landscape and can use that to search more efficiently. If the function has something resembling a smooth surface, meaning that nearby points have similar altitudes, then we can try to climb to the highest peak. We pick a starting point, measure the altitudes nearby and then move to the highest spot, repeating this process until we get to a point where the altitude of all the nearby points is lower than where we are standing. For many smooth surfaces, we can actually do better than just getting the altitude; we can also get a measure of the incline at each point so we can just follow the slope up from wherever we are standing until there is no more up. Or, because it's all math and not real topography, we can flip it over and slide down the slopes to the bottom, then flip it over again and be at the top.

Metaphorical hill-climbing will get you to *a* peak, but we still have the problem of not knowing if it is *the* peak. We could adjust for this by picking multiple starting points and seeing where we get from each one. We can modify the sliding-down version to include momentum, so that you don't get stuck on small bumps. We can employ a team of searchers who can tell when one teammate is standing on an anthill and thinks he has found a peak because all the points around him are down from where he is. None of these modifications guarantee we will reach the absolutely highest point, but they can improve the chances of success.

Now one might imagine we will eventually put together maps of all the interesting surfaces, just like we build up a library of maps of the Earth's surface. Only with math, our challenge is less like mapping the entire surface of Earth and more like mapping the entire surface of every planet orbiting any of the stars in the visible universe. In particular, one application of these hill-climbing, peak-finding techniques involves equations constrained by observational data such that every time one needs to analyze a new data set, one is exploring a new surface.

Equations constrained by data are where I have the most experience with optimization methods. In the simplest scenario, I need to find a straight line that best fits my data by adjusting the line's angle or slope and the point where the line reaches zero, called the intercept. Going back to Mark Watney's nutritional dilemma, his rate of eating in Calories per day would be the slope and the day when all the food runs out is the intercept. Our prior analysis imagined an ideal consumption of exactly the same number of Calories each day. In reality, food doesn't come in precise, equal units; Watney eats a lot of potatoes and some potatoes will be bigger than others. If Watney were to make a plot (like Figure 2.2) with days on the horizontal axis and total Calories remaining on the vertical axis, he could make a point each day to indicate how many Calories he actually has left. Those points won't all fall on a perfectly straight line, but we can find the line that best approximates the data and thus know how many days of food Watney has left.

Each combination of slope (eating rate) and intercept (day the food runs out) defines a candidate line for matching our data. Those

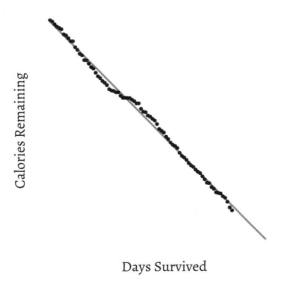

Figure 2.2: Observations of daily food consumption (points) and the line that best fits the data (line).

are the variables I can change for my optimization problem, while the hill I'm trying to climb is a measure of how well a candidate line fits the data. We can calculate our assessment by taking each observed value and subtracting the value that the line predicts for that observation to get an error for each observation. We square those errors so that they are all positive and then add them all up, giving us a notion of how well the line fits. We want to find the line with the smallest errors using our hill-climbing optimization. (As I mentioned, we can always flip the surface over, turning a minimization problem into a maximization problem.)

Intercept (Day Food Runs Out)

Figure 2.3: Topographical map of the surface defined by possible slopes and intercepts and how well the line they define fits the data.

When we just need a single straight line, optimization is fairly straightforward. Using the square of the errors makes the surface smooth and convex, meaning that it is roughly shaped like a bowl as in Figure 2.3. Sometimes the bowl is more of a plate, broad and shallow, making our job a little tougher, but we are still guaranteed to find the bottom. In fact, even if we actually need a plane or a higher-dimensional equivalent, the surface we are searching will still be a multi-dimensional bowl with the same useful properties.

But we had a choice when we decided that we wanted to find the solution with the smallest squared errors. We could have used the raw errors, or the absolute value of the errors, or the cube of the errors. Or we could decide we don't care about all the errors, just the biggest one, and then look for the solution that makes sure we keep that biggest error as small as possible. Each of these options would give us a different equation, even for the same potato data; in other words, each would give our landscape a different topography where we would need to conduct our search. Not all of these alternatives are as smooth or bowl-shaped, making the search more challenging and possibly necessitating some of the modifications we discussed earlier (Figure 2.4). Squared errors are thus often used for these kinds of problems because they make the search more straightforward.

Intercept (Day Food Runs Out)

Figure 2.4: Alternative surface defined by a different equation using the same inputs, potential slopes and intercepts.

2.4 Purity Is Optimality

Having applied optimization to our Martian scenario, let's see how it applies to sin. The Greek word in the Bible we translate as "sin," for example in Ephesians 2:1–2, "And although you were dead in your transgressions and sins, in which you formerly lived according to this world's present path," conveys the notion of missing a target. The equivalent Hebrew word, as in "they will stumble like blind men, for they have sinned against the Lord" (Zephaniah 1:17), similarly suggests a missed aim or deviation from the path. In other words, our behavior is being compared to some standard. If we are looking for an analogy to the math of optimizing, we might think about fitting a line to data. Maybe the line is the standard, our behavior is the data, and sin is the extent to which our behavior deviates from the standard. Just like our real potatoes won't fit a perfectly straight line, we probably don't expect our behavior to always exactly hit the ideal. At the same time, we can see that our behavioral data points are closer to that ideal than some other folks' and thus convince ourselves we're doing okay.

However, such a comparative assessment is not the picture of sin that the Bible describes. For example, consider "For the one who obeys the whole law but fails in one point has become guilty of all of it" (James 2:10). That's not a relative perspective of sin where one is fine as long as there are worse people, it's an absolute one. Anybody who has missed the mark in any way has missed the mark and that's it. To me, this is more similar to the case of finding the highest peak. For simple line-fitting questions, there is one highest peak and if you aren't on it, then you aren't on it. In this model, our behaviors provide the dimensions of input, and the output is God's assessment of that behavior. If our behavior corresponds to the highest peak of the output, then we are sinless; otherwise, we have sinned.

Of course, just as with our line-fitting example, we have a choice of other functions by which to assess our behavior. Other religions prescribe behavior for their faithful; some of their requirements are comparable to the Bible's morality, such as prohibitions on stealing or murder, while others, like praying toward Mecca or not driving on the Sabbath, set those religions apart. The laws of your nation or municipality provide another standard to measure your behavior against. Philosophical frameworks of ethics and morality, like utilitarianism, are yet another option. Debating the merits of these different standards is beyond the scope of this book. I am merely acknowledging that all of these represent alternative equations for taking possible behaviors and defining a surface from them so that you can try to choose the behavior that corresponds to the peak of that surface. In that respect, they are all equivalent.

If we have choices for assessing our behavior, why choose the standards from the Bible? While I think there is a lot of value in the morality the Bible encourages and plenty of common ground with other popular options, I'm not personally inclined to argue that the Bible offers the best option. For starters, we can quickly get into an infinite regress of asking what standard we are using to decide that the Bible's moral code is the best and why we chose that standard and so on. Also, I can't ignore the empirical observation that plenty of people lead functional, socially constructive, and happy lives following another moral code; those alternatives aren't completely bankrupt or vacuous.

Instead, having made the choice of faith discussed in the last chapter to know God as an axiom and explore the truth contained in that axiomatic system, I accept the particular behavioral evaluation function that God establishes. Naturally, it should be as clear as possible up front that this is the choice being made; I'm not advocating anything less than transparency. I just think that the sequence of which conclusions follows from which premises makes more sense this way.

This sequence is also consistent with how the standards of morality are presented in the Bible. They are presented within the framework of covenants. Rather than saying "You must do this because I said so!" God describes what a relationship with him entails, both the benefits and the conditions. Such relationships can then be built on informed consent, not blind obedience.

Having decided to hold myself to a biblical standard, I need to know what God is trying to optimize. In Isaiah, God says "I will make justice the measuring line, fairness the plumb line" (Isaiah 28:17). Micah informs that God wants us "to promote justice, to be faithful, and to live obediently" (Micah 6:8). Jesus, in his famous Sermon on the Mount, encourages us "above all" to "pursue [God's] kingdom and righteousness" (Matthew 6:33). Earlier in that Sermon he also praises the meek, the merciful, and the peacemakers.

One common thread through concepts like justice, fairness, and peacemaking is a sense of communal well-being. We are not simply finding the best possible versions of ourselves independent of everyone else, but the best possible collective version of ourselves. I can't even assess my own fairness with respect to how I treat myself; fairness is only relevant to how I treat multiple other people. Justice and peacemaking go even further and ask how I intercede in situations between two separate groups or individuals. In other words, I can work toward peace between myself and someone else, and I can also work toward peace between two other parties, potentially over a dispute in which I gain nothing either way. While we are each responsible for our own conduct, we are not being evaluated in a vacuum.

Concern for our neighbors has many benefits in the here and now. At the same time, it is also relevant to our discussion of that future banquet in God's honor. Not only will we be spending a long time in God's presence, we will also be spending that time together with each other. We might as well start developing an affinity for our fellow celebrants.

Another notable feature of these values we are called to optimize is the tension between some of them. If we were only to maximize justice, there would be little or no mercy, while maximizing mercy would yield very little justice. In mathematical optimization, it is common to have multiple constraints. The optimal solution across all of them might not correspond to the optimal solution for just a single constraint. In our rocketry example, maximizing just the length of the mission would call for sending far more food, but the additional constraints on total rocket mass once we take fuel into consideration mean we have to send less food than we might otherwise choose. Similarly, the Bible calls us to balance justice and mercy rather than purely optimizing just one or the other.

There's a popular idea that God as described in the Old Testament is all about justice, while Jesus is the one who embodies mercy. While this analysis rightly recognizes the tension between justice and mercy, it glosses over details that illustrate how Jesus and the God of Abraham, Isaac, and Jacob balance both concepts. For example, the book of Leviticus is a detailed accounting of the law God gave to the Israelites during the time of Moses. In chapter 10, right in the midst of these detailed regulations, there is a story of how Moses' brother Aaron and his sons either deviate from some of the specifics or at least have differing interpretations of them. And yet there is no evidence of God punishing them; to the contrary, the story concludes in verse 20 with Moses being satisfied that such variation is within acceptable tolerances.

Another Old Testament story of mercy comes from the book of Joshua. The Israelites are in the process of conquering the land of Canaan and believe they need to eliminate all of its current inhabitants. The conquering of Canaan is often held up, if not as an example of God's wrath, then at the very least of his extreme sense of justice. Yet Joshua also recounts in chapter 9 the experience of the Gibeonites, a

group who lived in Canaan. They convinced Joshua and the other Israelite leaders that they weren't local as a pretense to secure a treaty. Even
after the truth is revealed, Israel upholds the treaty and the Gibeonites
are spared. This mercy is never condemned, and indeed years later
when the Israelite king Saul violates that treaty, he is sanctioned for it
(2 Samuel 21).

Meanwhile, Jesus stands up for justice as well as mercy. He cleanses
the temple courts of merchants who are exploiting the poor (John 2).
His teachings on anger and lust, holding them up with murder and
adultery, are radical in their severity (Matthew 5). He also demonstrates how justice and mercy can be served simultaneously. When
he spares a woman accused of adultery from stoning, he is showing
her mercy while also standing against the injustice of prosecuting her
alone (John 8).

If we are content that the Bible is consistently interested throughout with optimizing justice and mercy, we might also ask why there are
so many rules that seem to have little to do with either. For example,
Leviticus has 13 verses about mold and mildew (13:47–59). Part of the
answer is that the laws in Leviticus and Deuteronomy were the code
for an entire system of governance. Modern governments are also simultaneously interested in morality and health regulations, so why
not the nation of Israel? There is also an element of justice to health
regulations, by providing the entire population with access to healthy
food and water rather than just a lucky few.

At the same time, I think we should also be careful not to assume
that every condition God establishes has some social benefit such as
preventing disease or facilitating communal living. For example, if we
want to communicate our participation in God's covenant, we need an
arbitrary sign whose meaning is agreed upon by both parties. In the
last chapter, our examples of signs with mutually agreed meaning included Paul Revere's lanterns and Jonathan's arrows. The most obvious
candidates for signs of accepting God's covenant are circumcision and
baptism, since they are explicitly described as signs of participation.
They don't need to optimize some other criteria; in fact, they function
best as signs if they don't. There may be richer symbolism associated
with them beyond just the single "in/out" bit, but that's additional
meaning layered on rather than a functional necessity.

The Martian actually reminds us of this element of communication also. The same circumstances that strand Mark Watney on Mars

also leave him without a way to contact Earth. His first solution is to use the camera and communications equipment from an old probe. That gear allows him to send still pictures but no video or sound, and he can't receive pictures or sound back. He can ask questions in writing, but he can't get answers. Ultimately he works out a code involving the rotational angle of the camera, which NASA can control from the ground. The code is completely arbitrary in terms of which angles mean what, but it works because both he and NASA agree on the meanings.

Watney and NASA agree on a couple of other things. First is the goal of bringing Watney home. If he wants to arrange his life to optimize something other than his proximity to Earth, such as the length of his stay on Mars or his freedom from other people, then his behavior would be completely different, and of course NASA could decide to minimize budget and not spend resources to rescue him. Second is the means of achieving that goal. If Watney wants to get home more than anything, but wants to do it his own way rather than showing up when and where NASA's ship would pick him up, he'll never make it.

2.5 Of Man's First Disobedience

Similarly, I think our optimization framework for sin helps us talk about how the origin of sin lies in disagreement with God. If we are thinking of sin as deviating from the path to an optimal version of ourselves, a path Jesus marked out for us by searching the multiverse of possible "us"es to find, then sin starts when we choose to optimize qualities other than the ones God invites us to optimize. By doing so, we are essentially redrawing the map of our lives, just like we changed the surface for our potato line problem from smooth terrain with a clear optimal point (Figure 2.3) to a complex network of crags (Figure 2.4) by choosing to optimize a different quantity. While God waits for us at what is the peak of a mountain on his map, we might see that point as deep in a valley and so head off in a completely different direction toward the mountaintops of our map. Or maybe the differences in the terrain are more subtle, such that we often are heading in the same general direction as if we were using God's map. But ultimately we're going to stray off the way to God and thus into sin if we start by choosing some other optimization goals.

Genesis 3 is the origin story of sin, and this is precisely the scenario it describes. Adam and Eve walk with God, and he leads them down the path to an optimal existence. The one condition of their arrangement is that Adam and Eve may not eat from one specific tree. This is not a hardship, as food is available in abundance. If anything, it may seem a bit arbitrary since it's just one tree among many, but maybe that's the point. Not eating from that one tree is how they communicate the single bit of information that says they wish to participate in the relationship God offers.

Then the serpent comes along and offers an alternative interpretation—a different meaning. "Is it really true that God said, 'You must not eat from any tree of the orchard'?" (Genesis 3:1). When Eve says that they cannot eat from that tree or they will die, the serpent responds "Surely you will not die, for God knows that when you eat from it your eyes will open and you will be like divine beings who know good and evil" (Genesis 3:4–5). Adam and Eve could have chosen to use their relationship with God to explore his intended meaning, but instead they decide to make their own meaning.

In choosing their own interpretation for why God prohibited eating from that tree, Adam and Eve also chose to use their own optimization goals rather than God's. They were no longer following God by his map; they were drawing their own map and forging their own path. And thus their sin was born as they began to deviate from the optimal version of their lives that God offered.

In response, God demonstrates both his justice and his mercy. Adam and Eve had knowingly agreed to a covenant with God and then violated the terms, and so it was just for God to cut them off from the tree of life since death was the stated consequence for the violation. At the same time, the knowledge of good and evil that Adam and Eve received after eating the fruit was itself a mercy. Having chosen to navigate life and morality on their own, they could have been completely blind. Instead, they obtain a sense of what will lead to human flourishing and what will lead to destruction. They can still choose what to do with that information, but at least they have a framework to start with and respond to.

We might then ask what Adam and Eve have to do with us; my main interest is in how to equate their experience with mine. Regardless of your state at birth, by now you likely have your own sin origin story. I have my own sin origin story; I have decided on more than one occasion that I am going to seek a life which optimizes the qualities I want to optimize. Theologically, conversations about Adam and original sin and so forth are stimulating, but pragmatically I'm on the hook no matter how those conversations play out.

The idea of choosing one's own qualities to optimize, to forge one's own path, to be the master of one's own destiny—these may all sound quite positive. Self-determination is a core virtue of libertine society in general and the American mythos I grew up with. I appreciate and respect the value placed on deciding one's own fate. A great number of injustices have been perpetrated precisely by taking away self-determination, and restoring self-determination has been an important force for justice. Therefore I am not advocating complete rejection of it, especially in the context of how we relate to each other, and I don't believe God calls us to that either. At the same time, just as God calls us to balance justice and mercy, he also calls us to balance self-determination with submission to his will.

That call to submission can be answered in the affirmative or the negative. Not attending God's banquet is an option. Choosing your will over God's will is another possibility. Unfortunately, the Bible paints a fairly pessimistic picture of that scenario. Hell isn't a place where demons devise elaborate punishments to deliver poetic justice for whatever you did wrong in life, at least not in the Bible; that is the karmic *The Far Side* version. Biblical Hell is a place where everything is up to you—absolutely everything.

In this world, we see glimpses of that reality. We also see glimpses of what life with God's will is like. Being able to experience both is crucial to making an informed decision about which version we want to experience going forward. If our will always won out in this world, we'd have little reason to think there was any other option. If God's will always won out in this world, God would not experience *Weltschmerz* and there would be no need for redemption or new creation.

Indeed, one message of the Bible is that if we just started out in a place where God's will always determined what happens, we wouldn't stay anyway. Adam and Eve wondered if the garden was greener elsewhere. The nation of Israel followed God to the promised land only to immediately ask to see other options. God didn't force them to stay; he allowed them to search the surrounding wilderness exhaustively for a better alternative. The narrative from Judges through 2 Chronicles recounts how each generation would want to see for itself if there were better ways than the one God laid out for them, would go looking, would find none and desperately plead for mercy, only for the next generation or the generation after to start the whole cycle over again. And in Luke 15, Jesus tells the famous parable of the prodigal son, a personal version of the same archetypal story.

Why should we expect the banquet to be any different? Won't we eventually want to see if there's a better party elsewhere? Possibly, but everyone there has had the opportunity to see from this world what God's will produces and what their will produces and has opted into God's will. That experience changes the dynamics; memories of this creation inform the next and make it different. Jesus himself illustrates this reality in that his resurrected body still bears the scars of his crucifixion (John 20:27).

The resurrected Jesus is said to now be sitting at God's right hand, with all things under his feet (Ephesians 1:20–22). The image is one of a sovereign on a throne. Yet if God's will does not always win out in this world, is it reasonable to call God sovereign? And if my sin means that I've genuinely stepped off the way God is calling me to travel, can I get back on? These are the questions we will explore in the next chapter as we try to define grace.

CHAPTER 3

Sovereignty in a Time of Spanners

Rahne Sinclair was found by grace.

The most personally moving fictional illustration of mercy and grace that I've encountered comes from an issue of the comic *X-Factor*. Written by Peter David and drawn by several artists with a range of styles, *X-Factor* tells the story of a detective agency staffed by "mutants," which in the universe of Marvel Comics basically means someone born with genes for superpowers rather than acquiring those powers from gamma bombs or arachnid bites. The book is notable for its rich and nuanced characters. One of them is Rahne Sinclair, also known as Wolfsbane because of her ability to transform at will from human to wolf and back. Rahne grew up in a remote part of Scotland and was primarily raised by a very conservative Presbyterian minister who thought that her lupine mutation was a sign that she was cursed by God. Rahne is eventually freed from this unhealthy environment, goes to school with other mutants, and learns to accept who she is. When *X-Factor* starts, she has graduated and is now working at a detective agency with the rest of the cast. Despite her childhood experiences, she maintains her faith in God, and her exploration of that faith is a big part of the character arc Peter David writes for her.

At one point, Rahne takes a break from the agency and goes off to appear in another comic book. Being one of many co-authors of a shared universe like Marvel Comics means sharing or relinquishing characters in service of larger narrative or editorial goals. In that other book, Rahne is put through the ringer; among other trials, she is brainwashed to become an assassin and ultimately winds up killing Reverend Craig, the father figure who raised and tormented her. Afterwards, she returns to the detective agency, traumatized and pregnant by a wolfen Norse demigod, because . . . comics.

At this point, Peter David could ignore everything that happened to Rahne in the other book and get back to the stories he had originally planned. Or he could have credibly given Rahne a crisis of faith and had her walk away from her biblical beliefs, a development that would have been sad to see personally but not incomprehensible or unrealistic. Instead, in a book that regularly defied expectations, Peter David had Rahne confront her guilt and explore an arc of redemption. In issue #237, at her lowest point, Rahne visited John Maddox, an Episcopal minister and occasional guest star in the book. She expected punishment to the point of literal self-flagellation, which Reverend Maddox appeared willing to facilitate. But Rahne finds that she can't do it and realizes Reverend Maddox never intended her to punish herself in that way. Instead, he encourages her to accept the grace to move forward from her sins and seek reconciliation rather than self-retribution, to restore what she tore down rather than destroying herself.

Retelling the story in these few short paragraphs hardly does it justice. Part of why it was so compelling is that I had spent years with these characters, grieving for and with Rahne over everything that had happened to her. To see her experience genuine forgiveness in God was no less affecting than if it had happened to a friend or family member in real life. And perhaps I was particularly receptive to it because I've had my own tendencies toward self-flagellation, if maybe not quite as literal as Rahne's.

3.1 Free to Do What God Wants?

I was also simultaneously struck by the graciousness illustrated in the construction of the story. As I mentioned, Peter David was handed some story elements by other writers and editors and had some choice in how to proceed. He chose what many of us might consider to be the hardest option, taking those elements and working them into the story he was telling, rather than asserting his right to tell the story as he had originally conceived it. Isn't that a helpful way to conceive of God's grace as well? Rather than insisting that we conform to a particular mold, God accepts us as we are and tells a story of our lives that weaves into his overall story for the universe—at least if we agree that we want him to do so.

J. R. R. Tolkien paints a similar picture of God's grace in his creation myth for the world of Middle Earth. The story describes the creation of the world as the composition of a great work of music, written by a God-figure Eru and performed by angelic beings. During the performance, one of those beings, Melkor, decides to introduce his own melodies and harmonies, distorting the sound of the piece. Rather than stopping the performance, or evicting Melkor for choosing a different path, Eru opts to adjust his composition as it is being performed to incorporate these new musical developments. In the end, the result is a piece of music that sounds like a cohesive whole, as if it had always been intended to include the elements that were introduced by Melkor.

Circumstances like these raise questions of whether every outcome is foreordained by God and if we bear any responsibility. One solution is to introduce free will and assert that we are agents who make independent choices. This reintroduces the possibility that we can be held responsible for our choices, because our own agency and no other force realized those choices. But once we add our own free will, then what becomes of God's will and God's sovereignty? In what sense can God claim to be in charge or have a plan if we can do whatever we please? Is God always playing catch-up, adjusting his plans to account for our choices? Can any such being claim any sense of sovereignty, or must he acknowledge that he is in fact secondary to the agents making the choices that he has to react to?

A conflict between control and freedom is popular in fiction. *The Matrix* and its sequels are all about control of humanity through an elaborate computer program. *Lost* is concerned with experiments and rules designed to exert order and control. *Numbercruncher*, a comic by Si Spurrier, P. J. Holden, Jordie Bellaire, and Simon Bowland, depicts a world governed by precise mathematics. In each story, independent thought or will or anything resembling freedom is portrayed as rebellion.

This tension appears to be present in the Bible as well. One example is from the life of Moses. Moses was from the nation of Israel and was born at a time when his people lived in Egypt. Moses wound up being raised in the household of the Pharaoh, but after a violent and lethal altercation he fled into exile to avoid punishment. He spent many years as a shepherd before God called him to become involved in the movement to free the Israelite people. As Moses is preparing to go speak to Pharaoh, he begins to have some doubts. From Exodus 4:10–14,

> Then Moses said to the LORD, "O my Lord, I am not an eloquent man, neither in the past nor since you have spoken to your servant,

for I am slow of speech and slow of tongue." The LORD said to him, "Who gave a mouth to man, or who makes a person mute or deaf or seeing or blind? Is it not I, the LORD? So now go, and I will be with your mouth and will teach you what you must say." But Moses said, "O my Lord, please send anyone else whom you wish to send!" Then the LORD became angry with Moses, and he said, "What about your brother Aaron the Levite? I know that he can speak very well. Moreover, he is coming to meet you, and when he sees you he will be glad in his heart."

In this passage, we can clearly see God asserting his sovereignty, reminding Moses that he has given Moses all he has, even the capacity to speak; if God is telling Moses to go and speak to Pharaoh, then surely God will have made sure Moses is up to the task. But then if all things must go according to God's plan, how does God justify getting angry at Moses? Isn't Moses just acting the way God made him? Or, if instead Moses has agency and free will, then what value do God's assurances have? If Moses can act independently, then doesn't that mean he has the capacity to screw up the mission, regardless of God's preparation? And then what do we make of the resolution, where God consents to send Aaron along? Was that God's plan all along? Was that a contingency option built into the plan? Or was God genuinely scrapping his plan for a new one in response to Moses' choices?

3.2 Parabolas to the Future

Once again, I think some math can help us answer these questions. Let's return to parabolas, a particular kind of mathematical model. Recall that the word *parabola* and the word *parable* have the same origin in a Greek word meaning illustration or model. It might seem a little uninspired to give a mathematical model a name that just means "model" but I'd argue that it's rather fitting, because on some level the parabola is the most fundamental mathematical model we have. Not in terms of mathematics itself, since there are plenty of foundational ideas you have to get through before you can even compute "1+1=2," let alone work with something as complex as a parabola. No, instead I mean that it is fundamental in terms of modeling the real world.

You may not consciously know what a parabola is, but your brain does. It can compute the path of parabolas automatically without you ever having to think about it. It does this every time you throw or catch something. That's because a parabola describes the path that an object takes when moving under the influence of gravity; it is the curved arc of that which initially goes up before finally succumbing and coming down again. Parabola refers to a group of shapes rather than a single arc, but all parabolas have the same mathematical form and all thrown objects follow parabolas. On the surface of Earth, all of these parabolas can be described in terms of the initial velocity of the object and the angle from which it was launched. Just knowing those two things tells you the path the object will follow. (On other planets, gravity will be different; the strength of gravity represents the third piece of information required to compute a path.)

And that regularity of behavior is what makes it possible to throw and catch. When you catch something, your brain tracks the path it is taking and quickly figures out where that path will wind up, then figures out a point along that path where your hand can intercept it. When you throw something, your brain works out how hard to throw it and at what angle so that it will reach the desired target. Some amount of experience may be necessary to fill in the details such as the strength of your particular muscles and the weight of the object in question, both of which factor into the computation of what force to impart to achieve the necessary initial velocity. But the evidence suggests that the basic calculation of parabolas is wired into our brains.

This psychological preference for parabolas may explain the popularity of the *Angry Birds* games. The parabola is the core element of those games. By manipulating the slingshot, you are choosing the initial velocity and angle that will define the parabola (gravity is constant again, this time decided by the programmers). Pull back a little more on the slingshot, and the bird launches faster and flies farther; pull closer to the ground and the launch angle gets steeper so the bird will fly higher. Then you release the slingshot and watch the bird follow a perfect parabola—at least until it crashes into a pig. Research suggests our brains find it very satisfying to watch an object follow a parabolic path because it works the way our brain expects; this satisfaction translates into our enjoyment of the game.

I wonder if this fascination with parabolas explains some of the mass appeal of various sports. A hit in baseball, a football pass or field goal kick, a basketball shot, a tennis volley—all of these are parabolas in action. Is it any wonder that those moments are the times when we all collectively pause, to more fully savor the satisfaction of subconsciously tracking where the ball will go? For in that moment, we possess the divine gift of knowing the future.

The parabola is not the only mathematical model to promise such foresight. Like parabolas, these models are determined by initial conditions. Once you know a few things about the system at the start, the math tells you everything that will happen afterwards; sometimes it is sufficient just to know a few details of the system at any point, rather than the starting point. Of course, it is possible for an outside force to change the system, but that really just means one needs to recompute from the new starting conditions. Think about a basketball shot that hits the rim instead of going into the basket; it deflects off and follows a new parabola, but that new parabola can still be tracked using the initial velocity and launch angle. And if you knew the location of the rim, you could have calculated that deflection based on the original parabola, the one defined by how the player shot the ball.

The other property these models share with parabolas is the smoothness. What I mean by that is small adjustments lead to small changes in the path. Imagine how hard it would be to learn to throw if the first time you threw a ball, it traveled one foot in front of you, and then the next time you threw that same ball from the same spot just a little harder, it sailed ten feet across the room instead of one foot one inch. And even worse, what if the next time you threw it a little harder still, it went one foot three inches? To get the ball to go where you want, you'd have to throw it at exactly the right angle with exactly the right velocity, and you'd basically just have to memorize which combinations of velocity and angle corresponded with which final destinations.

Given how useful these properties are, and given how strongly our brains are wired to expect the world to operate this way, it is little wonder that we make so many of our models to have those properties. More to the point, it's not surprising that we expect the world to actually work in this way. And with this kind of metaphor for how the world works, it seems fairly natural that those who believe in God would start to think of him in those terms.

If God does have a plan for the world, then surely it would be expressed in the natural laws that govern his creation. And since those natural laws are fully specified by initial conditions, then really his only opportunity to influence that plan is at the start. From there, we would seem to have only two options. Either everything proceeds as planned, or else there are other agents which can influence the system, in which case it will then be on a new trajectory requiring further intervention to get back to the original trajectory.

Peter David actually dramatizes this tension between control and freedom quite well throughout his run on *X-Factor*, mainly through the perspectives of two other members of the mutant detective agency. Lead investigator Jamie Madrox has the power to make multiple copies of himself, and with this gift comes the ability to see a situation from multiple angles. It makes him a good detective but it can be a liability as a leader. Life for Jamie is nothing but choices and because he can see the merits of all the options, he never knows how to choose. In the language of the last chapter, his optimization landscape is very flat, or maybe more accurately he can appreciate the contours of multiple optimization landscapes and the way their different peaks support different decisions. He is so free he doesn't even know where to start.

Then one day, she walks into his detective agency. Layla Miller. She knows stuff. Specifically, she knows exactly how the future plays out. She knows where to stand to avoid falling debris, which screws to loosen to thwart a criminal scheme, when the phone will ring for a crucial call. Her complete control over circumstances via subtle influence seemingly earns her the codename "Butterfly," apparently a reference to the so-called butterfly effect.

3.3 The Strange Attraction of Butterflies

The butterfly effect reminds us that not all systems in the physical world can be described by models that behave like parabolas. Surprisingly, it doesn't require terribly sophisticated mathematics to get a completely different kind of behavior, a behavior so counterintuitive it was initially called chaos theory. And the butterfly effect is usually the first topic when anyone wants to talk about chaos. Colloquially, the butterfly effect says weather systems are so complex and so sensitive that a butterfly flapping its wings in Japan can mean the difference between rain or sunshine in New York City. Jeff Goldblum's character Ian Malcolm famously illustrates a similar principle in the movie *Jurassic Park* by putting drops of water on Ellie Sattler's (Laura Dern's) hand. The first drop flows one way down her hand, the second a completely different way; according to Malcolm, small deviations in drop placement, the arrangement of the tiny hairs on the hand, or other conditions cause the differences in outcome. Nothing is exactly the same way twice, small changes get amplified into big ones, and thus everything is unpredictable chaos. Malcolm uses this idea to argue the dinosaurs in Jurassic Park can never be controlled—in fact, that control is an illusion.

And yet, as we shall see, chaos theory isn't quite as chaotic or hopeless as all that. Ian Malcolm has only told us part of the story. In fact, the mathematics of chaos theory reveal their own sort of order, which might just help us make sense of God's sovereignty and our free will.

To understand that order, we have to get into the mathematics a bit. Let's start with the simplest equation that illustrates sensitivity to initial conditions, known as the logistic map. The logistic map is used as a very basic model of population growth. (That a biologically motivated equation is chaotic and disruptive to the elegance of mathematics and physics will likely not be surprising to physicists, mathematicians or biologists.)

The most basic model of population growth would be one which says the population size tomorrow will be the population today multiplied by the average daily number of individuals that will exist tomorrow per individual from today. This is essentially the balance of the birth rate and the death rate, and if you want to get more complicated you can include immigration and emigration rates or other elements, adjusted for the appropriate time scale. If we are bothered by the notion of fractional births likely to be encountered when working day to day, we can think in terms of weeks or months or years; the behavior we're interested in here works out the same. As long as there is a net positive influx of new members at each time, the population will grow exponentially without limit. When this model was initially applied to population growth, some became concerned that the human population would grow unchecked and exhaust all available food and water supplies and other resources if left to its own devices.

Fortunately, other modeling options are available, including the logistic map. This model simply introduces the idea of a maximum population into our earlier scenario. In both scenarios, resources like food are fixed. The exponential growth model ignores this until the limits of those resources are reached, and then the population collapses. The logistic map model assumes that as we approach that limit, the increasing scarcity of resources will slow down population growth.

Under the logistic map model, tomorrow's population size (or next week's, or next year's) depends not only on the rate of new members and the current population, but also on how close the current population is to the maximum population. This last part balances out the exponential growth by providing feedback in the opposite direction. And it does so quite nicely. For example, if the growth rate is 2, meaning two people next time for every one this time, the population very quickly settles into a stable size of half the maximum population. It will reach this stable point no matter where the population starts—as long as it starts with at least one member, and isn't bigger than the maximum size (in which case, you probably need to adjust your estimate of the maximum size). This is obviously much better than uncontrolled growth, in terms of planning and resource management and so forth; in fact, it feels unrealistically stable, even downright boring.

Increasing the growth rate causes exactly what any parent would tell you to expect when you have more kids—chaos! It's not apparent right away; at first, increasing the growth rate from 2 just increases the stable population size. Instead of leveling off at half the maximum, it gets closer to 75 percent of the maximum. This all seems fairly intuitive relative to the models we considered earlier; small, smooth changes in the growth rate lead to small, smooth changes in the stable population size. But then something less intuitive happens when the growth rate gets around 3; now, instead of a single stable population size, there are two, and the population oscillates between the two every other time step. Okay, so that's a little weird, but hardly what you would describe as chaotic.

Let's increase the growth rate a little more. As we do, we see that those two stable points become four, and then eight. At this point, it may be hard to imagine what such a population would look like, with a size that oscillates between eight different values. Keep in mind that this is a particular population growth model with certain assumptions, like a constant growth rate and changes that occur at discrete time intervals. It is probably best understood as a model for the observed population size, if you took a census periodically over a long period of time, as opposed to a model that describes the exact mechanics of how the population size will change over time.

Eight stable points, while odd, are still a far cry from what anyone might describe as chaotic. There's still a very predictable pattern to the population size. Further, you might expect that if we increase the growth rate, we will go from eight to sixteen stable points, then thirty-two, then sixty-four, and so on. One might imagine that there will eventually be such a large number of stable points that it will look like there is no pattern, but if you waited around long enough you'd see it repeat.

Those are perfectly reasonable expectations, given what we've seen so far, but they are incorrect. After sixteen stable points, we start to observe what is called sensitivity to initial conditions. Now, the population size takes on different values with each iteration, without any discernible pattern of repetition or oscillation. Further, the exact values it takes depend very strongly on the starting size of the population. When the growth rate was lower such that the population size eventually settled into stable values, those values were determined only by the growth rate itself; no matter where you started you'd eventually get to the same point(s). Not so for a growth rate of 3.5; at that point, the starting population size also becomes important. Interestingly, if you continue to increase the growth rate, you will get back to a situation where there are small set of stable points, even as few as three. But increasing the growth rate still a little more and you'll be right back in a situation where there is no stability.

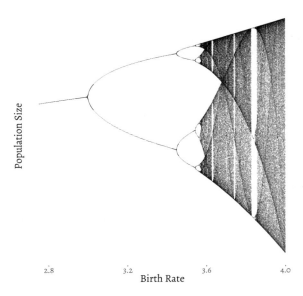

Figure 3.1: Each point on this plot represents the population size (vertical scale) at one unspecified time point for a given growth rate (horizontal axis). For some growth rates, there is only one point because the population stays that size constantly; two points indicate oscillation between two sizes; and so on.

This behavior is summarized in the plot shown in Figure 3.1. Different growth rates are represented on the horizontal axis. The population behavior is summarized along the vertical axis. When only one point is plotted for a given growth rate, the population remains stably at that size. When two points are plotted for a given growth rate, the population oscillates between those two sizes. When there are many points for a given growth rate, the population moves around among those sizes in no particular order, never repeating the same size twice.

That kind of instability, the sensitivity to initial conditions, led mathematicians to call this sort of mathematics chaos theory. Indeed, how else would you describe a system that appears to have no rhyme or reason to its behavior? It would be as if you threw that ball just a little harder than last time and it went sailing hundreds of yards farther; even if you were trying to reproduce how you had thrown it before, if you weren't exactly precise you could still wind up launching your ball onto the roof of the neighbor five houses down. If everything in the world worked that way, not only would no one ever be able to play sports, it would seem nearly impossible to get anything done at all.

Fortunately, there are plenty of systems with behavior that is much more regular and predictable. But even more fortunately for our purposes, the story of chaos theory does not end with the logistic map. Having found one mathematical model with this curious and unexpected property of sensitivity to initial conditions, we can look for others. Once we know what to look for, many other equations will turn up with the same kind of sensitivity. Some of them also demonstrate another property, behavior that settles into patterns called strange attractors. These patterns aren't quite as regular and repeatable as the two- or four- or eight-point oscillations of the logistic map, but in their own way they are stable.

Let's look at one such system that shows a strange attractor: the Hénon map. One way to understand how the Hénon map works is to see what it does with a circle. If we take all the points in a circle and apply these equations to them once, we see that our circle has been rotated 90 degrees and stretched into a sort of U shape, or perhaps a boomerang-like shape. Applying the equations again rotates another 90 degrees and stretches the shape even more. Figure 3.2 illustrates these first few steps of the transformation. You can almost think of it as a very specific and proscribed method for stretching taffy or kneading bread dough.

*Figure 3.2: In two steps, the Hénon map transforms a circle
to a boomerang and then a sort of headless giraffe.*

Now pick a single one of the points from our circle and follow it through many iterations. As you might expect trying to follow a single speck of flour as you knead bread dough, it quickly becomes impossible to predict exactly where our point is going to be. But we can also see that point doesn't just go anywhere, either (Figure 3.3). There does seems to be an odd kind of orbit that it stays within. It's not exactly an orbit like the planets follow around the sun, partly because it isn't as regular a shape as that but mostly because the point we were following doesn't go from one place to the spot immediately next to it in a smooth path; instead, it jumps all around. Nevertheless, we can still see that there are places it will go and places it won't, and that it stays within a bounded region.

This tendency of certain dynamic systems to stay within certain bounds despite perturbations, or what might be seen as bumps in a predetermined road, helps me to think about grace. More precisely, I find it easier to believe that grace can coexist with God having a purpose or will for how the world turns out. The metaphor of a bump in the road, a little deviation from the expected before returning to the intended path, conveys a similar idea. At the same time, a road is static; these strange attractors are dynamic. The stability of the pattern emerges out of the dynamic activity of the system, not in contrast to it. Thus I find strange attractors a useful additional metaphor when thinking about grace.

The unusualness of the shape, and the fact that our point is jumping around instead of smoothly following a path, is what gives strange attractors the strange part of their name. We can see the attractor part if we give our point a nudge in between iterations of our equation. With our parabolas, if we had nudged the ball in flight, it would proceed on a new parabolic path. But here, our point very quickly returns

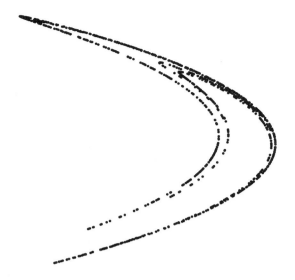

Figure 3.3: The trajectory for the bottommost point of the circle. Note that the points don't occur in any particular order, but the trajectory will stay within these contours. Many other points on the circle also wind up in these same contours.

to the same strange pattern it had been following before; it is attracted to that pattern. In fact, there is a very large region around that pattern that attracts points into the pattern. The exact places it will visit may differ because of the sensitivity to initial conditions, but it will still stay within the same pattern. Thinking in those terms, we can see that even our logistic map demonstrates a kind of strange attractor, it's just not as striking because it is in a single dimension. But for a fixed growth rate that exhibits chaotic behavior, the population size is still bounded within certain regions rather than ranging over all possible values.

3.4 There But for the Strange Attractor of God

What would this strange attractor phenomenon look like in a familiar physical system? In our ball-throwing example, no matter how hard we throw the ball, it will always wind up in our friend's hands, even if sometimes it bounces off the roof of the house five doors down along the way. Or if you throw a basketball in the general vicinity of the rim, it will eventually make its way through the hoop.

Alas, basketball hoops in reality are far less forgiving and thus we marvel at the few who can guide a ball through them consistently. The same strict requirements attend many physical activities; all the conditions must be just right to get a positive outcome. Our intuition for the more abstract trajectory of our lives is often similarly constrained. We have to go to the right college, so we can get the right job. We have to marry the one partner who completes us. Life becomes a series of make-or-break choices.

So what would a strange attractor look like as part of the trajectory of our lives? And if we desire God to be involved in that trajectory, what would a strange attractor look like as part of his will? When we thought everything behaved like parabolas, then it seemed as if either God had a plan and everything was following it, in which case there was little room for free will and little need for grace and mercy, or we as humans have free will, in which case we can sin and be in need of grace and mercy, but then God's plan seems to need so many contingencies and adjustments that it becomes hard to see it as a plan at all. Obviously lots of people have come up with different ways to reconcile these various ideas, but the one that makes the most sense to me is to think of God's plan as being something like a strange attractor.

Consider what happens when we think of God's will in strange attractor terms. On the one hand, it is absolutely a well-defined, prespecified plan. The behavior that led to strange attractors was completely defined by our equations; we didn't have to make adjustments as we went. And yet on the other hand, there is room for free choice in the system as well. We can get off the pattern, and eventually events will come back to that pattern. There are still consequences to that choice, in that the exact spots within the pattern that get visited will change, but overall the system stays in the attractor.

Now perhaps a system that returns to an attractor still doesn't seem like freedom to you, if it is not possible to stay outside the pattern. I can understand that, and so I think it's probably most helpful to apply the strange attractor analogy to the state of the entire world. You can make individual choices for your own life, including whether you want to choose axioms for your life that allow for the God of the Bible or not. Those choices have real consequences for how future events play out. But the world itself will continue on in the same overall contours it was always following.

Let's see if this perspective helps us to understand the story in Exodus any better. We saw God asserting his sovereignty over the world and claiming responsibility for how events play out; our model is consistent with this idea. We saw Moses choose to decline the commission to speak to Pharaoh on his own; our model affirms that this is genuinely a choice on Moses' part and allows for such choices. That makes it easier to understand God's anger at Moses' choice, since it is something Moses has genuinely chosen without God having always intended for Moses to act thusly; our model indicates that Moses' choice will have real consequences, which may be suboptimal for Moses and/or other people in Moses' sphere of influence, and thus represent a true sin which would displease God. One of those consequences is that Aaron will accompany Moses to lead the Israelites out of exile, and it is Aaron who will later facilitate the worship of the golden calf in place of God while Moses communes with God on his own. If Aaron hadn't been Moses' spokesperson, perhaps he would not have later been seen as having the authority to condone the forging of the calf. Finally, we know that the nation of Israel was freed from its exile in Egypt; our model proposes that outcomes such as this will be resilient to individual choices.

Further, I think this strange attractor notion is reflected in other passages of the Bible. In Genesis, Abraham encounters someone named Melchizedek who is described as a priest of God, despite the fact that the priesthood as it is usually understood was not instituted until later and despite the fact that Abraham is the father of God's chosen nation of Israel. I think it is easiest to understand Melchizedek if we think in terms of an attractor that allows for multiple starting points feeding into the same path.

In Numbers, we see the Israelites who left Egypt arrive at the Jordan River across from the land of Canaan. We are told that it is God's plan for them to live in Canaan, and yet they choose not to cross the river. The strange attractor model affirms this as a genuine choice, with the consequence that the Israelites wander in the wilderness for forty years and the generation of adults that chose not to cross the river don't live to return to Canaan. And yet, their descendants do return, cross the river, and wind up living in Canaan, just as God's plan indicated.

In Esther, the Jewish people, a subset of the original nation of Israel, are now subjects of the Persian empire facing another existential crisis. Really the entire history of Israel and its remarkable longevity in the face of multiple such crises seems to me to be best understood in terms of consequences of genuine choices within the context of a broader plan. In this particular crisis, a faction within the Persian court has conspired to have all the Jews killed. Esther, a Jew herself and a member of the harem of the Persian emperor, sees an opportunity to spare her people, albeit with some risk that she will fail and be killed with them. She seeks the advice of her uncle Mordecai, who tells her that "If you keep quiet at this time, liberation and protection for the Jews will appear from another source" (Esther 4:14). It's not hard for me to imagine Mordecai speaking of strange attractors, had he known the math.

Finally, in the Gospels, even Jesus seems to affirm the idea that individual choices do not negate God's plan. When Jesus enters the city of Jerusalem on what we now celebrate as Palm Sunday, he is met by cheering throngs. Some of his critics find this display of enthusiasm indecorous (or worse) and suggest it be wrapped up. Jesus informs them that if his followers were to keep silent, then the very stones would cry out to celebrate his arrival. One way or another, this party is happening.

And later that week, on the eve of his death, Jesus appears to contemplate the possibility of alternatives that don't involve crucifixion. This is a very challenging idea, but it is in the Bible and so if we are taking the Bible seriously we have to take it seriously as well. To me, it makes the most sense if Jesus genuinely has a choice in that moment, rather than perpetuating the illusion of choice for our benefit. And if Jesus is wondering whether there is an alternative, then it would seem that he must be comfortable with the idea that there is more than one way to achieve a given goal. How could Jesus consider the idea of an alternative if he knows that God's plan is as fixed as a parabola?

Such a balance of freedom to choose among alternatives and an overall sense of direction is also how *X-Factor* resolves its central thematic question. Layla Miller eventually accepts that absolute control of the future is not worth the sacrifices it demands of herself and her friends. In doing so, she discovers that there are multiple ways to achieve what is really important to her, most dramatically in an issue (#240) shortly after the one in which Rahne Sinclair found grace. And Jamie Madrox grows into a more decisive leader by realizing that even though he is his own multitude, the advice and the needs of his peers can provide some helpful points of orientation, getting him out of his own head. Thanks to the genre-shifting nature of the book, these lessons in grace allow the team to overcome not just the malicious choices of some bad actors but also spiritual forces of genuine evil.

In the last chapter, I said that what happens in this world is a mixture of what God intends and what creation intends apart from God, so that we might appreciate the distinction. I believe this strange attractor model of God's sovereignty and God's grace allows that statement to be coherent. Creation has the genuine freedom to choose other than God's will. At the same time, the system will tend toward those ends that God desires to see. That does not imply God is indifferent to our choices, allowing those ends to justify whatever means are used to reach them. Rather, God has the means to bring all things to a redemptive end regardless of how grieved he is by our choices.

A gracious universe is also a universe in which life is possible. Life is dynamic; every change holds the potential to make things worse instead of better. A universe that can recover from missteps, an organism that can tolerate error, those are systems that can persist, remaining coherent over time. Our hearts may be one such system. Muscle cells must contract in concert with each other to create a steady beat; nerve cells must fire all together to coordinate those contractions. Yet sometimes a few may go astray, firing just a hair ahead of or behind the rhythm. Nevertheless, the beat persists; those tiny deviations aren't amplified, they are absorbed by a system that tends toward consistency.

We can practice such grace in our own lives as well. Rather than making plans that require everything to go perfectly, we can expect and allow for disruptions. We can especially prepare for our fellow humans to make their own choices and perhaps even their own mistakes. We'll return to some more specific principles on how to accomplish that later on. To get there, first we'll take a look at Jesus, in whom was embodied God and all of the abstract qualities of his we've discussed. For that conversation, we'll use the language of physics, a scientific discipline where the precision and abstract beauty of mathematics has to deal with the reality of the physical world.

PART II

The Language of Physics

CHAPTER 4

The Kamala Khan Conundrum

Kamala Khan feels pulled in several directions. So much so that when she manifests a superpower, it's the ability to stretch and reshape her body at will.

Khan is a Pakistani-American teenager; she and her siblings are the first generation in her family born in the United States. Her family's traditions and practices differ from her classmates' both because of their Pakistani culture and their Islamic faith. The contrasts are hard to hide. She dresses differently, she eats different food, her familial conversations are peppered with Arabic and Urdu. She's not looking to abandon her heritage, but she is in that liminal phase of deciding who she will be as an independent adult.

And that's before she becomes a superhero, adding a whole additional layer of complexity to her life. She feels the burden of responsibility to use her extraordinary power for good. She worries what would happen if her friends or her family discover she is even more set apart from either of them than they already think. So she has to figure out how to protect them from the dangers that invariably crop up when one is a superhero while not revealing to them who she is becoming.

That's not to say her powers are purely a burden. Controlling her body's shape and size allows her to drastically change her appearance. At certain moments, this allows her to obscure her identity or even pass for someone else. Yet she explicitly rejects the possibility of fully exploiting her potential to reinvent herself permanently. For example, she chooses a costume that reflects her religious concern for modesty rather than one that creates more distance between her superhero and civilian identities.

4.1 Me, Myself, and I

Kamala Khan's adventures are featured in *Ms. Marvel* by G. Willow Wilson, Adrian Alphona, Ian Herring, et al. It's a relatively recent title from Marvel Comics and Khan is one of the more successful examples of a modern character integrating into an existing superhero universe crowded with characters established two or three decades ago. She's also the latest update of the Spider-Man archetype, the teenager next door just trying to be accepted as normal by her peers while adjusting to abilities that are anything but. And her concerns about maintaining multiple identities go all the way back to the earliest superheroes like Superman.

Superman is both the last son of Krypton and a son of Smallville, Kansas, trying to maintain his life as a newspaper reporter and his role as a superpowered protector of truth, justice, and the American way. How many times have Superman and Clark Kent had to be in the same place at the same time, requiring him to appear as one, make an excuse, dash off and change clothes at superspeed, then return in the other guise, wondering aloud "Oh, was Clark Kent just here? I'm sorry I missed him." Princess Diana must turn her back on Themysciran traditions of isolation because she feels responsible for protecting the entire world as Wonder Woman. The Black Widow has worried that her past as a Soviet spy will undermine her heroism with the Avengers. Peter Parker felt such stress about his superhero identity impacting on the lives of family and friends that at one point he thought the only way to cope was to walk away from it all and be Spider-Man no more. Kamala Khan resorted to making mindless copies of herself from magic clay so she could pretend that she was in more than one place at a time.

In our personal experiences, we might think about our identity as a spouse or a parent, and contrast that with our identity as a member of the workforce. We talk about them as if there is a tension between the two, that the primary dynamic is one of conflict. Younger people might express a tension between their identity as a student and their social identity. We ask questions about balance, about whether we can have it all.

If these stories and descriptions reflect how we think about the multiple aspects of our lives, how can we possibly conceive of Jesus maintaining both human and divine natures? And yet this is how Christians understand Jesus, that he is God incarnated in human flesh. As we discussed in the first chapter, part of the purpose of this incarnation is so that we can know God better by interacting with him the way we interact with each other. But while we can say that Jesus was both God and human, it can be challenging to conceive of how that might actually work. After all, much of how we talk about God is in contrast to humans.

In the last chapter, we encountered human free will and God's sovereignty, two concepts traditionally presented as incompatible. We also explored an alternative model that allowed us to describe those concepts in a way that doesn't require one to be defined as the opposite of the other. I believe we can accomplish something similar to reconcile Jesus' divine and human natures, this time by moving into the realm of physics. While physics relies heavily on mathematics, it also deals with tangible reality that we can experience with our senses instead of relying primarily on our minds. Likewise, for the Christian, Jesus is God made a tangible reality whom some experienced with their senses in the past, and whom we all may have a chance to experience with our senses in the future.

4.2 It's a Wave! It's a Particle! It's . . . a Photon!

While Jesus was on Earth, he described himself as "the light of the world" (John 8:12). Fitting, then, that we should examine different properties of light in order to understand Jesus better. Now, I wouldn't go so far as to claim to know for certain that Jesus intended all of the interpretation we're about to explore as some sort of secret coded message waiting for science to catch up so the full meaning could be revealed. Jesus was primarily communicating to the people actually listening to him at the time, and his intended meaning should be understood in that context above all others. At the same time, I find our present understanding of light provides a helpful conceptual framework for further exploring what Jesus was like.

In particular, we will look at how light informs our understanding of quantum mechanics. I know quantum mechanics has a reputation for being weird, scary, and complicated. Nevertheless, I'm confident that even if it took geniuses to come up with the theory, you don't have to be a genius to understand some of the core ideas. Simultaneously, I would also reassure you that even the great geniuses who spend their entire lives studying quantum mechanics don't fully agree on how to interpret some of the implications. In other words, I think you can get this, but you also shouldn't feel bad if it all doesn't click right away.

Just as we are trying to understand the nature of Jesus, we're trying to answer the question "what is the nature of light?" Light plays a central role in scientific observation, since detecting light is one of our senses and one we often rely heavily on. After all, seeing is believing.

Specific to science, light brings us information from distant galaxies, allowing us to study the physics of the universe on the largest scales. That light is often faint because it spreads out as it travels and it has traveled far to get to our eyes. If we can collect that light from a larger area and focus it, we can see further and clearer. And so developed the science of optics, the study of how light is reflected by mirrors, refracted by prisms, focused by lenses, etc. Better lenses and mirrors make better telescopes, and also better microscopes, since lenses that collect and focus light can also be used to magnify images. With improved telescopes and microscopes, we can explore the frontiers of the infinite and the infinitesimal.

How do mirrors and lenses work? If we imagine light as a stream of particles, basically tiny little balls, then mirror reflection seems fairly natural. The same math that describes how billiard balls bounce off the rails of the table could describe how light reflects off of a mirror. This stream-of-tiny-balls model also explains observations like the sharp, distinct boundaries of shadows.

Lenses on the other hand do not lend themselves as readily to an explanation in terms of billiard balls. In order for glass to be transparent, it has to let those balls pass through. But the most straightforward explanation for why the path of those balls would deviate from a straight line is if they were bouncing off of something.

Waves provide a different metaphor for light that can explain lens behavior. The ocean provides ample opportunities to experience waves, but the way ocean waves behave is a combination of several influences. In physics, it is helpful to study these influences in isolation first, just like when we were launching Mark Watney and we considered rocket thrust before adding gravity. A more helpful starting picture might be the ripples created by a tossed stone into an otherwise placid lake.

The first feature to appreciate about these ripples is that the ripples travel laterally but the water effectively does not. The water does move; the stone displaces some water, which needs to go somewhere and so pushes into the water around it creating a small surge upward. But then the stone falls and the water can return to its original spot, more or less. Meanwhile, the water surrounding it got pushed, so it surges into the water further out from it, but again only temporarily before flowing back to where it started. This surge-and-recede dynamic perpetuates so that the observable ripples travel but the water—and anything floating on the water—stays put. Alternatively, the energy of the stone throw is being transmitted through the water.

If there is an islet in our lake, the ripples will be refracted around the island. The changing depth of the water explains this change in the path of the wave. The phase speed of the wave, or how fast the crest moves, is influenced by how deep the water is because that influences how much water has to surge and recede to make a ripple. The amount of energy being transmitted cannot change, however, since it all came from the initial stone toss. In order to keep everything balanced, the frequency of the wave stays the same and so the wavelength changes; the path of the wave must also change in order to accommodate the new wavelength. Water immediately around an islet is shallower than water further out, causing the wavelength to change and the waves to bend around the islet. Water near the ocean shore is also shallower, which is why ocean waves tend to arrive at the shore at an angle rather than straight on.

For light and lenses, the chemistry of the glass and the air is the equivalent of the depth of the water. The path of the wave depends on the material; transmission through different materials results in different paths. By adjusting the thickness of the lens and the shape where it meets the air, one can arrange for all of those paths to meet at a specific point, the focal point of the lens. This is what happens in *Raiders of the Lost Ark* when the headpiece of the staff of Ra focuses diffuse sun beams on a specific map location. A wave model provides a convenient explanation for how light interacts with lenses.

A stream-of-tiny-balls model is still a more convenient explanation for how light interacts with mirrors, though. And yet both mirrors and lenses work very well, as continual improvements in telescope and microscope technology demonstrate. And so we have one of the great questions in physics: is light made of particles or waves?

Here's where the nerdiness of science, the ability to imagine different possible worlds and the consequences of their differences, comes into play. We can think about what a world with light waves would look like and what a world with light particles would look like and then design experiments that will have different outcomes depending on which version of the world we actually live in. One of these experiments is called the double-slit experiment, and you can do it in your own home.

Understanding this experiment involves another property of waves called interference. When we say that waves interfere with each other, we mean that two waves overlapping in space will reinforce each other in the places that they both go up or both go down, and cancel each other out in the places where one goes up and the other goes down. You can see this in our pond ripples if we toss two stones; where their waves meet we either get an extra high ripple or no ripple at all. In our surge-and-recede description, if water is surging from both waves in the same location, there is twice as much water coming together and creating a higher peak, but if water is surging into a spot from one wave while it is receding from that spot due to the other wave, the net effect is calm. Figure 4.1 demonstrates the result of two waves interfering to reinforce each other and cancel each other out at different points.

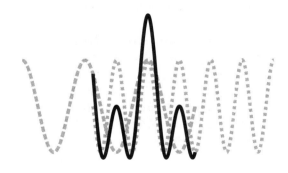

Figure 4.1: Two waves (gray) overlapping to create a third wave (black) that is twice as intense where the peaks of the two waves coincide and null where the peak of one wave coincides with the trough of another.

The double-slit experiment involves shining a focused beam of light through two narrow slits very close together and looking at the resulting pattern of light. If a beam of light is really a stream of little particles, the result should just be two lines of light made up of many tiny dots. Imagine pouring sand through two slits; the sand will just pile up underneath the slits in two lines. You can try it with sand to see what the particle result will look like, and you can try it with water to see what the wave result will look like; these are called controls in science because you have control of the outcome by virtue of knowing the properties of the materials in advance.

You can also try the experiment with a laser pointer to see how it turns out for light. An Internet search for a DIY double-slit experiment will get you some demonstration videos. (Go ahead; I'll wait.) Did you see two lines of light?

If you get the laser and the slits set up properly, what you should see is not two lines at all, but instead a whole pattern of bright and dim regions. This observed pattern is consistent and reproducible. A good model for explaining this pattern is to imagine two waves interfering with each other. The bright spots in the pattern are the places where two waves are reinforcing each other, and the dark spots are where they cancel out (see simulated results in Figure 4.2).

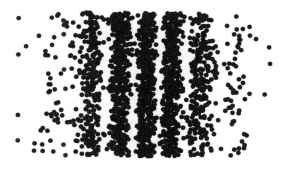

Figure 4.2: Results of a simulated double slit experiment. Each point is a detected photon; the relatively empty vertical spaces are places where interference results in very low probability of detection.

A wave model of light is also supported by the mathematical equations we use to understand how properties of light relate to each other and to other quantities we can measure. We currently understand light as a form of electromagnetic radiation, or what gets radiated when matter interacts via electrical or magnetic forces. The electromagnetic radiation equations are differential equations. Solutions to these equations are not numbers but whole other equations which will themselves have numeric solutions we can plot like we've done before with

Martian potato consumption and rockets. There are multiple solutions to these differential equations, corresponding to different combinations of electrical charges and magnetic poles. Some combinations produce equations for a standing wave where fluctuations in the electric field propagate in one direction and fluctuations in the magnetic field propagate in the same direction in such a way that the electric field induces the magnetic field, which induces the electric field, and so on indefinitely. These wave equations correspond well to the behavior of light, providing a theoretical basis for the observations of wave-like behavior we saw in our experiment.

Is there a reason to think light can't be both, like maybe a stream of particles traveling in a wave? Yes, because those concepts typically operate at different levels of organization. Particles are individual units, whereas a wave is a specific way of organizing many individual units. How can light simultaneously be the constituent pieces and the organized whole?

How can Clark Kent be Superman, when Clark Kent is so mild mannered and so uncoordinated that he can barely operate a revolving door? How can Peter Parker keep his friends and family safe when being Spider-Man involves so much danger? How can Kamala Khan push boundaries with her American teenager-rebel peers when respecting those boundaries is central to her religious faith?

Recall that in our pond wave, the water did not travel, just the pattern or the energy. Another way to visualize how a wave is a pattern apart from what it is organizing is to take a garden hose and move it up and down while water flows out. The stream of water appears to go up and down like a sine wave. It might be tempting to think that the individual water molecules are following a path shaped like that wave, and some clever videos with strobe lights really reinforce this perception. But after a little consideration, hopefully you can see that there is no force that would make the molecules turn upwards at the trough of the wave.

Each individual molecule in our water wave follows a parabolic(!) path from wherever it left the hose nozzle down to the ground, always falling, never rising. The wave we observe is not described or defined by the behavior of any individual water molecule. In fact, it would be impossible to get that kind of wave with just a single water molecule; if it were possible to watch that lone molecule, we would see it taking a parabolic path with no hint of waviness. Thus, we can only have a wave if we have a whole set of water molecules. We call the water molecules the medium in which the wave is traveling, or which the wave is organizing.

Which brings us to another big question about the nature of light: if light is the wave, what is the medium? We basically invented a concept named 'luminiferous æther' to be the medium that light organizes, then set out to find experimental evidence of it. The most rigorous such experiment sent light away from a source in two different directions, one with the movement of the Earth around the sun and one perpendicular to that movement. The light beams were then routed to meet back up. One of those beams was expected to travel faster than the other because of their relative orientation with respect to æther. The beams would then interfere because they wouldn't match up perfectly, and the specific interference pattern might tell us something about the æther. In fact, the beams overlapped perfectly, much to everyone's surprise, apparently indicating that there was no æther. What kind of wave doesn't need a medium?

Just when you thought things couldn't get stranger, we have one more experiment to discuss. The original version was a bit more sophisticated, but you can do this one at home too. The basic idea is to charge a soda can with static electricity, just like you might a balloon that you wanted to stick to the wall. You can use a paperclip and some tinsel attached to the can to gauge the charge status of the can. When it is charged it has surplus electrons and a net negative charge; this will cause the bits of tinsel to repel each other. The same phenomenon makes your hair stand on end when you have too much static; the individual hairs are negatively charged and are trying to get as far away from each other as possible. You can relieve the charge by grounding the can with your hand. Or you can get more creative.

Imagine a beam of light dislodging those extra electrons, returning the can to a neutral state and allowing the tinsel to relax. The electrons will require a certain minimum energy to knock them loose. If light is a wave, then the amount of energy it contains will be related to how intense the light is; a brighter light would have more energy. Thus knocking the electrons loose should just be a matter of getting a sufficiently bright light. And yet, if you get a regular flashlight and shine it on the can, the tinsel will remain repulsive, no matter how bright it is. However, an ultraviolet light will work just fine.

How do we explain this observation? The best explanation we have is that in addition to the wave properties that light clearly has, it still has the property of coming in discrete units, just as particles do. The quantum of quantum physics refers to this discreteness, and the individual units are called quanta. Those discrete quanta can only have a specific amount of energy related to their wavelength, which is why UV light works and white light does not; it has a shorter wavelength and thus higher energy. A brighter, more intense white light emits more of these discrete units, but each individual unit doesn't have enough energy to knock loose an electron.

4.3 Stop! You're Both Right!

It's been roughly a century since the most recent of all these experiments was first conducted, and in all that time the most widely accepted explanation is that the nature of light encompasses both wave properties and particle properties. We can't deny the interference patterns that light creates with itself, and we can't get around the discrete or quantum behavior of light. Instead, the best way to resolve what appears to be a contradiction is to instead embrace it, and realize that our metaphors of tiny balls and water waves were both inadequate or incomplete when it comes to describing light.

On the particle side, we have realized that there are other ways to get discrete behavior. Discrete entities on the subatomic level have a reality, just a different one than discrete entities on our human scale experience. On the wave side, we have found a model that can allow a wave to exist without a medium after all. It turns out that certain properties of light, and indeed of all subatomic entities, have a probability distribution, which is defined by a wave; these waves interfere with each other and change the probability of where a photon will show up in our slit experiment, for example. Ultimately, we've found a feature of reality that requires us to invent a new concept and create (or really coopt) a name for it.

Superhero fiction takes a similar approach to resolving its questions of dual identity. Rather than relieving the tension among the facets of their lives, many heroes redefine their roles around an integrated concept of themselves. Some come to that place early on. The Fantastic Four lived publicly as superhero celebrities basically from their origin story onwards; when the world doesn't need saving, they are using their powers, their minds, and their resources to make material improvements in the world as innovators and entrepreneurs. Jessica Drew, a hero known as Spider-Woman, tried giving up superheroing to have a baby, only to realize her child provided extra motivation to save the world. It helps these heroes found careers that complement their costumed exploits, or perhaps chose them as part of creating a coherent self. Similarly, Barry Allen upholds law and order as the Flash and as a forensic scientist for the police department and Carol Danvers bridges existing military command structures and superhero teams as an Air Force colonel and Captain Marvel.

Two of my favorite superhero stories take an even deeper look at the process of self-integration with rich, multi-faceted characters. David Haller is the son of X-Men founder Professor X, and he came into his own in the pages of *X-Men Legacy* by Simon Spurrier, Tan Eng Huat, Craig Yeung, et al. David is written as having dissociative identity disorder; each identity has its own superpower. As the story begins, David has them imprisoned in his mind and hauls them out of their cells when he needs to exploit a given ability. Over the course of a world-saving adventure, he realizes the value of employing grace to allow the various parts of himself to integrate organically. Whether that is a viable model for dealing with a genuine mental health concern, I cannot say, but I found it a moving portrait of how to deal constructively with the multitudes we all contain.

The other character is Multiple Man Jamie Madrox, the private investigator with the surplus of perspectives whom we already met in chapter 3. To get through the cases and crises, he has to learn to accept that he is somehow the sum of all of his disparate parts. Both David and Jamie go through a process of redefinition. They began with the categories they inherited from their families and from their peers in the superhero community. Reaching the limits of those categories was challenging at first, suggesting a problem with themselves. Over time, each discovers that the real problem is with the categories.

Kamala Khan is on a similar journey. As I'm writing this, she is still very much in the midst of it. Already there is evidence of progress and success. For example, she has discovered that her relationship with her parents is flexible enough to accommodate her powers and her desire to use them responsibly, rather than requiring her to be limited in ways that would prevent her from thriving. In that sense, it was her own understanding of the category of her parents' daughter that was inadequate, rather than the category itself.

Still, these are all stories, and fiction isn't always constrained by the same rules as reality. Integration and unification of identity are clearly the goal for understanding the nature of Jesus, but are those goals plausible? Just as we looked at various experiments that revealed properties of light, we'll need to look at the data we have for Jesus from the Bible.

The first thing that I notice is that the observations we have of Jesus are equally as challenging to reconcile. I find the story of the resurrection of Lazarus to be particularly illustrative here. Lazarus and his sisters Martha and Mary are described as close friends of Jesus. At one point, Lazarus falls ill, so his sisters send for Jesus, who had healed a number of other people throughout his ministry. The messengers reach him and appeal to his humanity, imploring him to have compassion on his friend. The response they get is unexpected; Jesus agrees to come, after taking care of some other unspecified business. He indicates that there is a plan in place that will maximize God's glory. When he finally arrives, Lazarus has already died; the narrative leaves little doubt that if Jesus had come right away, he would have found Lazarus alive.

Understandably, the emotions in that situation are intense. And yet, through their inner turmoil Lazarus' sisters recognize that Jesus might still have the power to to help their brother. They seem to be appealing to his divine nature, to exercise authority over life and death in a way that no human being would be capable of. And the immediate response they get is the shortest, and one of the most famous, verses in the Bible: "Jesus wept" (John 11:35). This is a very human, emotional reaction to the situation, when what was sought was a display of power. The Gospel of John does record that Jesus ultimately brings Lazarus back from the dead, apparently confirming his divine nature, but not without complicating our ability to understand what that means.

Or does it? Maybe what Jesus is really showing us is that our understanding of humanity and divinity is flawed. That fits with our ultimate premise, that Jesus represents God's ultimate effort to model for us concepts that we would otherwise have been unlikely to arrive at, in order to facilitate communication between us and God. So let's see what else Jesus teaches us and how that relates to what it means to be man and God.

You've probably heard the famous Alexander Pope line, "To err is human; to forgive, divine." It comes up in Edgar Wright's fantastic meditation on addiction, *The World's End*, where it is offered as a defense of humanity's right to be left alone. It's quite affecting to hear it used as a rallying cry and an expression of the value of humankind.

And yet, Hebrews 4:15 asserts that Jesus was tempted in every way, and is consequently sympathetic to the challenges of being human, but nevertheless succeeded in remaining sinless, as we discussed last chapter. Does that make him somehow less human, or does he demonstrate human potential being maximally realized? It's also interesting that Jesus regularly forgave sins, while also observing that it is God's place to forgive sins. Thus it would seem Pope was at least half right, and yet even then Jesus uses the act of forgiveness to challenge preconceptions.

In *The Matrix* one of the characters asserts that "to deny our impulses is to deny the very thing that makes us human." Personally, that always struck me as overly reductive, but it is certainly one model of what it means to be human and express our humanity. And yet, when Jesus fasted for forty days in the desert and then was tempted to turn the stones to bread so that he could eat, he declined and noted that "man does not live on bread alone, but by every word that comes from the mouth of God" (Matthew 4:4). There are few impulses stronger and more basic than hunger and the desire to eat, and yet Jesus seems to think that hearing from God supersedes even that need. Even independent of the Bible and any theological notions, I think there is merit to the idea that part of what it means to be human is to have control over our physical impulses, rather than being driven by them above all else; after all, even a bacterium can respond to physical stimuli.

In some societies, our human identity is strongly associated with self-determination and the assertion of our rights. While not denying the importance of these things, the Bible offers a somewhat different picture. "Instead of being motivated by selfish ambition or vanity, each of you should, in humility, be moved to treat one another as more important than yourself. Each of you should be concerned not only about your own interests, but about the interests of others as well" (Philippians 2:3–4). Treating one another as more important than yourself is not exactly the message of today's vigorous individualism, but I'm comfortable pushing back a tad on that cultural facet. And the verse certainly still allows that you will need to give some consideration to your own interests. It's more a matter of how we weight different things, and which interests are given ultimate value.

Woody Allen has a joke about how he doesn't want to live on in the hearts of his fans; he wants to live on in his apartment. There is now a movement within science to see if we can make that dream a reality, extending our present existence far beyond the one hundred or so years that seem to be the current limit of a human life. Aging is seen as a curable disease and carrying on indefinitely as the natural condition of life. This claim about the nature and purpose of humanity is particularly intriguing to consider in light of Jesus. On the one hand, Jesus' own life illustrates a rather different priority. He intentionally forfeited his own life for the benefit of others, instead of seeking to extend it to the maximum possible. And yet, there is also a sense in which Jesus' entire mission was to make eternal life possible for everyone. In one act, he affirmed the desire for our existence to continue, and yet challenged us to consider the cost of how that will actually be realized.

Thus the life of Jesus regularly challenges many of our popular notions of what is significant or distinct about humanity. This is particularly remarkable considering that far fewer people dispute his humanity than dispute his divinity. If Jesus was just a human, we would not be surprised if he didn't line up with our understanding of God's nature. That he can make us reexamine how we think about our own nature is notable regardless of his relationship to the divine, although to my mind it speaks to the credibility of his claim to be both human and something more.

If we do allow that Jesus was also God, then he also calls into question how we think about divinity. Take the story of Thor as told in *Thor: God of Thunder* by Jason Aaron, Esad Ribic, Ron Garney, et al. Thor is the Norse god of thunder; to Marvel Comics, that meant he was a public domain character with extensive brand awareness whom they could import into their narrative universe. In their universe, he is the individual from Norse mythology, and also a hero in the present day as a colleague of Captain America, Iron Man, and company. His actual status as a deity is often treated ambiguously, and can vary from story to story. For example, in the recent films Thor is essentially an alien from a society with such advanced technology it looks like magic to us.

In *Thor: God of Thunder*, he is explicitly a god and that status is based on the fact that people pray to him. The more prayers, the more power he has. At the climax of the story, all of the other godlike characters of the Marvel Universe, from the various Greek, Roman, Norse and other historical pantheons as well as fictional pantheons of other planets, pray to Thor, giving him the strength to overcome his foe. The implication is that gods only have the power we give them; when we stop believing, they go away.

This believer-dependent definition of godhood is very different from the model of God offered in the Bible. God is not God because we pray to him; we pray to him because he is God. This point is perhaps most strongly illustrated in the same temptation story I mentioned earlier. The tempter offers Jesus great power and wealth, if Jesus will only worship the tempter. Jesus declines, noting that one is to worship God and God alone. The tempter seems to think he can become like God if he is worshipped by Jesus, but Jesus indicates that this is not how worship or divinity works.

Another model of divinity is summarized in the concept of "the Force" from the world of *Star Wars*. Yoda teaches Luke that the Force is in every thing in the universe, flowing through them and binding them together. This seems reminiscent of pantheism, the idea that God is the sum total of the universe rather than separate from it.

This is not the picture of God Jesus offers. He does not claim divinity by virtue of all things being divine or part of the divine. Instead, he claims a continuity of experience with a personal entity who is distinct from all the other people Jesus teaches; why else would they need to come to know God through Jesus if they were already part of God? To me, the most striking claim of this continuity comes when Jesus says "I tell you the solemn truth, before Abraham came into existence, I am!" (John 8:58). This hearkens back to the name God gave himself when taking to Moses, translated as "I AM THAT I AM," which as we noted speaks to the axiomatic nature of God. Jesus' words seem to indicate he experienced that moment, and that his existence is similarly self-evident.

4.4 Playing in the Waves

Having looked at how Jesus challenges our notions of humanity and divinity, I want to go back to the nature of light and see if it has anything else to offer metaphorically for our understanding of divinity. In comparing the complex nature of light to Jesus, I find it most natural to connect the quantum discreteness of light with the humanity of Jesus, and the waveness with his divinity. The discreteness is fairly straightforward; humans come in distinct units, and Jesus is likewise separate and separable from the rest of us. (Amusingly, just as with quanta of light but not with tiny balls, the resurrected Jesus has the ability to be observed one side of a classically impassable wall and then other.) Waveness is a bit richer and requires more unpacking.

For starters, wave mathematics has one very interesting property. Remember the interference patterns we talked about earlier? One consequence of waves interfering in that way is that adding two waves together yields one wave (Figure 4.1). And for our purposes, adding three waves together yields one wave.

This gives us a useful way of thinking about the triune, or trinitarian, nature of God. It's a difficult one to grasp; the analogies that are often used, such as a yolk, a white, and a shell being three parts that add up to a whole egg, don't really capture what is meant by the Trinity. God is not Voltron; in fact, the early church rejected such a compartmentalized view of the Trinity as a heresy. But with waves, we have three waves adding up to one of the same kind of thing, a wave. Going a little further, if you have the single wave, there are techniques to decompose it into multiple waves, but the solutions are not unique and require some assumptions about the nature of those multiple waves. This would seem to mirror our difficulty in identifying exactly how God as the Father, as Jesus, and as the Holy Spirit relates differently to us and to each other, or in our need to be explicitly told about the Trinity in the first place rather than just being able to figure it out for ourselves.

Another handy feature of waves is that you can reproduce them in a variety of media. For example, think of sound waves, which transmit energy just like our pond ripples via a surge-and-recede dynamic, only there isn't a surface where we can see peaks. In a studio somewhere, a singer sings a song by intermittently forcing air out of her lungs, which displaces air around her, and so on in sound waves. Those waves are recorded by sensing when air surges around the microphone and creates pressure. The recordings are mixed and stored as digital files, which you then play in your house and hear the voice of that singer singing the song.

It is more than likely that not a single air molecule from that studio was in your house when you heard the song. The wave in your house is not made of the same stuff, and yet in another sense it is exactly the same wave with the same properties of amplitudes, frequencies, etc. This gives us hope for the process of sanctification, whereby we are called to be like God. Jesus provides us a proof-of-concept example, that it is possible for human stuff to reproduce divine qualities. And yet, we do not become God; there is a continuity of experience that defines God of which we are not a part. Likewise, there is a continuity to the sound wave in the recording studio that does not extend to our house, allowing us to talk meaningfully about the two different waves.

The third useful thing about waves is that you can take advantage of the interference patterns to make better telescopes. You've perhaps seen pictures of the very large radio telescope dishes that are used to detect signals from deep space, such as the one featured in the James Bond film *Goldeneye*. (Radio waves are a form of electromagnetic radiation, just like light.) The general rule is that the bigger the telescope, the greater the resolving power, because that large area allows you to collect more light or radio waves and thus see more distant objects whose light has spread further apart in travel. Maybe you've also seen arrays of smaller dishes that move together, like the ones seen in the film *Contact* based on Carl Sagan's novel of the same name. You can use the interference patterns of waves observed by each of those smaller telescopes to infer the image that you could have seen with a single large telescope big enough to cover the area occupied by all the smaller ones.

This ability to make a big telescope out of many small ones is quite handy, since it can be much more expensive to build a single large telescope than the equivalent array of smaller ones. It also handily paints a picture of how we can work together to understand God. Rather than trying to be the big telescope and see everything for ourselves, we can instead compare notes, see where our theological signals reinforce each other and where they cancel each other out, and infer from that combination a better picture of God than any one of us could see on our own. This is not equivalent to a lowest common denominator approach with a final image that is simply whatever is common to all observers. The inference from the combined signals is instead a careful and rigorous reconciliation of data from telescopes that are tracking together to look at the same part of the sky. With that understanding, I think we can get an encouraging model of how we can work together in the enterprise of theology.

In particular, this telescope array model informs how I think science and theology can interact. If God authored both the Bible and the natural world, then both are sources of signals from God that we can receive. Scientists and theologians studying those signals should be able to bring them together to resolve a clearer picture of God than either group could assemble separately. Again, that process will require thoughtful care to reconcile the data, and will be more challenging without the benefit of well-defined mathematics and physics models like we have for combining telescope data. And we can't just settle for finding the minimal points of agreement; we have to interpret both signals within their own contexts and in relation to each other. Still, we have successful examples from the past, both from the Bible itself and from the history of the church, so there is reason to think this approach will continue to be fruitful.

I believe this describes the approach of John Polkinghorne, for example. In his book *Quantum Physics and Theology* in particular, he outlines how the process of science and the process of theology overlap in terms of methods. Highlighting these shared approaches and in fact simply drawing the connections allows for more fruitful dialogue and the possibility of cross-fertilization. Polkinghorne even describes how the history of exploring the nature of Jesus and the history of exploring the nature of light are similar. However, he draws the line at connecting the concepts of quantum physics and the concepts of theology.

I can understand Polkinghorne's reluctance to apply quantum physics beyond the realm of subatomic particles, even metaphorically. The concept of quantum woo was coined to describe applications and analogies physicists find most dubious. I wonder if a significant stumbling block is the fact that so many quantum physics phenomena are beyond regular experience and counterintuitive, so they are described and even named using metaphors to more familiar experiences. Folks then see a connection between that familiar phenomenon referenced by the metaphor and a topic they are interested in and make the further connection to quantum physics.

At the very least, I think I caught myself doing that. I kicked around possibly including an analogy to quantum entanglement and the way God entered into creation via Jesus. Then it occurred to me that what I was really thinking about was a more conventional sense of becoming intertwined or entangled, and the only connection to quantum physics was the use of entangling as a metaphor for the phenomenon where two particles can have a joint probability function describing their behavior. And so, in the spirit of comparing Polkinghorne's 'signal' with my own to see where they reinforce each other or cancel out, I opted to heed his advice and not wade too deeply into quantum physics. Instead, I stuck with waves and particles as my primary conceptual points of reference, which perhaps still goes beyond where Polkinghorne would, but that's all part of having multiple perspectives to reconcile and integrate.

Having reflected on the nature of Jesus as both God and man and determined that, as with light, we need to let Jesus define our categories rather than be restricted by inadequate ones, we can apply those categories to our own lives. If Jesus is the ultimate expression of what it means to be human, then it is reasonable to orient our lives so that we are following in his example. This also aligns with our notion that Jesus sought out the best version of us across the multiverse of all possibilities and is leading us on the path to that version. In the next chapter, we'll continue discussing the physics of light as we explore the challenges and benefits of orienting ourselves relative to Jesus.

CHAPTER 5

A Conspiracy of Chronometers

Ender Wiggin does not feel pulled in any direction, which presents its own sort of problem. How do you orient yourself when you can't even tell "up" from "down"?

Ender Wiggin is the central character of Orson Scott Card's *Ender's Game* and several follow-up novels, as well as a recent film adaptation. In the imaginable future, humanity is visited by organisms, dubbed Formics, from another planet and that first contact doesn't go so well. The scenario everyone dreads in *Arrival* comes to pass: an inability to communicate due to drastically different languages and conceptual frameworks ultimately leads to violence. The humans successfully defend their planet, but fear that they've only just repelled an expeditionary force and even that required considerable resources and some luck. What happens if the visitors return with a main battle group?

That's where Ender comes in. In the years following the near-invasion, humans of many nations have united behind the twin goals of upgrading their military technology and training a generation of strategic geniuses who can employ those weapons most effectively. There is a belief that old tactics won't measure up; new approaches, fresh eyes, and lateral thinking are the order of the day. So they are going to take children in their formative years and train them in the context of new technology and everything they know about their adversaries. This way the children have the freedom to form new strategies before their minds are too entrenched in traditional modes of thought.

5.1 From a Certain Point of View

The military training of these children even goes so far as to remove them from Earth and train them on orbital platforms in space. A central feature of this training is the Battle Room, a zero-gravity arena where squads play capture the flag against each other to hone whatever tactical edges they can find. Ender's potential as a Battle Room warrior is initially overlooked because he is insubordinate and unimposing. But c'mon, his name's in the title of the book, so he's bound to have some unappreciated skill that will carry the day.

Ender's most famous contribution to the Battle Room is an organizing principle: "The enemy's gate is down." Ender realized that even lateral thinking was too Earth-bound. It suggests a sideways approach to your goal within a coordinate system defined first by the up/down axis of gravity, then the forward/backward axis of movement relative to your goal. But in space, there is no strong gravitational asymmetry to orient along, so why not use your goal to define your primary axis?

This reorientation of the Battle Room helped his squad in several ways. Advancing toward their goal suddenly seems as natural as falling down. They now have a common reference system in an environment that did not readily offer one. The soldiers were freed from thinking about their movement in earthbound terms that created artificial restrictions irrelevant to space combat. By comparison, think about how the large ships in *Star Wars* or *Star Trek* often engage each other the way naval vessels would, as if there is still a plane in space that everything must move along like the one defined by the surface of the oceans.

By providing this new frame of reference, Ender acknowledges two realities. The first is that he and his classmates were being held back by rules that made sense on Earth but were incoherent in space. The second and more subtle one is that casting aside those rules for complete freedom wouldn't be an improvement. In order for his squad to work together, they would still need a framework in which to operate. When they found the old framework didn't match the new context, they didn't ditch rules altogether; they found ones that fit the new context.

A similar paradigm shift occurred in physics as a result of studying light. For centuries, space and time were considered fixed, which is to say that everyone measuring the dimensions of the same object would get the same sizes and everyone measuring the duration of an event would get the same time. All speeds on the other hand would be relative; how fast you observed an object moving would depend on how fast you yourself were moving. The only speed that everyone would measure the same is infinite speed. Whether infinite speed is physically possible is a separate question, but you can use the equations of motion from this model of physics to work out mathematically that infinite speeds are the only ones with this property.

Studying light, however, wound up challenging this conclusion. It's not that the calculations were being done incorrectly, but rather that the models and equations were built on assumptions (or axioms) that did not correspond to the reality of our world. First, it was observed that light has a finite speed. This was not immediately apparent; light travels so fast that over human scales, it might as well be instantaneous. It was only when we started studying the world on the scale of the solar system and the galaxy that we could start to observe the consequences of light traveling at finite speed. The electromagnetic equations that describe light as a wave confirm this conclusion, since a wave that is everywhere all at once is no wave at all.

By itself, a finite speed for light is not revolutionary. However, what we also observe is that the speed of light is measured the same by everyone, regardless of how fast they are moving. The experiments to study the æther that mediates light waves that we discussed last chapter were among these observations. In addition to failing to find evidence of æther, these experiments also failed to find any evidence that the speed of light depended on relative motion the way other speeds do. This was perhaps the most famous and most significant example of the value of negative results, of knowing with precision what we don't believe about the universe. If we don't believe that the speed of light depends on relative motion, then something else about our model of physics must be wrong as well.

Ultimately, the observation that the speed of light is both finite and fixed led to a new framework for understanding space, time and motion called special relativity. No, wait, come back! You survived the quantum physics chapter; you can handle this one as well. I know special relativity, along with its cousin general relativity, has a reputation for mental gnarliness rivaling that of quantum physics. This is at least partly because both theories are counterintuitive, being based on observations at scales far removed from daily experience. Quantum physics comes into play when things get very small, and as we noted earlier, special relativity was only developed once we started considering a galactic scope. But this is precisely why these theories are valuable to us for expanding our conceptual repertoire for thinking about God.

Likewise, moving Ender and his friends to space proved fruitful and necessary to understanding how to deal with the Formics. Expanding their conceptual horizons by learning to operate in a context other than the surface of Earth enabled them to conceive of tactics and strategies that would never have occurred to the greatest military minds of the previous generation. Ultimately, Ender's perspective shifted so drastically that he was able to entertain the possibility that the Formics weren't even the bloodthirsty enemy they seemed to be.

Broadening one's horizons and changing one's perspective have positive and negative associations. On the one hand, doing so can spark creativity or expand our capacity for empathy. On the other, there is a concern, at least in Christian circles, that one can go so broadly into a pluralistic experience as to wind up in pure relativism. And since special and general relativity have relativity in their names and spread in popular awareness around the same time as postmodernism, I can see where those topics in physics might make some Christians uneasy, especially when applying them via analogy.

While special relativity predicts that the outcome of certain measurements will depend on the context of the measuring, it is also a theory with absolutes. We are not giving up a more absolute model for a more relative one, we are simply changing which quantities are absolute and which are relative. And we are doing so because the model better reflects the reality in which we live, which provides an absolute point of reference of a different sort. At the same time, we also cannot completely escape relative motion. It is a part of everyday experience that is consistently modeled in special relativity and the theories that preceded it.

5.2 Highway Speedometry

Although we've demonstrated the merits of going to space for a new point of view, let's come back to Earth for a bit to deal with some familiar examples of relative motion. Nearly all of us have had the experience of driving on a highway and being passed by another car going in the same direction. Let's say that I am driving 55 miles per hour and you are in the next lane going 60 miles per hour (mph). Clearly you are going to pass me. But you won't look like you are passing me at 60 mph; you will look like you are passing me at a leisurely 5 mph. Yet your speedometer will clearly read 60 mph. This discrepancy between my observation and your speedometer isn't just a trick of faulty human perception. Any measurements made of your speed from my car, using a radar gun or a stop watch and a ruler or any other scheme, will give a result of 5 mph.

Both measurements of your speed are correct. We just have to understand that these measurements were made relative to different frames of reference. I measured relative to my car, which is itself moving. The speedometer of your car is essentially making its measurement with respect to the road.

(We might prefer to say that your speedometer is actually measuring how fast the road is moving relative to your car, rather than the other way around. Although really the speedometer is just measuring the speed at which the wheels are turning and using the circumference of the tires to express that speed in terms of distance instead of revolutions. This is why your speedometer would be inaccurate if you put different rims on your car with a significantly different diameter than the stock rims. But for our purposes, it is reasonable enough to say that the speedometer is measuring speed with respect to the road; feel free to substitute a stationary police officer with a radar gun for your speedometer if that provides a clearer picture of which speed is being measured relative to what.)

Okay, so measuring speed is a little trickier than it first seems, but maybe that's just a practical issue of having to use wheel rotations or backseat rulers. Fair enough, but consider that even the direction of movement is relative. Let's say that in my car I was driving 55 mph east. After you've passed me, what do I look like to you? To you, I am traveling 5 mph . . . west. I am sure you would acknowledge that I am in the eastbound lane, but from your perspective I am moving away from your car in a westerly direction. What else can you conclude but that I am moving west?

Perhaps we can salvage what appears to be a trip straight into total relativism by choosing a particular reference frame as being more correct in some way. We mentioned measuring our speed with respect to the road; the road isn't moving, so surely that's a more objective frame of reference from which to start. That would make a lot of sense, except that the road isn't moving only with respect to the surface of the Earth. However, the Earth is spinning on its axis and it is traveling around the sun. That means the road is moving too.

And it gets worse. The sun is moving as well. It, along with all the other stars in the Milky Way, orbit around the center of the galaxy. And the galaxies themselves move. Worst of all, space itself is expanding, making it truly difficult to establish a point of absolute rest from which to measure the real speeds and directions of all movement.

So it looks like we are stuck with the idea that motion is indeed relative. This means that there is no way to distinguish between the measurements made with respect to my car and the measurements made by your speedometer to decide which one has measured the "true" speed of your car—both measurements are correct and neither is privileged. And remember, this relativity of motion is not a consequence of special relativity; it has been a part of our physics models for centuries.

It is easy to see how one could draw an analogy from relative motion or the relativity of measurements to moral relativism. Like measurements of speed, we can see how moral judgments are made from specific contexts and perspectives and need to be understood as such. The circumstances of the Formic incursion are used to justify exposing children to stressful and horrifying training scenarios in *Ender's Game*. Examples from history are especially easy to come up with, not least because our forebears are not here to contradict us. We can point to child labor or disenfranchisement of various populations or any number of other past practices which were either justified on moral grounds or at the very least weren't prohibited for being immoral, and which today we would describe as immoral. Or at least those of us who live in Western societies that have outlawed child labor, granted voting rates to all adults, and otherwise abolished whatever practice you have in mind. The fact that I have to qualify my statement in this way further speaks to the contextual natural of moral judgments. We already encountered this possibility in chapter 2 when discussing choices of objective functions to optimize. We noted that one can choose different principles to maximize for a moral life, including the one defined in reference to God, which then provides the frame of reference for assessing one's behavior.

Moral relativism can also take the form of assessing one's morality relative to the people around you. To be clear, I think this is a perfectly functional way to behave or operate; however, if one chooses to use a biblical framework as the basis for one's moral choices, then it is hard to reconcile with what the Bible teaches. Consider the widow's offering in Mark 12 which is small relative to other gifts but lavish by Jesus' standard, or the Pharisee in Luke 18 who is boastful of how he compares to others, to his detriment. It is often easy to assess ourselves by what's going on around us, just as it is easy to assess how fast we are going on the highway by comparing our speed to the speed of other cars. I can't be going too fast if there are other cars going faster than me; I can't be too bad of a person if other people are worse. We might like to think that we can look at a speedometer to determine how fast we are going, but we've already established that the measurements from the speedometer are equally relative and no more or less correct than the measurements made relative to other cars. Are we naive to think that it should be any different with morality, that any speedometer we might choose is really just another kind of relative assessment?

Here's where I think special relativity comes in. As I mentioned earlier, in prior theories, space and time were absolute and only infinite speeds were measured the same from all frames of reference. In special relativity, we trade absolute space and time for an invariant and finite speed of light. I think these properties and their consequences are useful for understanding the role that Jesus plays in the biblical notion of morality. But first we need to understand a little more about what we mean when we say the speed of light is not relative to motion.

Let's get back on the highway, only now we need to go faster, so imagine it's an interstellar highway. I am flying my spaceship at 168 million mph. You are passing me going 335 million mph by your speedometer, and since it is dark in space you have your headlights on. A "stationary" interstellar highway patrolman clocks the light leaving your headlights as traveling 671 million mph, the speed of light in a vacuum. From our earlier analysis, you might expect that if you measured the speed of the same light you would get an answer of 336 million mph, and if I measured it I would get a speed of 503 million mph, due to our various relative motions. What would actually happen is that you and me and the officer of the law and everyone else will get the same answer of 671 million mph.

5.3 Only the Light Deals in Absolutes

How does it happen we get the same measurements for the speed of light? Now we get to the counterintuitive part that gives special relativity its reputation for being very hard to understand, so don't be too bothered if it is hard to wrap your head around the first time. Notice that our measurement of speed involved measurements of space or length, the width of the window, and measurement of time or duration, how long it took to travel from one side of the window to the other. The outcomes of our measurements of space and time are affected by how fast we are traveling when we make the measurements. Those adjustments work out just so that all measurements of the speed of light give the same result.

Thus, in reality when I measured the speed of your car from my car, my measurements of space and time themselves were influenced by the speed I was traveling. The differences are subtle enough that they don't matter with respect to the precision of our 55 mph result—but they do matter to the GPS devices we might be using to navigate our cars. GPS relies on very precise time synchronization between the satellites and the receiver devices, because the receiver figures out where it is by observing how far it is from a variety of satellites. Those observations rely on the time it takes for a signal to get from the satellite to the receiver, which means they both have to agree on when the signal left the satellite. That synchronization can be problematic, because the satellite and the receiver are not in the same reference frame and so their measurements of time durations will differ. But fortunately, thanks to special relativity we can compute very precisely how the measurements will differ and take that into account, which allows the GPS receiver to very accurately figure out where it is. If these special relativity adjustments were not made, your GPS would not work as well as it does (any issues you might have with the accuracy of its maps or directions are an entirely separate issue that physics cannot help you with).

Measuring the speed of light the same is most natural in a geometry that unites space and time dimensions into a four dimensional coordinate system called spacetime. Spacetime intervals in this coordinate system are also consistently measured no matter how fast or slow the measurer or measuring equipment is moving. This might be thought of as another example of the situation with particles and waves in the last chapter. Our preexisting intuitions from human-scale observations may not always be adequate; here, our separate categories of space and time are replaced with a single category of spacetime. In this case, we can even retain the useful property of consistent intervals, just in a somewhat different form.

It is probably a coincidence, but it is still notable that our language already treats space and time as interchangeable. Just like the Battle

Room squads before Ender, we have coopted our sense of three dimensions of space that are very comfortable and applied them to time. The future could be above or below, but our thinking is so oriented to movement on a surface that the future is invariably in front of us, the past behind. We talk about durations as lengths of time. And anyone whose sense of morality is more similar to our ancestors' than our own is described as backwards (i.e., of the past), even though morality doesn't actually follow a linear progression.

The linguistic substitution runs the other way too, describing space in temporal terms. It is not uncommon to ask a distance question—"How far to the next exit?"—and get a time answer—"2 minutes." Before interstate highways, railroads or airplanes, distances between cities might be reckoned in days. We can't travel through space without also traveling in time, which at least partially explains the conceptual connections. Regardless of the explanation, these features of our language turn out to be consistent with reality in unanticipated ways.

As we saw, combining spatial lengths and temporal durations into spacetime intervals yields a physics in which the speed of light is invariant. The geometry of spacetime itself seems to be calibrated in such a way that any attempts to measure the speed of light will give the same answers. If we are thinking about Jesus as the light of the world, perhaps Jesus has a similar special status when it comes to morality. Prior to Jesus, the law as recorded in the Old Testament and other Jewish texts and traditions was the standard for moral behavior. Jesus came to fulfill the law (Matthew 5:17), in a sense establishing himself as the standard for moral behavior, a shift just as revolutionary as the one from invariant space and time to invariant light speed.

Consider that Jesus is widely regarded as a good, moral teacher. Christians obviously hold him in high esteem. Islam counts him as a prophet. The Dalai Lama has described him as enlightened. Plenty of atheists and agnostics acknowledge the moral value of his teachings or his example. It is practically a cliché to emphasize his goodness in the process of denying his divinity. Whatever problems folks might have with Christianity, it's rare to come across someone who thinks that as a man he was bad, evil, or immoral. It is almost as if everyone's morality is calibrated so that they evaluate Jesus as good.

This is also a theme in the Gospel accounts of Jesus' life. The earliest story from his childhood, in Luke 2, recounts a trip to Jerusalem with his parents for a holiday celebration. As his parents start the journey home with the rest of the pilgrims, a preteen Jesus stays behind to talk with the religious teachers. Eventually his parents realize what has happened and they are reunited. They express concern about his choice and point out how worried they were when they realized they didn't know where to find him, but his explanation apparently satisfies them. Already it is clear that Jesus' priorities are different, without necessarily being wrong.

Throughout his adult life, as recorded in all four Gospels, various religious and political factions attempt to find something they can use to accuse Jesus. They ask him all sorts of questions that they think are no-win, Kobayashi Maru scenarios, and every time Jesus finds a way to navigate through the rhetorical traps, leaving his would-be accusers with nothing to use against him. As an example, one group asks him whether Jews ought to pay taxes to the Roman government that controlled the region. The expectation was that if he said "yes" they could paint him as a Roman sympathizer, costing him credibility with his Jewish followers, and if he said "no" then he was encouraging people to break Roman law. Jesus asks whose picture is on a Roman coin, and when he is told that it is Caesar's, he suggests that they "give to Caesar the things that are Caesar's, and to God the things that are God's" (Mark 12:17). There's a lot of common sense there that's hard to argue with; in fact, it borders on tautology. And yet he doesn't explicitly affirm the legality of Roman taxes nor endorse a boycott of them; there is also a lot of room for discussion about what actually belongs to either party. Jesus handles all of these verbal confrontations in a similar manner, thwarting attempts to find substantial grounds to condemn him.

In another memorable incident, someone comes to Jesus to ask him some questions, and addresses him as "good teacher." Jesus begins by asking the man why he called Jesus good (Mark 10:18). It feels like an odd reaction to a show of respect; Jesus seems to be making a point of calling attention to the question of whether in fact he is good. He doesn't necessarily deny that assessment, but he wants to make sure we understand why we are reaching it.

Finally, even in the process of putting him on trial and ultimately putting him to death, his interlocutors have a hard time finding a charge that will stick. They resort to bringing in ringers to offer false testimony (again, according to the Gospel accounts) and even they can't keep their stories straight enough to manufacture a credible accusation (Mark 14:56–59). Pilate famously washes his hands of the whole business, reportedly because he wants nothing to do with the execution of an innocent man. The impression from these stories is that Jesus has been condemned without clearly established guilt.

The explanation for this inability to find fault with him, according to the Bible, is that Jesus did in fact live a sinless life, and was the only person to have done so. For the sake of argument, let's say that is true. Is there anything analogous about light? It turns out that yes, there is—light has no mass. That is why it can travel at the speed of light. Anything with mass cannot reach that speed; it's not just really hard, it's impossible. So what happens if we think of being sinful (having committed one or more sins) as having mass and being sinless as equivalent to being massless?

5.4 Space & Time & Momentum & Energy

Recall that spacetime is such that measurements of length and duration made at different speeds will yield different results. Relativity affects the measurement of other quantities also. It implies a particular relationship between momentum and energy, for example. Observers moving at different speeds will measure energy and momentum differently, but like space and time, the two can be combined in a way that is consistent across all reference frames.

Momentum summarizes an object's current motion, or lack thereof. It is a function of mass and speed and represents how resistant the object is to changes in motion. Slower objects and less massive objects are easier to affect than faster and more massive ones. Think about stopping a small child running amok versus tackling an adult running back going at the same speed. Or think about catching a baseball tossed by that same child versus catching a 100 mph fastball.

Bear in mind that speed and motion are relative, which is why different observers will assess momentum differently. You could catch that baseball much more easily if you were running alongside it at 100 mph. In fact, it would be no different than picking up a ball lying still on the ground. Meanwhile, a catcher running at the ball at 100 mph would find it even harder to catch than the catcher crouching behind the plate.

Since momentum involves motion, it needs to be described in the three dimensions of space. Although an object will be moving in one particular direction, that direction can be broken down along the three different axes. If I'm driving east in my car, the car's momentum may have a positive value along the east/west axis and 0 in the north/south and up/down directions. Meanwhile, Ender Wiggin in the Battle Room may be moving in such a way that his momentum has positive components along all three axes; maybe he's floating down toward the gate while also drifting in a south-southeasterly direction. The point is that momentum is strongly associated with space.

The energy of an object likewise connects most naturally with time. Energy quantifies an object's capacity to do work, which involves change over time. The object needn't be presently doing work to have energy. Consequently, energy isn't associated with any particular direction or separable along the different axes of space. In other words, at any given moment we cannot know how the energy an object possesses will be used; it could be used to do work in any direction at some future point. But we do know that work will occur over time, hence the association of energy with time and not space.

The combination of space and time into spacetime thus implies a connection between momentum and energy. And indeed, as we stated, the two are connected in such a way that while different observers will measure the separate quantities differently depending on their motion, a joint energy-momentum measurement will be the same for all observers. The particular details of how momentum and energy interact imply that any object with mass can never travel at the speed of light. Notably, this connects the geometry of momentum and energy, which is one of those geometries where parallel lines meet that we discussed in chapter 1.

Remember when we were sending food to Mars and we ran into the problem that at some point adding more fuel to the rocket in the hopes of being able to carry more food actually meant that we were burdening the rocket more than we were increasing carrying capacity? Diminishing returns also factor into why an object with mass cannot travel at the speed of light. We are not talking about the same phenomenon in both cases; the details of the effects are different and thus the math is different. But the intuition that you can't just keep pushing and accelerate without bound is reasonable to carry over.

In our momentum and energy situation, think about an object moving at some fixed speed (according to some specific observer, natch). To get it moving faster, we need to increase the energy of the object. The object will now have higher momentum, which we described as a capacity to resist change in motion. Thus the higher momentum means it will take even more energy to make the object move faster still. At which point we will measure its momentum as even higher, meaning we need even more energy to speed it up again.

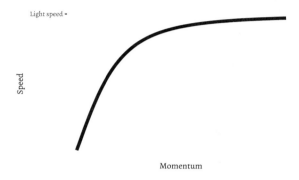

Figure 5.1: At familiar speeds, momentum and speed increase proportionately with each other, but eventually momentum continues to increase while speed approaches but does not reach an upper limit.

The function relating momentum and speed is graphed in Figure 5.1. For a while, the two increase together as we would expect because our intuition is based on experience at low speeds. But as our object gets close to traveling at light speed, it becomes harder and harder to get it to go faster. And the graph approaches but never actually reaches light speed. For an object with mass, actually reaching light speed is impossible.

5.5 The Burden of Sin

All of this discussion of momentum, energy and mass was meant to be a metaphor for sin. Let's make that a bit more explicit. Our "speed" is our righteousness and all of the other qualities we are trying to maximize as followers of Jesus, as detailed in chapter 2. Our "mass" is the sins we have committed. Our "momentum" is our resistance to change our behavior, a function of both our righteousness and our sin, for after all when we are behaving morally it is easier to continue to do so, and when we behave sinfully it is easier to persist in our sin. "Energy" is the capacity to do good works.

In this model, the moral perfection of Jesus is the optimal point of righteousness we are supposed to be reaching if we are choosing to follow Jesus. But this level is impossible to reach for anyone who has sinned, just as traveling at light speed is impossible for any object with mass. The diminishing returns aspect of trying to reach light speed resonates with biblical accounts of what it is like to be in the presence of God's sinless righteousness; the closer we get, the more aware we become of the burden of our sins. Isaiah reacts to the presence of God by saying, "Woe me! I am destroyed, for my lips are contaminated by sin" (Isaiah 6:5).

On the other hand, with enough "energy" or good works, it is possible to get as close to the speed of light you want. It is tempting to think that our good works can cancel out our sins, like credits and debits in a ledger. But that is not what the Bible actually teaches. It encourages good works and invites us to work at the process of sanctification, or approaching optimal righteousness in our own lives. But if we have any sin in our life, then we will only ever be able to approximate that righteousness, never fully achieving it in this lifetime, just as no amount of energy can cancel out the effect of an object's mass on its ability to travel at light speed.

This model also explains why folks who don't believe in the Bible can be just as good, if not better than, folks who do. With good works, it is possible to get close to being righteous. And the relativity of momentum and energy has analogues in our moral relativity as well. Depending on how fast we are going, how righteous we consider ourselves, we may come to different conclusions about the righteousness of others.

Now, you may have a notion that mass and energy are related. The energy of an object can be quantified with respect to motion, which we call kinetic energy, and it can be quantified with respect to mass. This works to a degree in our analogy as well. We can equate energy with works in general, expressed as righteousness (motion/speed) or sin (mass). Still, for any given action we might want to say it is either sinful or sanctifying, while the mass-energy relationship is not binary in the same way. That probably means we are reaching the limits of our metaphor (although we will also add some nuance to the good/bad binary in chapter 11).

You may also have a notion that mass can be converted to energy, and vice versa. Here it's typical to invoke the famous equation $E = mc^2$, where E stands for energy and m stands for mass. The c stands for the speed of light, which you may remember is quite large and squaring yields an even larger number. (This is actually a reduced version of the energy-momentum relationship I mentioned earlier that only holds when momentum is zero; i.e., when an object is at rest.)

Thus there is hope for redemption in our metaphor. Matter can be transformed! In particular, many transformations can yield photons, a massless form of matter that travels at the speed of light. Those photons preserve many of the properties of the previous form of matter. So too we can look forward to being transformed, leaving behind our sin but retaining the essence of who we are.

Of course, that's only good news for those of us who have already accepted the possibility of sin by choosing God's metric for our morality. I'm describing how I understand biblical morality to work, but just as speed and space and time relate to each other differently when space and time are absolute instead of the speed of light, so effort and good works and guilt relate differently under different systems of morality. I think the biblical approach is worth considering, not least because of the possibility that it applies to everyone regardless of what they believe, but you may see differently. Still, I think there's one more facet of our metaphor more broadly applicable because it deals with how we relate to each other, and we all have to do that regardless of beliefs.

We also observe that mass is what gives rise to gravitational attraction. In our metaphor, I think this speaks to the self-reinforcing quality of negative choices. Matter will clump together because of gravity, leading to a more massive clump, leading to greater gravitational pull, leading to more matter being pulled into the clump, and so on. Likewise, behavior with negative consequences tends to attract more bad behavior, either in ourselves or others, creating a cycle that requires significant work from which to break away. When we are hurt by the choices of others, we have a greater tendency to cause hurt ourselves.

Finally, you may have heard recently about the Higgs boson. The physics model explaining mass involves the Higgs boson and the Higgs field. The Higgs field exists everywhere in the universe, and when matter interacts with that field, it acquires mass. The Higgs boson is a particular kind of matter predicted by the Higgs field description of mass.

What I find interesting about the Higgs story is that, if we extrapolate to our metaphor of sin, it resonates with the idea that sin is relational, arising out of interactions. We might wish to think of God as the omnipresent Higgs field, and us as the individual bits of matter. This might suggest to you that sin only exists because of God, and in a sense I think that is an accurate representation of the biblical teaching. Sin is only sin with respect to our relationship with God, and by extension other people. It is not meaningful to talk about sin outside of the context of those relationships.

And that brings me back to Ender Wiggin, no longer floating in the Battle Room but now confronting the Formic beings he has trained his whole life to defeat. He recognizes that how he interacts with them has moral significance. And he also starts to appreciate an unintended consequence of the way he was trained. He was removed from an Earth-bound perspective in order to better understand how Formics see the world. That understanding is supposed to help him defeat them. Yet he observes, "When I truly understand my enemy, . . . then in that very moment I also love him."

The Bible offers a similar observation. Although we chose to be enemies with God, he chose to know us and show us love. "And you were at one time strangers and enemies in your minds as expressed through your evil deeds, but now he has reconciled you by his physical body through death" (Colossians 1:21–22). If that is true, and I believe it is, then I think it only reasonable to get to know him in return. And so in the next chapter we will explore a definition of love through the physics of entropy.

CHAPTER 6

The Entropic Principle

In Gotham City, Batman exerts the force, to a soundtrack of *Biff!*s and *POW!*s. Some believe he is also attracting supervillains who desire the infamy that comes from squaring off with him.

In *The Dark Knight*, Batman's two antagonists clearly exist as a response to his crimefighting approach. The previous film, *Batman Begins*, demonstrated Batman's flair for "theatricality and deception." The Joker employs those same tools in the service of crime, positioning himself as the funhouse mirror version of the Caped Crusader. Two-Face's connection to the Dark Knight has more of a two-sides-of-the-same-coin vibe. Harvey Dent starts out as a fellow crimefighter, operating within the law as a district attorney, but when he experiences his own personal tragedy he becomes disillusioned about heroism and justice.

6.1 The Many Faces of Entropy

The Joker and Two-Face are connected to each other as well, via their personal histories and various plot machinations. More esoteric, but also more relevant to our discussion, is that they both represent aspects of entropy. Entropy is a concept from thermodynamics, a discipline within physics. Up until now, we've basically been dealing with the physics of individual objects, photons and cars and baseballs and rockets. Thermodynamics is concerned with how objects behave when large numbers of them are aggregated together.

The classic setup for thinking about thermodynamics is a box full of air; turns out they can do more than just entertain toddlers and cats. Air is made up of many, many small molecules that are imagined as essentially a bunch of tiny little balls. In theory, the equations of motion should allow us to model the movement of each individual molecule-ball. In practice, it is impractical to track trillions of trillions of molecules, each of which can potentially collide with any other molecule at any given moment and influence its path.

Instead of tracking individual molecules, thermodynamics is interested in their aggregate properties. For example, each individual molecule is moving around because it has kinetic energy. We can't measure the energy of each one, but we can measure the average energy; we call that quantity temperature. And just knowing the temperature tells us a lot about the behavior of our box of air.

Entropy is another of these aggregate properties, relating to temperature and heat transfer, or how energy flows. There are actually several equivalent ways to define it, which we will explore with the help of the Joker and Two-Face. You've probably heard about entropy and the 2nd law of thermodynamics, commonly paraphrased as the tendency of systems to go from order to disorder. This version is not exactly wrong, but it can be misleading if we aren't clear on what we mean by order and disorder. We don't want to run the metaphor in reverse from our intuition of order to entropy and arrive at the wrong conclusions.

How should we think about order? "A place for everything and everything in its place" is probably a good reference. Relatively few arrangements are considered organized or ordered. Numbers are a great example; 1, 2, 3, 4, and so on is the natural way to order numbers. Your DVD collection could be grouped by genre or sorted alphabetically and your books could be arranged by the Dewey Decimal system or the Library of Congress system or the Book Industry Standards and Communications system, but once you've chosen a scheme there is a lone unique arrangement that satisfies the criteria. Conversely, there are many ways to be disordered—25, 5, 77 or 21, 10, 15—that are equivalent in the sense that they are not ordered, just as there are many ways your friends could shuffle your DVDs that would all be equally irritating. In some circles, this is known as the Anna Karenina principle, inspired by the quote "Happy families are all alike; every unhappy family is unhappy in its own way" from Tolstoy's novel.

I have also found it helpful to think about entropy and order in terms of symmetry and asymmetry, because those words carry less colloquial baggage that can give us the wrong intuition. Symmetry refers to the ability to swap things around and get something equivalent to what you started with. A popular version is mirror or bilateral symmetry, where an object or arrangement of objects is balanced left and right. A convenient example is a person; broadly speaking, we could swap a person's right-hand-side and left-hand-side and get an equivalent person. But one of our goals is to go beyond human-centric concepts, and so we need a more general version of symmetry.

Our box of air is also symmetrical, to a much greater extent than we are. You can swap around the molecules into all kinds of different arrangements and the result would be indistinguishable in terms of what we can measure like temperature. An asymmetrical box could have all the molecules squeezed to one side and the rest just empty space. Now there are far fewer equivalent arrangements because we've ruled out all the options where some molecules are in the now-empty side.

Asymmetrical arrangements are useful precisely because changes matter. When an asymmetrical system changes to a qualitatively different arrangement, there is an opportunity to do something useful. For example, imagine our box changing from the squished-to-one-side state to the all-spread-out state. This transition will generate a net movement from one side of the box to the other, akin to a gust of wind. We could harness that wind with a turbine and generate electricity until the box reaches the all-spread-out state, at which point the turbine will stop spinning.

Asymmetry is thus a structured or organized arrangement that can be qualitatively distinguished from other arrangements. These distinctions between arrangements imply that changes are meaningful and potentially useful. Symmetry by contrast is a state with a number of indistinguishable arrangements, rendering changes meaningless.

Whether we think about entropy in terms of order and disorder or symmetry and asymmetry, we need to be careful about two things. One is that thermodynamic entropy deals specifically with the ordering or symmetry of molecules. An unsorted DVD collection may be more disordered or more symmetrical than an alphabetized one, but the differences between the two are at the level of macroscopic objects. At the molecular level, there likely is no difference and so the thermodynamic entropy will be the same. We can apply our definition of symmetry to various levels, making it useful metaphorically, but we can't work backward from it to thermodynamic entropy.

We also need to be careful because our intuition of what makes something ordered or symmetrical may not always be accurate. For example, when you mix objects of different sizes you can get some counterintuitive results. Think about a bag of chips, with big pieces, little shards, and crumbs. You might think that having pieces of all sizes mixed up with each other is the most symmetrical. But by our definition, it is more symmetrical to have all the crumbs together at the bottom. In that arrangement, they have more options to switch places with each other and yield an equivalent arrangement then if they are filling in the gaps between the bigger pieces where there is less space to move around. That's why crumbs settle during shipment. Yes, this does leave us with discernible organization of separated big and small pieces, but the way to further increase symmetry is to break the big pieces into small pieces rather than getting them to intermingle.

With these concepts of symmetry and asymmetry put in terms of meaningful changes, and with the appropriate caveats, hopefully we are better equipped to discuss entropy. A low entropy system has relatively few equivalent ways in which its molecules could be arranged and yet still be thought of as in the same macroscopic state where temperature and other aggregate measures yield the same results. These molecules are ordered or asymmetrical. A high entropy system has many equivalent ways for its molecules to be arranged and yield the same aggregate measurements; the molecules are disordered and symmetrical.

In *The Dark Knight*, Batman's butler Alfred describes the Joker as one of those men who just "want to watch the world burn." The Joker is an agent of disruption. His favorite tools are fire and explosives, both of which take asymmetrical, structured things and raise their thermodynamic entropy before reducing them to symmetrical rubble and ash. There are many ways to strew bricks about to make rubble, but comparatively few to make a functioning hospital, to use one example of Joker's mayhem.

Thinking in terms of many equivalents and few equivalents leads naturally to a treatment of entropy in terms of probability. If the lower entropy equivalents are few in number, then they are less likely to occur as a result of just poking around at random. This is the essence of the second law of thermodynamics, which says that the entropy of isolated systems will increase with time. In other words, if left to their own devices, systems will wind up in the most likely states, which are also the high entropy ones. Understood this way, it almost verges on a tautology, which explains why many scientists consider it one of the least likely principles to ever be contradicted by new observations.

The equation for entropy expressed in terms of probability is

$$S = -\kappa_B \sum_i p_i \log p_i$$

where S is entropy, p_i is the probability of a particular arrangement of a system, κ_B is constant relating energy and temperature whose value is measured experimentally, and $\sum$ and log are math operations ($\sum$ is a Greek 's' for "sum" and log is the reverse of raising a number to a power such as squaring). Here we get, via mathematical analogy, yet another way of thinking about entropy, this time in terms of information. A fundamental equation from information theory is

$$H(X) = -\sum_i P(x_i) \log P(x_i)$$

where Pxi is the probability of a particular message. Even without understanding all the details and notation, hopefully you can appreciate that these two equations have a similar form. The similarity was so striking that the quantity referred to as $H(X)$ in the information equation came to be called information entropy.

To understand $H(X)$ a little better, we turn to the Joker's partner in crime, Two-Face. When we first meet Harvey Dent, he appears to use a coin to obtain a classic information bit, a single this-or-that answer, to make decisions. Then we learn he's using a two-headed coin, and so a flip provides Dent no information at all; he always knows what the outcome will be. The quantity $H(X)$ is a measure that applies to message sources, and as a data source, this coin has low information entropy. The probability it will land "heads" is 1. Using our equation and the fact that the log of 1 is 0, we get an entropy of 0 bits; that's the most information we can get from flipping a coin. This matches our experience; seeing the coin come up "heads" tells us nothing that we didn't already know before the flip.

Later, thanks to the entropy-increasing chaos of the Joker, one head of the coin becomes scarred (as does half of Harvey Dent's head, hence "Two-Face"). That face of the coin is heated and melted, allowing individual metal atoms to swap places without distinguishable changes, meaning that the heated coin has higher S entropy. Now the probability of unscarred "heads" is ½ and the probability of scarred "heads" is ½. Substituting these probabilities into our equation yields a higher information entropy as well: 1 bit. In fact, it gives the highest value you can get for a single this-or-that outcome, which is why we call such an outcome one bit of information. Thus we have a connection between an increase in the symmetry type of physical entropy associated with the Joker, and the information entropy associated with Two-Face; no wonder they are a perfect pair in the film!

Now, that's a neat instance of cinematic synchronicity, but it's hardly definitive. Likewise, the similarity between the two entropy equations seemed like perhaps a cute bit of mathematical symmetry but unrelated to the physical reality underlying those equations. Scientists have come to appreciate that the reason the equations look the same is because they are in fact capturing closely related phenomena from different angles.

The relationship can also be understood as follows: the thermodynamic entropy S of a system represents the amount of information necessary to encode the full arrangement of its molecules, given the equivalence category it is in. If there are many different possible equivalent arrangements, then more information is needed to specify exactly which one the system actually occupies at the moment. At the other extreme, if there is only one possible state, then you may need as little as one bit of information. In our box of air example, the version with the air squished to one side needs less information because we can categorically eliminate all the positions from the empty side.

6.2 Eternal Sunshine of a Spot in the Sky

Now, ostensibly light is the focus of our discussion on the language of physics. Yet we've gotten this far discussing entropy without it. There is a connection, and to understand it we have to ask what it is that we receive from the sun every day.

A few minutes outside in the daytime will suggest that the answer is some combination of light and heat. The value of the light for seeing is pretty obvious. We humans tend to rely on our eyes as a primary mode of perceiving the world around us. In other words, it is a key source of information about our surroundings. That's already kind of a neat connection, and it has biblical resonance. "Your word is a lamp to walk by, and a light to illumine my path" (Psalm 119:105) ties together information from the word and illumination. But I want to push a little further and get to entropy as well.

What we experience as the warmth of sunlight on our skin can be described more generally as a kind of energy. This energy was stored in the sun, is carried by photons to Earth, and feeds into all the energy pathways we use here. The sun heats the air, creating temperature differences that manifest as winds, which we can convert into electricity using turbines. The sun heats water, causing it to evaporate; when it condenses in clouds it eventually comes back down as rain, and when that rain falls on hills and mountains it creates running water, which we can use to turn turbines and generate electricity. And of course we can make electricity more directly from sunlight using solar panels. Plants and algae do something similar, and we can access that energy by eating them, or eating the things that eat them, and so on. Or we can wait until those plants and algae and the organisms that ate them convert to oil and natural gas and get energy from them that way. Surely this energy is the greatest gift that the sun has to offer.

And yet, from another perspective, our net energy gain on any given day is zero. If you were to measure all the energy coming from the sun to the Earth in a 24-hour period, and then measure all the energy radiating from the Earth during the same period—in the form of heat escaping during nighttime hours as the Earth cools, or reflected light, etc.—you'd see that the two amounts are the same. Upon reflection, this makes a certain amount of sense; if it weren't the case, the Earth would heat up. (Actually, this is exactly the concern with global climate change: recent changes in the atmosphere have reduced the amount of heat radiated back into space, causing the planet to get warmer because the energy input is higher than the output.) So, is there any property where we can observe a net difference between what we get from the sun and what we send back into space?

Yes! As you might suspect, the answer is thermodynamic entropy. If you measure the entropy of all the photons coming to the Earth from the sun, it will be lower than the entropy of all the photons leaving the Earth over the same period of time. After a fashion, the sun gives us our daily dose of asymmetry.

One easy way to think about why this must be so is to consider colors. Sunlight spans a fairly wide spectrum including all the colors we can see, which is why sunlight can make rainbows, and also other colors we can't see, like ultraviolet. Most of the light from the Earth is actually in the infrared range that we can't see. The energy of light is connected to its wavelength or color; ultraviolet and visible light has more energy than infrared light. We get high energy photons from the sun, and give off low energy photons. If the total energy is balanced, that must mean we give off more photons than we take in. More photons means more ways of arranging them, which means higher entropy.

Another way to think about the entropy difference between the input from the sun and the output back into space relates to direction. All of the photons from the sun come in a fairly narrow band, about half of a degree of the sky as seen from Earth. By comparison, the Earth radiates photons in all directions. There are more ways to rearrange those photons and still have them cover the same range of directions than there are to rearrange the photons from the sun and have them remain within the same narrow band. Thus the photons leaving the Earth have a higher collective entropy.

To understand the organization that the sun provides, let's discuss the same energy pathways we mentioned earlier in terms of entropy instead. For example, consider the heating of air to create wind. When the air is calm, it is because it is well-mixed and all at the same temperature. This is a relatively high entropy state; there are lots of different ways to organize the air molecules to get the same well-mixed situation. But when some of the air is heated so that there is a temperature differential, an asymmetry, this is now a relatively lower entropy state. The warm air molecules can only be in the warm area, and the cold ones in the cold area, limiting the possibilities. This temperature differential creates wind because the most likely way for the system to change is for the hot air to spread into the cold area (and vice versa to a lesser extent; cold molecules don't move as much) and get into the higher entropy state.

How does the sun create these temperature differentials? The answer is surprisingly simple—the sun is just in one place in the sky and not all around us. If the Earth received photons from all directions at the same time, there would be less wind because the air would be heated more evenly. (Differences in how different materials like water and rock heat up and cool down would still provide temperature differences that could create wind, but these are really just further examples of organizing asymmetry.) But we don't get sunlight from all directions, we receive it from one specific place in the sky. Life on this planet depends on the fact that the sun is one spot and that there are colder spots where the sun isn't.

Having received wind from the sun, we use it to turn turbines and create electricity, essentially taking some of that low entropy, or asymmetry, and storing it in a battery. A charged battery is in a low entropy state, with the negative and positive charges separated; a spent battery is in a higher entropy state as all the charges have balanced out and are thoroughly mixed. A similar analysis applies to the water cycle; separating some water from the oceans into clouds is a lower entropy arrangement than if all the water were in the ocean, and again results from the fact that only some of the Earth is heated at any given time. Tides are also useful for creating electricity, and are another consequence of the sun's (and to a lesser extent, the moon's) influence coming from a specific location.

At this point, you may be wondering about the second law of thermodynamics, the one that says something about entropy always increasing. If it's a law, why do I keep talking about things becoming more ordered or achieving lower entropy states?

I hope for your sake that you have some experience with the act of tidying or organizing, so hopefully it is not completely foreign that something can become more ordered over time rather than less. This turns out to be perfectly consistent with thermodynamics, which dictates that an *isolated* system always increases in entropy. An isolated system does not communicate with any other system, preventing it from receiving any input. As we've seen, the Earth doesn't qualify because it gets input from the sun, and indeed the sun and the Earth together don't even really form an isolated system. If we consider all the parts of the system, the total entropy is increasing. Remember that the Earth is giving off high entropy photons every day, thus increasing the entropy of the solar system and ultimately the universe.

Returning to our recasting of energy-centric accounts of what the sun provides as entropy-centric narratives, let's talk about plants and animals and people. Plants absorb the low entropy photons from the sun, via a molecule called chlorophyll. Those photons enable the plant to convert high entropy substances from their environment, like carbon dioxide and water, into more structured, low entropy compounds. By this process, plants are able to use the order from the sun to build and maintain their own highly organized, asymmetrical structures. If a plant were cut off from the sun and had no low entropy input, then it would proceed to a higher entropy state that we recognize as death and decay. By virtue of access to sunlight, however, the plant is able to keep itself ordered. It should be noted that in all of this process, some high entropy molecules also are produced, such as the oxygen that the plant gives off; this keeps everything consistent with the second law of thermodynamics. The universe gets more symmetrical, but the plant stays asymmetrical.

The asymmetry of that organized state of the plant can then be transmitted up the food chain. Animals and people eat those plants, taking in organized molecules and using them to maintain their own ordered, living states. The same notion applies to the consumption of animals by other animals and people. You can observe this for yourself. What we eat comes in a variety of distinct shapes, colors and structures, indicative of organized states, and what we put back into the world is—without putting too fine a point on it—fairly disorganized, being generally uniform in color and texture, and unstructured. (Meanwhile, the carbon cycle is complete when we take some of the carbon we eat and exhale it as carbon dioxide, which is then incorporated back into the molecular structure of plants, making baby's breath perhaps the most aptly named of all the plants.)

From this picture, we get a useful definition of life and death. Defining life turns out to be surprisingly tricky, at least if you have particular ideas about what is alive and what isn't, and you want to preserve those categories while giving a succinct, coherent definition. For example, try coming up with one that includes bacteria but excludes viruses, ideas, and fire. The physicist Erwin Schrödinger popularized an entropy-based definition. He clearly needed such a definition, since his (hypothetical) cat played in a box of air that may or may not have been poisoned, leaving him uncertain whether his cat was alive or dead. He defined life as the process of keeping yourself ordered by making use of the asymmetry in your environment; conversely, death is the process of giving your internal asymmetry back into the environment.

Now, by this definition the sun is not alive; it is not utilizing the asymmetry from its environment to maintain its own asymmetrical state. But it is relinquishing its internal asymmetry into the environment, and so in some sense it can be thought of as dying. Astronomers and astrophysicists will sometimes talk about stars in terms of death, dying, or being dead, and also sometimes as having a birth. While perhaps intended as illustrative anthropomorphisms, it would seem that there is a kernel of more literal truth in those descriptions.

The entropy-based definition of life also implies that life is related to the flow of information. We can think about utilizing order from the environment as processing information because of the connection between information and entropy. To be alive is to consume messages from low entropy sources, sources that are consistent and predictable in what they provide, like a two-headed coin. It also means that we act as a high entropy message source, communicating signals that are more variable than the ones we consume. Conversely, in death we can serve as a low entropy message source.

In other words, we take the information from those low entropy sources and store it, and at death release it. That might sound like a contradiction of what we've said already about the connection between entropy and information. We said a message source that transmits less information has lower entropy. So you might think it confusing that storing information would be associated with maintaining our bodies' low entropy states; wouldn't that mean more information and thus more entropy?

Remember that information entropy pertains to message sources. When we are taking information in and storing it, we are not acting as a message source. A storage medium needs to be in a low entropy state so that it can reliably repeat the same message that was stored in it.

Imagine writing a reminder on a piece of paper, and then when you read it later it says something different. And then the next time you read it, it says something different again! That would make it a high entropy source and a terrible storage option. You want it to be a low entropy source, to read the same every time. Message communication and information storage are separate concepts.

Thus it is perfectly consistent to say that in life, we consume messages from low entropy sources and store the information from the messages. As a message source, based on what we put back into the environment, we are high entropy; this is independent from our role as information storers. It is in death that we act as a low entropy source, putting into the world the information we stored from those low entropy sources. And all of those sources can ultimately be traced back to the sun, whose low entropy photons make life as we know it possible.

6.3 The Dying and Living of the Light

Having discussed entropy and information and their relationship to sunlight, we are now ready to consider how that informs our understanding of Jesus. To start, we go all the way back to the beginning, when the world was described as "without shape" (Genesis 1:2), which sounds an awful lot like an unstructured, high entropy state. Creation introduces asymmetry so that transformations become meaningful, the universe becomes dynamic, and life becomes possible. We don't know precisely what the very first moment of the universe looked like or how it came to be that way. The earliest state of the universe we can describe had intermediate entropy and proceeded to higher overall entropy states, which nevertheless show signs of macroscale organization.

The key to understanding this observation is not conflating all forms of organization and actual thermodynamic entropy. The famous cosmic microwave background radiation actually indicates that kinetic energy was distributed symmetrically with little structure, which is not the lowest possible entropy state. With respect to mass and gravity, however, this even distribution is low in entropy because matter will tend to go from such an arrangement toward more clumps and clusters. Raising entropy with respect to gravity creates opportunities for kinetic energy to be gathered and put to further use. In other words, creation stems from a balance of the attractive force of gravity and the tendency of kinetic energy to spread everything further apart.

From there, let's look at some of my favorite bits in the Bible, the first chapter of the Gospel of John. It also provides an account of the beginning of the universe, albeit in more abstract terms. "The Word was with God in the beginning. All things were created by him, and apart from him not one thing was created that has been created. In him was life, and the life was the light of mankind" (John 1:2–4). How intriguing that the world is described as being created by the Word, or alternatively by information. As we noted earlier, processing information is a way to go from a disordered state to an ordered one, and here we see the source of that information identified as the Word of God. And then we see the connection to light and life, just as the light from the sun brings the order needed to preserve life here on Earth.

I want to reiterate that I am not asserting that these Bible passages offer a detailed account of the exact process by which the world came to be as it is now or was then. In particular, I would expect there to be particulars of the mechanism of universe-formation that can't be directly mapped to verses or phrases from the Bible. Detailed scientific accounts, in terms we would recognize today, would have been incomprehensible to the original audience, so I wouldn't really expect to find them in the Bible. The purpose of both the Genesis and John passages is primarily to indicate that God's agency was involved; figuring out the exact details of the mechanisms he used are left as an exercise to the reader. I would expect to see general themes that can be expressed in different ways to different people at different times. Here the theme is what we need and how God provides it, and I find it striking that we can talk about that in terms of Λόγος (*logos*), the Greek concept rendered as "Word" in most English translations, and that we can talk about it in terms of order, information, and entropy.

And the connections don't stop there. As we explored with our description of the sun's activities, the low entropy photons, or light, from the sun are required to sustain life on earth. And recall that this can be viewed as an influx of information. So when we read "Man does not live by bread alone, but by every word that comes from the mouth of God" (Matthew 4:4) we can appreciate a new sense of what that means. An ongoing input of order and information are indeed necessary to sustain life biologically.

Then we get to the death of Jesus. Put simply, Jesus died so that we might live, just as the sun is exhausting itself to sustain us. In addition, we described death as a process of disseminating stored information. Likewise, the death of Jesus was a key reason why the gospel message spread as widely as it did.

I think this entropic perspective helps us get our heads around one of the more challenging ideas of the gospel—that we are called to die just as Jesus did. Jesus said, "If anyone wants to become my follower, he must deny himself, take up his cross, and follow me" (Matthew 16:24). That's strong language, and yet most of his followers have not literally been crucified, nor faced a martyr's death of any sort. It doesn't take much reflection to realize that if every Christian died in that way, Christianity probably wouldn't have made it past a couple of generations at best. But I don't think that gets us out of having to take that command seriously.

Or consider the words of the apostle Paul, who encourages believers "to present your bodies as a sacrifice—alive, holy, and pleasing to

God" (Romans 12:1). An animal presented for sacrifice would have been killed and either eaten or burnt up. Grain offerings would likewise be consumed in one fashion or the other. So what exactly would it mean to be a sacrifice and yet remain alive?

That's where our definition of death comes in. First of all, we have the idea of putting order out into the world around us, even at the expense of introducing more disorder into our own lives. At times, that might mean literal cleaning or organizing of a home or a neighborhood for people who could use that sort of help, or building homes, or otherwise providing for regular material needs. Or in that vein, it could mean restoring order after a disastrous disruption, either natural or human-inflicted. It could mean working to restore relationships, which represent a kind of social order, or helping people order their minds through teaching. I don't mean to suggest that you get too hung up on exact entropy considerations for every action you take, but I think the question of whether you are bringing order or disorder to the lives of those around you is a helpful heuristic for guiding your behavior.

Another way to frame that question is to consider whether you are consolidating more power or resources for yourself (creating asymmetry), or working to distribute them to others (making your life more symmetrical so that others can have a useful asymmetry). A low entropy state can occur when something is sequestered, such as warm air being separated from cold air; mixing them raises entropy. The Bible is filled with commandments to take care of those with fewer resources, often represented by widows and orphans but sometimes just named as the poor. The law in Leviticus has provisions to prevent exploitation of the poor through practices such as charging excessive interest. The custom of Jubilee, in which land that has been bought and sold reverts to the original owner, prevents consolidation of too much land and wealth. The prophets regularly decry neglect of the poor and needy. Malachi warns that God "will come to you in judgment. [He] will be quick to testify against those who . . . exploit workers, widows, and orphans, who refuse to help the resident foreigner" (Malachi 3:5). The princes of Israel are denounced by Ezekiel because "they have devoured lives" (Ezekiel 22:25).

That Ezekiel verse is especially intriguing to me. The image of devouring someone is a powerful one, and connects strongly with the idea of eating as a means of taking up order from the world around us.

When we enrich our own situation at the expense of others, there is an entropic sense in which we are eating their lives. This also helps me understand a related and equally visceral element of the Bible. There are several individuals whose deaths very specifically involve their corpses being eaten. Perhaps most notable of these is Jezebel, queen of Israel, who is told her body will be eaten by dogs in 1 Kings 21; the actual realization of that event is recorded in 2 Kings 9.

This seems like a rather grisly detail to fixate on; we might think the Bible would be easier to accept without elements like it. And yet, Jezebel is apparently guilty of precisely this crime of "devouring lives." She and her husband are condemned for their exploitation of their subjects. The prophecy about her death comes directly after they murder someone to gain possession of his property. The circumstances of her death strike me as a potent reminder that, one way or the other, we will all wind up giving of ourselves so that someone else's life can be more ordered. Better then to do so voluntarily than in such a drastic and permanent fashion.

This is the recommendation of John the Baptist. His preaching centered on repentance in preparation for the coming of Jesus. When his followers asked how they should change their ways, he offered three specific suggestions. "The person who has two tunics must share with the person who has none, and the person who has food must do likewise" (Luke 3:11). "Collect no more [taxes] than you are required to" (Luke 3:13). "Take money from no one by violence or by false accusation, and be content with your pay" (Luke 3:14).

None of these are particularly radical, although they probably spoke pointedly to the tax collectors and soldiers noted in the crowd. They don't represent extraordinary sacrifice, nor do they require grand gestures. What they have in common, though, is an emphasis on equality. Instead of concentrating power or possessions for oneself, we are encouraged by John to ensure that our resources are distributed equitably.

Much of Jesus' ministry for which John was preparing the way can also be described in terms of ordering. Consider the various healing miracles. A diseased or dysfunctional organ or limb is most likely in a relatively higher entropy state than its healthy and functional equivalent, or at least went through a higher entropy state like Two-Face's scarred coin and face. So healing represents a type of symmetry-lowering organization. The feeding miracles represent a distribution of order, since as I described earlier we get life-sustaining order from the food we eat. I'd include his teaching in this category as well. I'd further observe that Jesus avoided opportunities to create disorder, eschewing violence and discouraging the sort of civil unrest or strife that many expected him to instigate or at least endorse.

And how do we remember his death? We practice the sacrament, or ritual, of communion. We eat bread and drink wine that represent his body and his blood, which brings us back to the idea of consumption as a way to obtain order. If you are unfamiliar with the practice, it may seem like an odd or even unsettling bit of symbolism, but I think an entropic treatment helps illuminate the significance.

The repetition of communion is, I think, also quite important. In order to go on living, we must continually have a low entropy input to keep our internal entropy low. The constancy of sunshine is one reminder of this; the daily need to eat food is another. How wonderful, then, that God offers to provide exactly this.

In Matthew 7, Jesus tells a parable about two builders. One man builds his house on a bedrock foundation; rock is ordered and asymmetrical, with a structure that would be changed if the molecules were shuffled. Another builds his house on sand; sand is highly symmetrical, being synonymous with shifting. When a flood comes, things don't go well for the sand house but the bedrock house is preserved by virtue of its stable foundation.

And who is the bedrock builder? Anyone "who hears these words of mine and does them" (Matthew 7:24). In other words, anyone who receives information from God, through Jesus, and uses it to order their lives.

Building on solid rock seems like such a good idea, it's hard to imagine why anyone would build on sand. And yet, when it comes to God, that's exactly what we do so often. Think about what makes the sun a source of low entropy messages for the Earth—it's in just one small part of the sky. Think about what makes a rock a solid building foundation—it is constant, unchanging. Think about what makes a message source low entropy—it provides the same messages time and again.

Aren't these exactly the qualities of God that we find so irksome? We want God to be whatever we want him to be at any particular moment. We want him to be infinitely malleable, like sand. And yet he inconveniently insists on being the same. He is a fixed point; there are things he stands for and things he does not.

This does not mean that God is simplistic or necessarily boring. A low entropy message source is consistent in the messages it sends, but that places no limit on the length of one of those messages. There can still be depth, richness, and nuance to a particular message from such a source; in fact, that message could go on forever! God could store an infinite number of bits, as we posited in chapter 1, which would mean a message of infinite length. The low entropy nature of the source simply means that every time we go to it, we get a predictable answer.

Which is great news! That means the source can be known! And that's exactly what we said our goal was with God; to know him. If God was a high entropy message source, he would be unpredictable, unknowable.

And yet time and again we go back to the sand. We can push it around and make it into anything we want. But saying you can build everything with sand is another way of saying you can build nothing with it. You can spend an entire Sisyphean existence pushing sand around, chasing something new, only to see it slide back to where it was. How wonderful then that the message of the sun, entropy, and life reminds us that what we need is something consistent and unchanging.

The book of 2 Samuel provides a variation on this theme. In chapter 14, we read, "Like water spilled on the ground, which cannot be recovered, so we must die. But God does not take away life; instead, he devises ways so that a banished person may not remain estranged from him" (2 Samuel 14:14). First, we get another image of a high symmetry state, in this case spilled water, connected with death. Then we get a reminder that life is dependent on being connected to God.

This is reiterated elsewhere in the Bible, where being cut off from God is reckoned as the worst possible fate. "Wicked men will be cut off, but those who rely on the Lord are the ones who will possess the land" (Psalm 37:9). Nahum tells us that those who plot wickedness will be cut off the way that wool is shorn from a sheep (1:2). Habakkuk likens death to someone with an insatiable appetite, always consuming (2:5). And in John 15, Jesus likens himself to a life-giving vine to which branches must remain connected to thrive; unconnected branches wither and are consumed in fire.

Vines also provide another service to branches. Remember that being alive means consuming low entropy messages and producing high entropy ones. We've described our calling as living sacrifices as being a low entropy source for others, but to fulfill the living part we need to do the opposite. Well, the vine is the place where the branches can send their high entropy messages. I believe this is an indication that God needs to be both the ultimate source of our low entropy messages and also the sink for our high entropy ones.

Remember that messages from a high entropy source are more unpredictable. That requires more grace, as we defined it in chapter 3. Fortunately, God's grace is sufficient for us. Sometimes, that grace will be extended to us through other humans. We shouldn't always expend the grace of others when we can avoid it, but at some point we will all need to receive grace, and we will all have opportunities to extend it. In both cases, we need to draw on God's resources so that no person's grace is exhausted along the way.

The idea of being consistent or predictable in how we relate to others is stated fairly explicitly in the Bible. Both Jesus, in Matthew 5:37, and James, in James 5:12, tell us to let our "yes" mean yes and our "no" mean no. These are the tools for communicating a basic bit of information. We should make sure that we are dependable in how we use them. We also need to assign them their conventional meaning, so that our intentions are clear.

Recall that information lacks intrinsic meaning; meaning is supplied externally via interpretation. It is thus possible to exploit this nature of information to pursue a curiously open form of dishonesty. One can say one thing, but secretly intend some meaning other than the usual one we've collectively agreed to attach to those words.

Many of us learn this exploit as children, even if we wouldn't describe it in terms of information theory. We call it sarcasm. We say one thing—"This is the best book I've ever read!"—but internally intend a meaning at odds with what those words are usually understood to mean. Often the message sender can communicate this flipped meaning to the receivers via tone or context, so that the communication is still clear. However, we sometimes exploit the ambiguity to appear to send one message to one audience, while perhaps revealing our true intentions to another with the extra bit of a concealed wink or crossed fingers. That's not say there's never any place for sarcasm as a rhetorical device, but we should consider whether we are using it to communicate clearly or to keep information to ourselves at the expense of others.

After all, there's a reason that hidden meanings are a common motif in literature associated with evil, often manifest as the devil himself. Marvel comics employ this story element regularly. Multiple characters, from Loki the Norse god of mischief, to demonic figures like Mephisto, appear in the shared Marvel universe as tricksters looking to con the heroes. Loki in particular is usually depicted as a character who will always tell you the truth, but he does so in a way that masks his intended meaning to achieve his own purposes. Kieron Gillen, Doug Braithwaite, Richard Elson, et al. captured this well in *Journey into Mystery*, in which a young Loki is the protagonist. The story illustrates how tricksters can be entertaining in their cleverness, especially when they try to outwit each other, as Loki does to Mephisto in that story. Such trickery isn't terribly heroic, though, and often has consequences; without spoiling the end of *Journey into Mystery* completely, I will just note that it is thematically consistent with Luke 17:33 and our entropic, information-theoretic notion of life and death.

This form of deception goes all the way back to Genesis and the Garden of Eden. In a way, what the serpent tells Adam and Eve is true. When they eat the fruit, their physical bodies do not stop functioning immediately; that is to say, they do not die. And their eyes are open so that they know good and evil in a way that they did not before.

Yet from an entropic perspective, eating the fruit does result in their death. It causes them to be cut off from God, the source of life-preserving asymmetry. This is symbolized by their lack of access to the tree of life. They will still have food and sunlight, but as we all know, those are imperfect solutions. And with the increased effort required to obtain food, the entropic benefits of it will be decreased. Thus the serpent conceals the fact that, once they eat the fruit, they will begin the process of dying.

Fortunately for all of us, that isn't the end of the story. Genesis talks about the day when that serpent would be defeated. Traditionally, that defeat is understood to be the ultimate miracle of Jesus' time on Earth—his resurrection. By reversing his own death, Jesus once again illustrates his role as a bringer of order.

Earlier we said that, in his death, Jesus called us all to die to ourselves. Doesn't his resurrection undermine this, by doing the opposite? My take is that it doesn't, because we defined dying to ourselves in terms of serving others. Jesus did not reverse his death at the expense of anyone else. Instead, he did it to initiate a reversal of the dying process that began when we cut ourselves off from God. He also did it to demonstrate that God alone can serve as the inexhaustible source of life-giving, entropy-lowering asymmetry, displaying another facet of his status as the ultimate axiom.

Since lowering entropy is connected with the flow of information, we can thing about dying to ourselves in information terms. The Bible, the observable world, and the person of Jesus all represent ways in which God provides information to us. Ultimately, Jesus even died so that this information, in the form of the gospel, could be distributed more widely. This implies that sharing the gospel, rather than keeping it all to ourselves, is a way in which we can die to self as well.

Actually, that realization is part of what motivated the writing of this book. For any folks who aren't Christians reading this, I appreciate that the last thing you may want to hear is an encouragement for people to pester you about religion. It is my hope that we can distinguish between sharing information and pestering. Christians have an obligation to make the information available, but what people choose to do with it and how they choose to respond to it is up to them.

Really, sharing the gospel is just another way in which the nerdiness of being a Christian comes to the fore. Here I appeal to John Hodgman's definition of a nerd as someone who is passionate about something. One way that passion manifests is a desire to share what one is passionate about; we want others to experience the same joy and satisfaction we experience from the object of our interest. As Christians, we should endeavor to share in that spirit, and as nerds I hope we can be willing to give space for other nerds to share their passions.

It's not just sharing the gospel that I think we need to be concerned with. I see this notion of dying to self via information as a call to transparency and openness in all facets of our life. I know my own inclination is to withhold information whenever possible. That may be fine when I'm planning a surprise party for my wife, and it may be appropriate at times in the interest of propriety. But if I'm being secretive for my own selfish gain, this perspective on dying to self encourages me to consider openness instead.

So we can die to ourselves by allowing some symmetry into our own lives to bring asymmetry to the lives of others. We follow God's example as the vine and "carry one another's burdens" (Galatians 6:2), bearing away what prevents others from flourishing, and "comfort those experiencing any trouble with the comfort with which we ourselves are comforted by God" (2 Corinthians 1:4). Of course, to be living sacrifices we need to maintain enough order to go on living ourselves; the goal isn't to be completely consumed, but to reach a balance with those around us. We can make sure that we are distributing our resources more symmetrically. We can be open and straightforward with our information. Hopefully, all of these sound worthwhile and perhaps even familiar. Rather than thinking of them in terms of death, maybe you'd file them under another name: love.

Well, biblically those two concepts are rather strongly linked. John puts it most succinctly. "No one has greater love than this—that one lays down his life for his friends" (John 15:13).

Earlier, Jesus had told his disciples that they would be known by their love. Now that we know what love is, we can explore how the followers of Jesus relate to each other. For that, we will move from the frictionless sphere of Jesus' ideal humanity to the messy specifics of everyone else's. Which means we are going to need the language of biology to talk about how the church operates, for good and for ill.

PART III

The Language of Biology

CHAPTER 7

The Genome Made Flesh

Ensemble casts make television shows work. Serial storytelling, week after week for years, needs variety of character and plot to stay fresh. *Orphan Black* has an ensemble, with an interesting twist. A large portion of that ensemble is played by one woman: Tatiana Maslany.

Orphan Black is about a group of women from all over the world who discover they are all clones from the same donor. Different mothers gave birth to them, different families raised them, but they all started out from the same genes. To sell that reality, all of the clone characters are played by Maslany. Wigs, make-up and costumes provide some visual cues about who is who, aided in some cases by different accents. But what's truly impressive is the way Maslany imbues each with a distinct personality reflective of their diverse upbringings.

Actors act, so playing different characters comes with the territory. There have been other shows designed to showcase their actors' range or just give them a chance to experiment and have some fun. Spy shows like *Mission: Impossible* or *Alias* readily lend themselves to disguises, undercover operations, and all manner of subterfuge. *Quantum Leap* and *Dollhouse* use science fiction to create character-of-the-week premises for their stars—respectively, time-traveling consciousness inhabiting different bodies and escorts with programmable minds. Or sometimes a character will have an evil twin or an identical cousin just for fun.

Orphan Black feels different, though. It's not a character-of-the-week format; a half dozen or so clone characters recur over the course of the series. Remarkably, there are even extended scenes in which three or four of them appear together, interacting verbally and physically. By allowing the clones to interact, these technically demanding sequences highlight the similarities and differences between the clones.

The clone narrative is a useful device for exploring the roles of nature and nurture in human development. In this fictional realization, the characters are nearly identical physically and significantly divergent in personality and behavior. Reality doesn't split so neatly into nature determining biology and nurture determining psychology, if for no other reason than the interactions between biology and psychology. Not to mention whatever possibility exists for genuine freedom apart from the influence both nature and nurture provide. However, my point is not really to critique the science of *Orphan Black* but to illustrate a central question of both biology and theology.

Last chapter we talked about symmetry and asymmetry. When a system is fully symmetrical, everything is interchangeable and so nothing changes; any rearrangement has no material effect. Asymmetrical systems have differences, gradients, structures, some aspect that has the capacity to meaningfully change and thus do some work. So the trick is to find asymmetry to use.

All of us start out in a relatively symmetrical place, as a single cell. Eventually that cell will divide into two, four, eight, and so on. Still, all of those cells have the same DNA, which creates another sort of symmetry. Yet we know that eventually we wind up with a wide assortment of cells, tissues, and organs, none of which are interchangeable. Where do they all come from?

The same question arises for Christians. We all believe in the same God, we all follow Jesus, we all read the same Bible. Yet clearly Christians aren't being stamped out on an assembly line. How do we wind up so different? And perhaps even more importantly, should we?

7.1 Me, My Cells, and I

I'm not the first person to notice this thematic connection between biology and theology. Song of Songs, a poem celebrating the passion between a bride and groom, has been interpreted as a metaphor for God and the nation of Israel. The apostle Paul uses the human body as a metaphor for the Christian church. When he was writing, the church was solidly in the "getting the gang together" phase. And just like the eponymous teams in films such as *Ocean's Eleven* or *Guardians of the Galaxy*, it seemed almost impossible to imagine that everyone would actually be able to tolerate each other long enough to accomplish the most trivial of tasks, let alone their rather auspicious goal of saving the world. Sometimes it can feel like the church never really left that phase; we still see evidence of the same odd-couple dynamics that lead some to question the viability of the whole enterprise. It is little wonder then that Paul felt the need to provide the early church with a metaphor for understanding how they could possibly fit together when it seemed like they were all pieces from different puzzles.

Wisely, Paul doesn't attempt to enforce homogeny as a solution to the lack of coherence and unity. Requiring everyone to be the same is one way to smooth over differences. Instead, Paul advocates for diversity and achieving cohesion through complementation. He illustrates this ideal in 1 Corinthians 12 with a body metaphor presented in terms of limbs and organs, a macroscopic level of subdivision that is widely understandable. I believe the metaphor is just as valid and just as rich now after all we've learned about cell and developmental biology.

We generally think of ourselves as a cohesive, indivisible unit, named "I." That's perfectly sensible, eminently functional, and possibly necessary for mental health. But if you reflect for a while on the tens of trillions individual cells that make up your body (give or take an order of magnitude or so; precise estimates are surprisingly challenging), that "I" concept starts to get a little fuzzier at the very least. Each cell could theoretically be autonomous. Like a heist crew or a special forces unit, each has specific skills and a particular job to do. And like *Orphan Black*'s clone club, they can accomplish things together that would be inconceivable for any single one to even contemplate. In fact, contemplating is one of the things they can only do collectively!

As usual, we need to talk about the science a bit to see how it works for our metaphors. In math and physics, it is often useful to simplify and apply a certain level of abstraction to get to core concepts and relationships. Simplicity is a goal in biology as well, but the details and specific cases will become increasingly important. We won't be able to summarize key ideas in a single equation that can be readily visualized in a graph. Instead, we will have to spend more time getting to know our cast of distinct characters, namely different types of cells and the parts they have in common.

Let's orient ourselves to a stereotypical cell by working our way in from the outside. First, we'll encounter the membrane, a barrier that keeps the insides on the inside and the outsides on the outside. There are two layers of molecules called fatty acids making up the membrane.

The fatty parts face each other in the middle portion of the membrane; they would feel oily or greasy if we got enough together for a macroscopic amount we could sense. Like oil, they don't mix with water, and a significant portion of us is water. The acid parts of the fatty acids in one layer of the membrane face the outside of the cell, and the acid parts of the other layer face the inside.

Membranes are effective barriers because they are a sandwich of fatty parts in between two sets of water-compatible acid parts. Molecules that interact well with water will tend to interact with the water outside the cell or with the outer layer of acid parts of the membrane. Passing through the membrane would require interacting with the fatty parts in the middle, which is not chemically optimal. Likewise, molecules that interact well with oil will first have to interact with the outer acid parts, which is again suboptimal.

Thus we have our first biological asymmetry. There is a clear boundary defining the inside and outside of each cell. The barrier to flow makes it possible to accumulate certain chemicals inside the cell in amounts proportionately greater than outside, or vice versa. These chemical differences between the inside and the outside make it possible for the cell to accomplish some of the work it needs to do.

Asymmetries will play a key role in allowing our cells to differentiate into different types as we develop. As we'll see, what goes into a cell from the outside affects how it develops, so controlling the flow in and out is important. That concept will also be relevant to our metaphorical application.

So how do we get into a cell? There are gates permitting transit. These gates are proteins (more on them shortly) that only open for specific molecules that are useful to the cell. Think of a door with a fingerprint scanner instead of a standard keyed lock, where the "key" is not a separate thing you carry but an integral and unique part of yourself. Only instead of a single door with a single scanner connected to a database of approved prints, there are many doors, each with a scanner that recognizes a single fingerprint. And those doors are mainly like automated revolving doors, in the sense that when they open they don't just make a hole for whatever can get through, but rather actively transport molecules in a directed fashion.

Assuming we have the correct 'finger,' a gateway protein will open and transport us in. Inside the membrane is a water-based solution of many different chemicals, including proteins and sugars. The molecules dissolved in this solution will jostle around, bumping into each other as they meander from here to there. There are also protein scaffolds to help organize the inside and serve as conduits along which other proteins carry inbound and outbound payloads. Some of those payloads are the cell's equivalents of incoming food and outgoing waste. Others are products that the cell makes to contribute to the body's function as a whole, including molecules that communicate developmental signals.

The interior of the cell also has compartments set apart by more membranes. Many of these compartments are involved in the process of making proteins; breaking up the interior into compartments in this way keeps the protein-making equipment concentrated together for more efficiency. Other compartments like lysosomes break down complex molecules into spare parts. And there are compartments called mitochondria that are the core of the energy processing pathways.

7.2 Digitally Encoded Digits

The most relevant compartment for our purpose is the nucleus, which stores the DNA representing a complete copy of our genome. That DNA represents information that the cell needs to carry out its various functions. This includes information to guide development from a single cell to a ten-trillion-member strong community known as you. We want to understand how DNA is involved in that development, and more generally how processing common information can yield different results. So we need to understand how the information in DNA gets put into action.

It's become *de rigeur* to talk about DNA in terms of a language whose alphabet has four letters: A, C, G, T. Those letters represent four structurally interchangeable chemical subunits that make up DNA molecules. They occur in a linear chain, making it natural to represent a DNA molecule as a sequence of letters, GATTACA and so on. Chemically, DNA does very little. It doesn't participate in reactions that would change its composition. Doing so would erase the information it stores. To function as a stable, copyable storage medium it has to be relatively inert.

The inert information stored in DNA gets implemented into action via proteins. The messages of DNA sequences get decoded into proteins via a two-step process. First, a working copy of a single gene from the DNA is transcribed into an RNA molecule, which is practically DNA with one small chemical difference that makes it somewhat less stable, and thus good for these disposable copies. DNA inside the nucleus is an exhaustive and expensive reference book that stays at the library because if anything bad happens to the only copy then the cell is in big trouble. So RNA copies of small, relevant sections are made to be taken outside of the nucleus to work with; if anything happens to them, then another copy can be made.

The actual proteins are then translated following the sequence of the RNA. Proteins are also single chain molecules made of modular units called amino acids. The RNA "letters" are read three at a time, and the corresponding amino acid is inserted into the protein sequence. As this process goes along, the protein folds up into a complicated 3D shape that enables it to fulfill its function as a structural element or facilitating a chemical reaction.

There are twenty different amino acids, making it easy to represent them via single alphabet letters also. And since proteins are also linear chains, we can write out a string of letters to indicate a protein sequence as well: CENESONTPASDESLETTRES. Between the linguistic metaphors implied by transcription and translation and this notation, we can hardly think of proteins as anything but a sort of language.

If we cannot get away from the language analogies, we can at least nuance them. Amino acids are complex and chemically active units unto themselves. A single amino acid can contribute significantly to the function of a given protein. And because proteins fold into complicated three-dimensional shapes, the critical amino acids for interaction with another protein or other molecule can be far apart in the linear sequence but close in the final structure.

These are not the properties of letters that have no individual meaning and only matter within the immediate sequence of the word they belong to. These are more like the properties of words within the context of sentences and paragraphs. Each word has meaning even apart from any other words, although of course context can modify or clarify that meaning. And the key words of a sentence or paragraph needn't be adjacent to each other. For example, in the famous garden path sentence "The horse raced past the barn fell," "horse" and "fell" are the subject and the verb and thus the most important parts despite appearing at opposite ends. Thus, if we must think of DNA or protein sequences in language terms, let's think of them as sentences and paragraphs, with all of the potential for complex syntax, conditional nuance and detailed discourse.

Every cell starts with the same DNA information and the potential to make all the same proteins and thus perform the same functions. And cells do share a large number of activities that take advantage of the same shared genome information; they all use the same proteins for their core energy metabolism and for transcribing RNA and translating it to make proteins. Other cell activities are associated specifically with being a skin cell, or a heart muscle cell, or a brain neuron. In addition to the information that gets transcribed and translated into proteins, DNA also contains control information related to cell types. In broad terms, you can think of those control sequences as saying, "If I am a skin cell, I will make genes 4, 8, 15, 16, 23, 42, and 108; if I am a brain neuron, I will make genes 451, 1138, and 2099."

Of course, cells don't really know that they are a particular cell type. Instead, they have a combination of context and heritage. Context is especially important early in development, and may be provided by maternal cues, environmental conditions, and signals from other cells on their way to becoming you. As development progresses, cells have more heritage and that becomes relevant. Skin cells beget more skin cells, not muscle cells or neurons.

Again, we start out as a single cell whose primary job is to divide from one to two to four cells and so on. After a few days of this, there are a couple of hundred cells (it takes a while to copy your entire genome) roughly in a ball; at this point, the cells start to have different functions. There is a notion of outside, the edge of the sphere, where cells will develop into skin and hair, and a notion of inside, the interior, where cells develop into internal organs. In other words, after several rounds of cell division, there are asymmetries that arise from the interactions between cells that did not exist for one cell by itself. And once those asymmetries are present, further asymmetries can be defined.

One cellular activity is making and releasing chemicals that act as signals to the other cells around them. As those signal molecules spread from their origin, they become less concentrated, creating a gradient, another form of asymmetry. Those signals can control which proteins get made, and can do so in a concentration-dependent fashion so that cells receiving more signal make different proteins than cells receiving less. Among the proteins controlled by those gradients are those which make other chemical signals that can make more gradients. The first gradients specify major axes (just like Ender Wiggin in the Battle Room) such as head-foot, back-front, and left-right. A subsequent gradient can establish something like an arm, with cells at the high end becoming the shoulder and those at the low end becoming the hand. A further gradient indicates the thumb-to-pinky orientation of the hand.

Let's talk about that last example in more detail. The signal chemical in question is a protein dubbed Sonic hedgehog. As arm development progresses to the point where the hand is ready to form, some of the hand cells start making Sonic hedgehog protein. Cells closest to that side of the hand become the pinky, while cells at the other end where there is no Sonic hedgehog become the thumb. Intermediate concentrations along the way signal formation of the other fingers.

This mechanism explains why some people wind up with more or fewer than the typical number of fingers. If the cells making Sonic hedgehog make too much of the protein, the concentrations across the hand wind up differently. More cells toward the thumb end receive enough Sonic hedgehog signal to start making a finger instead of a thumb, but there are also cells receiving no signal and so they still make a thumb. There is no mechanism to count fingers, there are simply mechanisms to make different fingers in response to different amounts of signal.

Interestingly, the same Sonic hedgehog protein is used at other times and other places to signal spinal cord development, tooth development and lung development. This is where context and combinations of signals is key. When Sonic hedgehog is made in the hand, those cells have already received other signals that indicate they are part of the arm and not, say, the mouth. It is really the combination of those other signals plus Sonic hedgehog that results in finger growth; Sonic hedgehog plus different signals prompt different development pathways.

Overlapping and intersecting gradients can establish major axes and large-scale body plan features like limbs. On a smaller scale, there is a need for repeating features that are distributed spatially but don't need to be arranged precisely or in an exact number. For example, as those fingers develop, the skin needs several features. Some cells need to grow hair, some need to become nerves, some need to be actual skin cells, and so on. Which ones become hair follicles, say, is not critical, as long as there are hairs everywhere and they don't all clump up too close together.

Coordinating the growth of some hair follicles while preventing all the skin cells from turning into follicles requires coordination between cells via a series of signals. The first signal is received by all skin cells on the surface, at which point some of them respond by starting the process of follicle formation. Those cells that start first generate a second signal that inhibits follicle formation and is released to the cells around them. Essentially, it's a game of 'shotgun;' whichever cells call 'follicle' first get to be follicles and the other cells follow different developmental paths. There are subsequent signals to further complete the follicle, and other structures elsewhere in the body have their own signal combinations, but the basic principle of interacting positive and negative signals ensures that all the different necessary tissues and organs develop.

In a way, developmental biology has features of chaotic dynamics and strange attractors that we saw earlier. As with chaotic dynamics, there are certain degrees of freedom; each skin cell has the opportunity to respond or not to the call of becoming a follicle. Development does not require that any one cell make a particular choice in that regard. And yet the interplay of positive and negative feedback provides some high level stability of outcome and structure, just as with strange attractors. Once again, the emergence and continued existence of life thrives on grace.

To this point, we've covered how context matters to human development and contributes to the variety of cell types even when each cell has the same genome. This is also the explanation we get in *Orphan Black* for the differences between clones; the environments they grew up in, the encouragement or discouragement they received along the way—these are the factors that led to one clone becoming a suburban soccer mom while another became a lesbian molecular biologist. But heritage is also critical to human development and function. In this case, I don't mean one human's heritage from her parents, but each cell's heritage of the parent cell from which it divided.

Once certain skin cells start down the path to making a follicle, there is no turning back. Those cells will continue to divide, but all of the resulting cells will remain follicle cells; they cannot change careers and become nerve cells or part of a blood vessel, even if skin needs those cell types too. The way that heritage is communicated is not directly in the DNA sequence, since all of them have the same sequence. Rather, annotations of the DNA molecule preserve a record of a cell's heritage and influence which sequences actually get made into proteins in that cell and its descendants.

The DNA in a single cell, if stretched out so that the ACGT sequence were fully linear, would be about two meters long, basically as long as you are tall. Yet cells are microscopically small, so obviously they don't have room to keep all of that sequence unrolled. DNA can be wound up around proteins called histones in an arrangement not unlike a rolled up scroll of the sort parts of the Bible used to be written on. Just like a scroll cuts down on the storage space needed for a manuscript, winding DNA around histones allows it to be packed tightly in the nucleus. But, just like you can't read a scroll that is rolled up, DNA around a histone can't be transcribed into RNA and translated into protein.

Thus the particular choice of which parts of the DNA sequence to wind up and which to leave unwound and accessible influences which proteins a cell makes and thus what activities it can contribute to the body. And that information about which DNA sequences to leave unwound are passed on from one cell to the next as development proceeds. The information encoded in the sequence is called genetic information, and the heritage communicated through development is called epigenetic information because it is a layer on top of the genetic information. The genetic information is not altered or erased in terms of its ACGT sequence, it is simply annotated.

One consequence of epigenetic information is that you can't tell everything about a cell just by reading the ACGT sequence of its genome. That's true of people as well. In a way, our DNA is like a set of axioms in that they set some boundaries and they are only fully appreciated once we start interpreting them by proving theorems, which in this case is decoding them into proteins and seeing what activities those provide for cells and bodies. And also like a set of axioms, they are incomplete and do not answer every question we might wish to answer biologically. We are certainly not less than our genome, but we are also more than our genome.

7.3 Your Changing Church Body

We started talking about genomes and biology partly to understand how the church, its members, and the Bible are related. So now let's consider the implications of all these biological ideas for how we are to function together as the body of Christ. The first thing that stands out to me is the pattern of growth. The church began with a single individual, Jesus. Just as the single cell represents all of the necessary potential to become a fully formed human, so Jesus represents the fullness of human potential that he wants his church to realize.

To realize that potential, Jesus began his ministry by recruiting a small core group of disciples to labor with him. While the Gospels regularly mention larger crowds who followed Jesus and listened to his teaching, he focused his attention on this group of twelve. It was these twelve who would then spread out and start churches elsewhere, which in turn sent missionaries out to start more churches, and so on. These subsequent movements replicated this same pattern of growing from individuals or small groups that expanded as circumstances allowed.

There are clear advantages to this approach, in the sense that often one or a few can go places and do things that a large group cannot. The challenge is for those folks to be flexible and able to do many jobs, because they are all that there is. The apostle Paul captured this idea when he wrote "I have become all things to all people" (1 Corinthians 9:22). In the same way, your cells can't specialize too quickly in development; they need to be able to maintain that potential to do a wide variety of jobs in the future.

Even in the first century as the church spread, we begin to see the signs of specialization in response to context. One group of churches was developing in and around Jerusalem, among the Jews. Other groups were developing in Turkey, Greece, and Rome, in the context of the Greek, Roman, and other cultures of those nations. The practices of those churches began to diverge, since communication was slow, making it logistically difficult for them to keep synchronized; the local environment was bound to be influential. When the leaders of the different churches discovered that they had different practices, the immediate response was to think that one group had to change to fall in line with the other group. Ultimately, however, those leaders mutually decided to recognize that their core principles could in fact be expressed in different ways depending on the context.

This does not mean, however, that anything goes. Think about our cells: they have a wide latitude to express different genes in their particular contexts, but they can't just invent new genes on the spot. For the church, the Bible serves the role of the genome. Even as those early churches were discovering how to best express their principles in their different contexts, they agreed on the texts that would guide them in their decision making. Everything that they did had to arise from those texts and be consistent with them, otherwise they could not claim to be part of the Christian church, the body of Christ. But they had freedom to determine what that looked like in their environment.

If we push a little further on the idea of the Bible as the genome of the church, we come to an interesting observation. There is no single cell that expresses every single gene in your genome. There are some core genes that they all use, such as the ones that are involved in making proteins from DNA. Every cell needs to be able to do that. But other sequences are only used by certain cell types. And even then, they aren't all used all the time; some play a role at one stage of development, while others are relevant to mature cells, and still others only come into play in response to a certain external signal or condition.

Likewise, the church, rather than the individual Christian, is the unit that expresses the entirety of the Christian genome. After all, the Bible is a pretty big book, making it practically challenging to keep the whole thing in mind all at once. Even when we are trying to live according to the Bible, we tend to be thinking about a few verses or a group of ideas rather than the entire Bible. Rather than trying to pretend that we can do otherwise, we can embrace that arrangement as the way things are meant to operate.

Of course, there are some fundamentals that will be common to all Christians. Every Christian should be able to read the Bible themselves, just as every cell needs to be able to read the genome and put it into action. Every Christian needs to be connected to the overall church, just as every cell needs to be able to interact with the other cells. But some of the functions within that church can be divided up among us all. And this seems to be exactly the idea that Paul is getting at when he talks about us all being members of the same body but having different gifts and different purposes.

How do we discern what those purposes are? We can take some cues from our cells. Remember the two factors that influence the role that each cell plays in our bodies: heritage and context. On the one hand, we are born with particular skills, gifts and abilities that are further influenced by where we come from. It is natural to use the model of our parents, influential leaders, and those who have preceded us in a particular role to inform the way that we lead our lives. On the other hand, we need to take into consideration the balance of functions, to ensure that all of them are represented. The council of those around us are valuable in considering these questions, and we have a responsibility ourselves to communicate clearly about how we can contribute so that others can adjust accordingly.

We've primarily been discussing purpose and membership within the context of the Christian church, but many of the same principles apply to any group of people working together toward some common end. Companies, clubs, and even casual social circles all tend to be composed of people who each bring something a little different to the table, and it is in the group's best interest to see those individuals engaged in personally satisfying ways. So even as I'm trying to illustrate for you what it looks like to be part of a church so you can potentially make an informed decision about joining if you haven't already, hopefully you'll find some relevant ideas about group dynamics and individual fulfillment within a group that are applicable somewhere in your life.

While exploring what the Bible has to say about group dynamics, we've looked at the writings of Paul, but they aren't the only place in the Bible where diverse skills are relevant. In Exodus, the Israelites are given detailed instructions for building a tabernacle in which to worship God. Individuals are mentioned by name, like Bezalel and Aholiab, for specific jobs because they have the necessary skills. The construction of Solomon's temple later in 1 Chronicles similarly requires numerous artisans with expertise in metalwork, textiles, and various other crafts. Individuals are able to complete these tasks precisely because they have both aptitude and training for them.

Elsewhere, we see individuals take up different tasks because the job needs to be done. The book of Judges is all about leaders called to lead because the people of Israel need them, not because they are obvious candidates. Recall Gideon's rigorous confirmation of his calling because he did not believe himself to be an obvious leader; Jephthah is an outcast because of his parentage and Deborah is underestimated for her gender. David was a youngest son, a shepherd, and not the son of the king when he was anointed to be king of Israel. The prophet Amos was a shepherd and explicitly not "a prophet by profession" (Amos 7:14). Jesus' disciples we mentioned before included fishermen, a tax collector for Rome, and a political insurgent, hardly a dream team for a new religious movement. And yet each of these and more rose to the occasion because they recognized a need.

Rising to the occasion in response to a need is not limited to biblical narratives. Farm boy Luke Skywalker and scoundrel Han Solo would scarcely be mistaken for the knights or soldiers of classical heroic tales, yet both saved a galaxy when called upon. Scrawny Steve Rogers was determined to play his part for the Allied cause in World War II, only being transformed into Captain America after demonstrating a willingness to do whatever was asked of him. And in real life, thousands of us every day heed the call of doing what needs to be done, in ways big and small, so that the collective enterprise of society can carry on.

Sometimes, our heritage and our context come together in unexpected ways. Our inherited skills and passions may find uses we've never anticipated until we are in a context that provides an opportunity to express that application. Moses thought himself underqualified for leading Israel out of Egypt, having been in exile for decades, but his particular heritage as both an Israelite and an Egyptian courtier provided him a unique perspective and opportunity. Ezra was a priest and a scribe in exile who was granted an opportunity to apply his learning on a large scale as the leader and teacher of Israelites permitted to return to Jerusalem by the Persian empire. Even Paul himself redirected his zeal for God's truth from the persecution of Jesus' followers to the propagation of Jesus' teachings.

The role of context and heritage in the development of our church bodies helps to explain why we don't all wind up looking the same, either individually or as congregations and denominations, even though we all read the same Bible. At the same time, it highlights the reality that the Bible does not fully determine everything about our Christian practice and beliefs, just as our genome does not fully determine our biology. That doesn't mean any aspect of our Christianity that is not fully determined by the Bible is wrong. It is simply a recognition that the Bible isn't a complete rule book for every decision we might have to make, which is fine since it neither claims to be nor needs to be.

In fact, the Bible explicitly allows for the reality that it does not fully determine all our choices. Earlier we discussed circumcision and the ultimate conclusion that it was fine for some believers to observe that practice while others didn't. In a previous chapter, we saw that eating meat dedicated to idols was acceptable depending on context. The freedom to make these choices would not be possible under a fully deterministic religion.

We can also recognize the practices of our various Christian traditions that are not explicitly biblical. There are commonplace matters like the way we organize our Sunday services and the songs we choose to sing. There are theological concepts such as God's omniscience or the doctrine of original sin. Different traditions vary on these matters precisely because they are not fully determined by the text. Our decisions in these matters are informed by biblical principles, but the history of the whole church, our denomination, our specific congregation, and our personal experiences also play roles.

Such variety and lack of specificity might be problematic if perfect obedience were required. Mercifully, as we have seen, God has built grace into the system. Grace makes it possible to leave some decisions undetermined in advance without leaving a trap for everyone who guesses wrong. And thus grace enables us to follow Jesus in different and diverse ways rather than requiring a one-size-fits-all approach.

One benefit of allowing specialization and diversity is that the complexity of tasks that can be addressed increases. A bacterial colony, even with a comparable number of cells to a human body, can't accomplish anything resembling singing a song or running a race, let alone designing computers or landing on the moon, because each individual cell has to worry about where its next meal is coming from. By contrast, most of your cells never have to give that any consideration because everything they need will just be delivered automatically, precisely because there are some cells that focus exclusively on passing that food around. The tradeoff is dependence; if the food deliveries stop coming, your heart cells are in big trouble.

The church as a whole can similarly accomplish projects no individual Christian could undertake. Humanitarian relief efforts, systematic theologies, and elaborately choreographed worship celebrations are just a few of the opportunities to realize the full potential of God's creation collectively. Even the very presence of the church on every continent is a testimony to the coordinated efforts of linguists, teachers, fundraisers, and other faithful servants playing their part in God's global mission. In order to focus and specialize on our particular roles, we need to rely on others to take care of tasks we don't have the time, skill, or opportunity for. That might mean having help from Sunday school volunteers in teaching our children, relying on scholars to help us understand the historical context of a Bible passage, or deferring to scientists about the best way to interpret particular data. We all do this to a greater or lesser extent already, even outside of the church context; few of us grow all our own food and make all our own clothes and build our own homes and manufacture our own cell phones, etc. If nothing else, I simply think it is worth being a little more aware and appreciative of just how much we depend on each other.

This dependency reminds me of another biological observation, namely that the larger and more complex a body's anatomy becomes, the harder it is to circulate everything the body needs and the more effort that needs to be put into it. The most basic multicellular organisms, like slime molds, have no circulatory system to speak of; between their small size and the natural mixing tendency of the world (remember our discussion of entropy) that's taken care of automatically. Plants have circulatory systems, but no pumps; even the tallest trees are simple enough that basic fluid dynamics will get everything where it needs to go with appropriate channels. Animals have more complex body plans, requiring hearts to actively distribute blood so that it gets everywhere it is needed and valves to regulate flow.

This would seem to have interesting implications for the church at large. There is no denying the size and complexity of the global Christian church in the present day. At the broadest scale, it is large enough to qualify for needing active circulation. We should be mindful of the need to have this role be filled within our body, and to ask in what ways our local church, our regional associations of churches, and our denominations can contribute. What expertise do we have locally that could benefit other communities in our region? What lessons can we learn from the collective church in South Korea or Zambia or Brazil? How does our denomination cooperate with other denominations on humanitarian projects that are mutually valued? All of these questions and others like them are already discussed, and I also think this is a particular aspect of a healthy body that could be highlighted more explicitly.

Inadequate circulation—sharing of resources, ideas, skills—is just one way for the church body to be unhealthy. Understanding how our biological health can go wrong is another way our body metaphor can help us understand how to live together as fellow followers of Jesus. Exploring diseases is the topic of our next chapter.

CHAPTER 8

Spleens, Strains, and Autoimmunity

Traditionally, the core of the Justice League is a trio of characters: Batman, Superman, and Wonder Woman. Any one of them could break the League apart if they so desired. Every one of them has suffered wounds in the past that might justify wariness of others. Instead, their commitment to each other has a healing influence that makes the League work.

As a boy, Bruce Wayne had everything: devoted parents, a bright future, and enough wealth to make any dream a reality. In an instant, his family and his future were taken from him. And so was born Batman, a vigilante determined to prevent crime from doing the same to anyone else. But in that same moment was born a deep suspicion; Bruce Wayne would find it difficult to trust anyone, lest they take from him or are taken from him. This doubt will eat away at Batman's relationships even with fellow superheroes, driving him to plan ways to take down even his closest allies should the need arise.

As an infant, Kal-El had nothing except the rocket ship that carried him away from his doomed home planet of Krypton. On Earth he would be taken in by the Kent family and raised as their son Clark. The sacrifices of both his Kryptonian birth parents and adoptive Earth parents taught Clark to view others selflessly and optimistically. He also strives for justice, not to spare anyone his own fate but instead to give as many people as possible the same opportunities he had.

The dynamic between Batman and Superman is already rich with story potential. Adding Wonder Woman as a bridge between the two adds even deeper levels. Like Bruce Wayne, Princess Diana was a child of privilege, wanting for nothing in her youth. Yet she set it all aside to become an immigrant like Clark Kent, living in a world not her own because it needs her. Having grown up in a female-only Amazonian paradise, she might have exceeded even Batman in distrust of men. Instead, she chooses love and truth over fear and hate and so brings out the best in her teammates (a quality Gal Gadot demonstrates well in her film portrayals of Wonder Woman).

If we are going to further develop our body analogy, guardians of humanity like the Justice League have natural parallels to the immune system. I studied the biology of communicable diseases as a graduate student in a public health school, so immunity, infections and vaccines are of great interest to me. Everyone who studies infectious diseases learns about the eradication of smallpox; I had the privilege of hearing about it from Donald Henderson himself, one of the leaders of that effort. It was a remarkable triumph for public health, and at the time we expected many similar successes thanks to vaccines, antibiotics, improved sanitation and other advances. Three decades later, smallpox remains the sole pathogen taken out of circulation, raising questions about why that effort succeeded where others have not. (Polio is close to being eliminated, and may have been when you read this.) The efficacy of the vaccine relative to how contagious smallpox is, the driving leadership of Henderson and others, and a confluence of global political will all played a part. But the factor that most stood out to me when I first heard the story was the obvious nature of the infection: when you have smallpox, everyone knows it and stays away.

One of the last things Jesus told his disciples is that the world would know they were his followers by the way that they loved one other. That was to be the marker of a health church body, and would make it attractive to others. But what happens when the church isn't healthy? What does smallpox for a church look like, a disease that repels people rather than drawing them in? Well, if a healthy body is a useful analogy for how we can get along, maybe an unhealthy body can suggest some patterns to avoid.

8.1 Internal Crisis

While external concerns might first come to mind, whether we're talking health issues or threats to the Justice League, not all problems start on the outside. For example, we mentioned Batman's plans for dealing with his teammates. Occasionally a mind control plot or evil doppelgänger infiltration will require Batman to tap into his emergency kryptonite or some other contingency. At the same time, the very existence of these contingency plans and the distrust they imply will create tensions for the League when the others discover what Batman has been up to. As a result, the Justice League can sometimes be their own worst enemies.

Likewise, there are many ways that our own bodies can create problems for us. Cancer, diabetes, dementia—these are all too familiar failures of our bodies to function as they should. Globally, you are more likely to die from heart disease or a stroke than any other single cause.

Probably the most obvious disease state is the lack of some particular cell function, cell type, tissue or organs. At the lowest level, there are diseases like phenylketonuria or cystic fibrosis, where the lack of a single protein activity has significant consequences. In the case of phenylketonuria, what's missing is the ability to break down a particular amino acid, one of the modular parts of proteins, leading to imbalances in the chemical makeup of cells. In the case of cystic fibrosis, one of the gatekeeper proteins in the cell membrane doesn't do its job properly, resulting in mucus that is the wrong consistency, which makes it hard for several organs to do what they need to do and impairs the lungs' ability to absorb oxygen. Even just those singular deficiencies among the whole host of things that the human body does can have profound consequences.

On the other extreme, the lack of an entire organ can be fatal. Yes, there are some organs that your body can cope without, such as the gallbladder, appendix, or spleen. But even in those cases, there are consequences or complications that can arise from not having them. Despite what was once thought, even the appendix contributes to the optimal functioning of your body, specifically the immune system. Likewise, you can function with a partial liver, only one kidney, or reduced lung capacity, but these are not ideal conditions for optimal present and future health. And then of course not having a heart or a brain can be fatal.

For these disease conditions, I think the implication for the church is clear—a healthy church needs all its parts. And as in the previous chapter, the same can be said for any organization or group of people, even if the exact needed parts may vary. How that breaks down for smaller groups such as individual congregations or local chapters of a fan club is less clear, as there will obviously be smaller groups that practically cannot have the same diversity of gifts, personalities, experiences, etc. as each other or as larger bodies. But even at the smallest sizes, I think diversity along as many dimensions as possible should be considered beneficial.

Of particular concern to me is the representation of the scientific and the nerdy within the church. I think these are folks who have valuable contributions to make to the church, and to keep them at arm's length intentionally or inadvertently is to diminish the body as a whole. That's not to say those groups are completely absent from the church, nor that they are underrepresented or undervalued in every congregation. And of course we can't artificially enforce their recruitment or participation. I would simply submit that those are dimensions of diversity worthy of consideration amongst many others where the church should consider whether it adequately reflects the population it serves.

Missing community elements figure into several Bible accounts. The book of Judges is a series of stories in which Israel struggles for lack of leadership. The reign of King Josiah brings to an end a season of dysfunction in the kingdom of Judah once the written law is rediscovered and the priesthood can operate properly again (2 Kings 22–23). Paul's letter to Philemon concerns itself with ensuring that Onesimus is allowed to serve to his fullest capacity. At the largest and smallest scales, when the people of God are not whole, then the entire body cannot reach its potential.

Pain is an essential physiological function whose role in health is often underappreciated. Individuals who cannot feel pain are more susceptible to serious injuries and infections because they don't sense the early warning signs to pull their hand from the fire or seek treatment. We might lament the presence of pain in our lives, and indeed some experiences of pain seem divorced from this purpose. But overall, pain is a form of communication; if we could somehow rewire our perception to interpret the message of pain as a more neutral or abstract sensation, it would cease to be effective communication.

Within the context of the church, we need to ensure that we remain collectively sensitive to what ails and harms the church and creation at large. Essentially, we need to cultivate our sense of *Weltschmerz*. We should make room to "weep with those who weep" as Paul exhorts in Romans 12:15. Of course, a fully functioning nervous system also communicates messages of pleasure and well-being. Sensing that which brings flourishing to our church body and to the world is another way to avoid harm, and so we also heed Paul's advice to "rejoice with those who rejoice" from the same verse.

Sensitivity to communicated messages plays a role in other diseases as well. Cells are frequently communicating with each other; we saw in the previous chapter how that facilitates development. Intercellular communication continues throughout our lives. Cells need food and one main source is sugar, making it important that your blood maintains appropriate amounts at all times. Insulin is a chemical signal made by your pancreas that controls whether your body puts more sugar into the blood, or takes it out and stores it for later. More insulin means store more sugar.

Diabetes is the disease that results when this cell-to-cell communication breaks down. There are two kinds; type I diabetes is inherited and is the result of the pancreas not being able to produce insulin. What is interesting about type II diabetes is that your pancreas still makes insulin to a certain extent, but the cells receiving that signal stop paying attention, as it were, and your blood sugar levels become unregulated. All of the functionality is still there, it's just not balanced the way that it should be.

Metaphorically, I think the lesson of diabetes is a reminder of the bidirectional nature of effective communication. A message never sent is a message never heard. At the same time, we need to be mindful of how we present our messages such that they do not become overexposed and eminently ignorable. It's an easy situation to find oneself in, passionate as we are about our faith and zealous to see God properly glorified. I suspect many nerds can sympathize as well, having lost audiences because we got a bit carried away in our enthusiasm for a particular fictional world or scientific discovery. I do not wish to deny anyone their zeal or enthusiasm, but I do think we sometimes need a reminder that our goal should be expressing a message which can be received and responded to rather than just satisfying our own desire to be heard.

Similarly, we should also take care to remain sensitive to the passions of others when they are shared. As the parable of the sower (Matthew 13; Mark 4; Luke 8) reminds us, the responsibility for responding to a message ultimately lies with the receiver. It may take an effort sometimes to hear with fresh ears something we have listened to many times before, but being receptive to what others have to offer is a way in which we can be gracious to them. We want to avoid making our "hearts as hard as diamond" that prevents us from obeying "the Torah and the other words of the Lord" (Zechariah 7:12).

When I was in high school and college, sharing my passion for biology frequently led to people encouraging me to pursue a cure for cancer. Given its public health significance, and the lengthy and visible effects it has on people, that's not surprising. Cancer is a broad class of diseases, but there is one thing that all cancers have in common. Cancerous cells grow and divide out of sync with what is beneficial to the rest of the body.

We touched on cell division briefly last chapter. Early in development, our cells are dividing as quickly as possible to grow from a microscopic cell to something our parents can hold in a timely fashion. But for most of our lives, most of our cells don't divide that rapidly, if at all. There are DNA sequences and proteins that regulate how often a cell divides. Sometimes, a mutation occurs in one of those regulatory sequence or proteins within a single cell, allowing that cell to divide more rapidly. Since that cell passes on the mutated version, its progeny cells divide quickly too and before long there is a large mass of cells where one doesn't belong: a tumor. Sometimes the mutation reduces the effectiveness of a "don't divide" signal, sometimes the mutation enhances the strength of a "divide" signal; but one way or the other, all cancers result from a shift in the regulation of cell division.

If we stick with the metaphor that the genome is to a cell what the Bible is to a Christian, then the picture of cancer corresponds to a scenario where the Bible is distorted in order to achieve rapid growth above all other considerations. That is not to say that growth is inherently bad or wrong, or that any congregation, denomination or movement that is large or growing is somehow going against the Bible. At the very beginning, the church experienced very rapid growth relative to its size and there is no indication that was inappropriate. And just because rapid cell division is primarily a feature of early development does not mean church growth at that pace was only appropriate at the beginning, both because we don't need to be slavishly beholden to the body analogy and because even in an adult there are cells that need to divide rapidly. Hair follicles and the immune system are cell types that divide regularly, and since many cancer treatments target rapid growth indiscriminately, patients on those treatments lose their hair and have reduced immunity.

Still, growth in and of itself is not the ultimate goal. For one, growth needs to be balanced with differentiation, specialization, and circulation, as we've discussed, to make sure that all of the needs of the new members and the congregation or church as a whole are being met. When growth is the ultimate goal, it makes individuals a means to an end rather than an end unto themselves, and that is never a good idea. Further, a focus on growth tends to put a focus on numbers, which are naturally ordered and thus easy to compare, but numeric comparisons between groups aren't always healthy or helpful. That's not just a church thing; the health of any community needs to be considered in context and not simply based on its relative size to every other community. And I say that as someone who does statistical analysis for a living; it's not that I don't value quantitative evaluation, but rather that experience has taught me to be careful and thorough in such analysis rather than focusing on a single, reductive value.

King David took a census of his army in 1 Chronicles 21. He was apparently motivated by pride in his military might or a desire to assess his nation's loyalty to himself. His advisors warn against it, and when he follows through God expresses his disappointment. And remember Gideon from Judges? Following God's guidance, his first act as a military commander is to send most of his forces home. These stories remind us that absolute size is not our highest priority. Of course, there are plenty of population counts in the Bible, including the book of Numbers that features two censuses. Counting and growth are not intrinsically bad, they just need to be balanced.

The book of Numbers also famously includes a biblical account of an actual physical affliction and a public health intervention to deal with it (chapter 21). Disease and illness are a common human experience and so appear frequently in the Bible. As we have seen, the regulations in Leviticus in many cases have health implications in addition to any possible spiritual significance. Some of the prophets performed miracles of healing, as did Jesus and his disciples. The blind were made to see, the deaf to hear, the lame to walk. Leprosy is a common biblical malady, although most translations are quick to point out that these were not necessarily cases of what we now call Hansen's disease. There are also instances of what is described as demon possession; make of these what you will, but in terms of the way their symptoms impact the lives of the afflicted, they fit the pattern of all the other conditions.

As presented in the Bible, disease and differences of ability can be isolating in way or another. So-called lepers were quarantined because of the highly contagious and highly visible nature of their condition. Those who couldn't walk were literally left behind by everyone who passed them by. The possessed are sometimes depicted living on the margins of society. Healing these people restores them to fellowship with the rest of human kind.

Differences in sensory perception also have the potential to be isolating, especially when a channel of communication, such as sight or sound, that used to be available to someone has been altered or eliminated. Nowadays we have a variety of cultural and technological options, from eyeglasses to wearable computers and implantable sensors, for supplementing our biological senses or providing alternative communication channels, such as sign language or Braille. In the biblical eras, there were far fewer options. Thus, when Jesus could provide a biological option for those who wanted it, such as giving sight to those who were blind (e.g., Luke 18, John 9) or hearing to those who could not hear (Mark 7), that was significant. Suddenly, these people had new means by which to connect with others, and also to experience the rest of the natural world.

8.2 Crisis on Infectious Earths

Hansen's disease brings us back where we started with communicable diseases. When we think about getting sick, this is probably what first comes to mind. Some of us experience genetic or developmental diseases from very early on, but for many of us, catching a cold or getting chickenpox or coming down with a "stomach bug" is our first experience with being ill. Before we can even remember, we are vaccinated against a whole suite of infections we likely know only by reputation, such as mumps or rubella. Every year, our doctors and our news reports remind us about flu season.

And those are just the tip of the iceberg. We check for ticks to avoid Lyme disease, wear insect repellent to ward off West Nile virus, and keep an eye out for bats with rabies. We wear condoms to prevent gonorrhea, syphilis and HIV. If we in the West travel abroad, there are pills and shots and water advisories so we don't get malaria, yellow fever, or cholera. Pregnant women don't scoop cat litter because of toxoplasmosis, misshapen canned goods are suspected of harboring botulism, and rusty nails are a vector for tetanus. And you probably haven't even heard of Chagas disease, Marburg hemorrhagic fever, Nipah virus, or schistosomiasis.

One could be forgiven for thinking that the microbial world, from *Acinetobacter* to Zika virus, is out to get us all. We'd find a sympathetic listener in Batman, who we mentioned sees conspiracy behind every negative outcome. In one specific sense, Batman is not paranoid, because so many rogues really are out to get him, his teammates, and the world. At the same time, Batman needs the optimism of Superman and the love of Wonder Woman to remind him not to give up on everyone. For every Joker, Lex Luthor, and Darkseid, there are millions of people worth fighting for rather than against.

Likewise, we are only recently coming to appreciate all the ways that micro-organisms contribute to our health. In addition to the trillions of cells descended from that first zygote we discussed last chapter and that we traditionally think of as "us," our bodies are hosts to entire ecosystems of viruses, bacteria, and microscopic eukaryotes. These tiny life forms are with us from birth, initially passed on from our mothers and subsequently enriched by our interactions with other people and with our environment. They are not merely harmless, failing to cause disease, but actively beneficial.

What's more, they vastly outnumber the microbes capable of making us ill. Our bodies host trillions of these beneficial organisms constantly. Over our lifetimes, that's innumerable interactions with possibly quadrillions of individual micro-organisms. By contrast, the number of times microbes make us sick likely number in the dozens all told, each episode initiated by as few as one individual cell or virus particle. Imagine if every person alive was actively looking out for your well-being save one; you'd probably think pretty favorably of your fellow humans.

Naturally I don't want to downplay or deny the seriousness of infections. To be sure, an encounter with the wrong microbe can be harmful and even fatal. Handwashing, vaccines, and all the preventive measures mentioned above are prudent and warranted. My point is simply that such experiences are the exception rather than the rule. And since we don't consciously perceive our interactions with beneficial micro-organisms, we need to be reminded of their presence and their benefits.

With that perspective, let's consider the three categories I mentioned: viruses, bacteria and microscopic eukaryotes. Viruses are inert packages of DNA (or RNA) wrapped in protein. Bacteria are single-celled organisms that bear only the most rudimentary resemblances to our own cells. Microscopic eukaryotes, which can be either unicellular or multicellular in organization, have cells organized in the same ways that ours are, with multiple distinct compartments like a nucleus and mitochondria. The diseases that they cause are diverse and oftentimes distasteful, but fear not: we will not overly concern ourselves with their symptoms so much as their mechanisms of infection.

8.2.1 Viruses

I mentioned earlier the challenge of defining life, and cited viruses as an example of an edge case. They do possess the kind of genetic material we normally associate with living organisms, and they pass those genes on to descendants. But they are always dependent on the kindness of strangers to provide the machinery and raw materials to produce those offspring. Many are just genetic material packaged in a protein shipping container, sometimes with a few additional proteins but not enough to make a new virus particle even if they were surrounded by the component nucleic and amino acids. They can't move on their own and show very little evidence of responding to their environment in the ways we expect living things to do; by comparison, plants are practically Olympic athletes. Viruses are biological information distilled.

The protein packages of a virus generally contain a forged key for one of the membrane gatekeeper proteins we mentioned, tricking the cell into letting them in. Once inside, the protein package is broken down or falls to pieces. The genes inside do their best to fly casual, so that they will eventually be picked up by the gene-copying and protein-making pipelines of the cell. There are a variety of mechanisms for this, depending on whether the virus carries its genes around in DNA or RNA, but the core idea is the same. The cell it has infiltrated will make more copies of the virus genes, and will make more protein boxes for those genes to go into. The genes are packaged up and sent out from the cell to infect others. Sometimes this is a subtle process, a trickle of viruses that can persist indefinitely while the cell also goes about its normal business. Other times, the infected cell is given over so fully to the making of viruses parts that it neglects all of its other duties, until it either starves to death or bursts at the seams from the volume of viruses.

Under the metaphor of genes-as-language, it is tempting to think of viruses as a warning against outside or foreign ideas. And indeed, ideas are powerful and thus potentially dangerous. It is even possible to be so fully consumed by an idea that it takes over your life. Among many tales of obsession, I think the film *Inception* depicts being consumed by an idea most powerfully. *Inception* is about a crew of infiltration experts who invade minds rather than money vaults, sometimes to plunder and sometimes to probe defenses. And sometimes they plant information in a mind rather than plucking it out, eventually raising the question of whether the only thing more devastating than failing to achieve that goal is succeeding because of the life-changing effect of the idea.

It is also the case that our own genomes contain rather a lot of virus genes. Sometimes a virus can be so good at convincing a cell that the virus' genes belong in the cell that the cell winds up integrating them directly into its own DNA, which then gets passed on to any cells descended from it. We can recognize these viral genes in our human genome; they still contain signatures of their origins. But they are also irrevocably part of us.

And so it also is with ideas. They have to come from somewhere; we don't all conceive of every single thought *de novo* no matter how creative a person we may be. Rather than trying to deny these outside influences, I think we would be better served to learn well how to recognize them and feel comfortable acknowledging their origins. If they are of value, if they are consistent with how we have chosen to engage with the world, then we can hold onto them and redemptively transform them as necessary. If they aren't, we leave them on their merry way. This is the same pattern we observe biologically, where incorporated viral sequences have been employed to our benefit in some instances. After all, they are merely information that can always be reinterpreted in a new context.

In terms of our metaphor between genomes and the Bible, I am not proposing that there are passages in the Bible that don't belong. But even the Bible shows the influences of the culture around it, such as when Paul uses terminology from Greek philosophy to express ideas in way that would make sense to his Greek audience but perhaps not to writers and readers of earlier Hebrew portions of the Bible. The most popular example is in Acts 17, a narrative account of Paul's encounter with Greek scholars in which he alludes to Greek poetry and theology, reframing their ideas in a way that expressed Paul's message about Jesus. That is not to say that Paul is reducible to a rehash of Greek philosophy. But just like everybody else, his language needed its metaphors from somewhere. And so he encourages reflection on "whatever is true, whatever is worthy of respect, whatever is just, whatever is pure, whatever is lovely, whatever is commendable, if something is excellent or praiseworthy" (Philippians 4:8) it is of value, without any caveat that it must come from the Bible.

Again, discrimination is important. The Bible also warns regularly about false or harmful ideas. Prophets like Jeremiah, Ezekiel, Micah and Zephaniah spoke against false teaching. Jesus describes false prophets with the metaphor of wolves in sheep's clothing (Matthew 7:15). The brief New Testament letters of 2 Peter, 2 John and Jude are all almost entirely warnings against false teaching. Clearly this is serious business.

Still, we acknowledged in the last chapter that not all of our Christian tradition flows explicitly from the Bible. Following the example of Paul, Christian teachers and writers from St. Patrick and Augustine to C. S. Lewis and J. R. R. Tolkien and into the present have brought ideas and texts from contemporary culture alongside the canon of scripture, while not explicitly adding to it. Transforming and redeeming the ideas we encounter is thus not inherently problematic; we simply need to be mindful of the process, where the ideas are coming from, how they compare to the scripture we have agreed is of value, and whether we are overly consumed with repeating and passing on ideas that are not worth our resources.

One other facet of viruses strikes me as worthwhile metaphorically. Recall that they are genes that do little more than make copies of themselves. Our own genes also make copies of themselves, but accomplish a great many other things besides. Like the ninth-wall-breaking "Ten Dollar Solo" from *Commentary! The Musical* or Peter Schickele's delightful "If Love Is Real," viruses are about nothing except themselves. Let them serve as a reminder to us, then, that our lives ought to be about something more than themselves, that the things we create should mean something that goes beyond the self-referential. Commentary and metafiction have their place, a rich ecosystem of created content and meaning on which to comment.

8.2.2 Bacteria

Unlike commentary and viruses, bacteria are self-sufficient creatures. They can do all the things we noted that viruses cannot. Most significantly, this means that they are not obligated to hijack the inner workings of our cells to get by. They can get along just fine without bothering us, and in fact many of them do precisely that. While clusters of bacteria can coordinate and communicate, arguably individual bacterial cells are even more independent than our genomic cells who rely heavily on each other.

We don't tend to talk about it much in polite company, but each one of us is a teeming bacterial colony. If you thought the ten trillion or so cells that make up your body were a large number, there are comparable numbers of bacterial cells inside your gut. (Strictly speaking, they are considered on the outside, in the sense that the inner edge of a donut hole is still outside the donut, but since we mercifully can't see our digestive tract, we commonly think of it as inside.) You may find that an uncomfortable thought because we are generally trained to think of bacteria as gross, bad, or nasty, but they are there and have always been there since you were born.

These beneficial bacteria help you digest your food, breaking down some of the bigger molecules that our own proteins can't handle. In this sense, our genomic cells are actually dependent on those bacteria as well as each other. Bacteria also protect us from infection by harmful bacteria, basically by occupying all the spots where those bad actors might seek to invade. We are still exploring the full medical implications of our relationship with these tiny allies, but it has the potential to be quite significant in ways both obvious—changes in gut bacteria may influence overall metabolic health—and counterintuitive—gut bacteria may influence our mental health. But the overriding implication is that our natural relationship with bacteria is not adversarial but mutually beneficial.

That is not to say that bacteria do not cause illness. There are plenty of diseases caused by bacteria, from ear infections to tuberculosis to meningitis, and these can be quite serious. So-called flesh-eating bacteria are a real and serious, if mercifully uncommon, public health concern. I would be doing you a disservice to minimize these, or to leave you with the impression that you won't ever need medical treatment for bacteria just because they are natural. I simply want to reiterate that these very real disease scenarios are the exceptional cases, rather than the norm.

Because bacterial cells are so different and because we depend on them more than they depend on us, the metaphor they suggest to me is of our relationship with the rest of creation. Actually, I'm not even sure that is a metaphor so much as a microcosm. Each of us supports an entire ecology and engages in a complex and mutually beneficial relationship with other living organisms that are decidedly other, and yet not without similarities. Just as we need them to live and thrive, so we are dependent on so many other species on the planet. And just as with our hosted bacteria, when things get out of balance for other species, there are deleterious effects not just for them but for us as well. So if nothing else, what I think we should take away from a reflection on bacteria is the idea that our natural relationship with the other living creatures on Earth should not be adversarial but symbiotic.

The picture of creation as God intended in the Garden of Eden is one of harmonious relationships. Adam and Eve cultivate the garden, attending to the needs of the plants even as the plants provide them food. The book of Isaiah describes an ideal kingdom where "a wolf will reside with a lamb" (11:6) and even "a baby will play over the hole of a snake" (11:8). Proverbs informs us that "a righteous person cares for the life of his animal" (12:10). And in 1 Kings 17, ravens bring the prophet Elijah bread and meat when food is scarce. Granted, human interactions with other living creatures are not always mutually beneficial, going back to the temptation by the serpent in Eden and plagues of frogs and locust up through contemporary animal abuse and manmade extinctions, but the overall impression from the Bible is that we are to live at peace with our fellow organisms to the greatest extent possible.

8.2.3 Microscopic Eukaryotes

Finally we come to the third class of micro-organisms we host, the microscopic eukaryotes. There are a wide variety of these; the primary thing they have in common is that their cells are more like ours—meaning they have a nucleus inside of a membrane and all the other membrane compartments like mitochondria inside the primary outer membrane. Some of them are unicellular, including yeast and amoeba species. There are even multicellular organisms like skin mites. As with bacteria, we only tend to think about these kinds of creatures when they are making us ill, but the reality is that we live with them all the time and the vast majority cause no harm.

Actually, there is one context where we think positively about these microscopic eukaryotes, and also bacteria. We call them pro-biotics. "Probiotics" is just a marketable name for certain bacterial and yeast species that provide health benefits like digestive regulation and disease prevention. And probiotics contain active cultures of those species, which is linguistically convenient for our purposes.

The church also coexists with a variety of active cultures. And metaphorically, the eukaryotic components of the microbiome serve that role well. In our church body metaphor, each member is an indi-vidual cell. These microscopic eukaryotes are cells very much like us, they just organize themselves around a different genome. They live their lives according to a different word.

Of course, history is rife with conflicts between people who live their lives according to different words. And the Bible, representing a sample of that history, is no exception. Likewise, there are microscopic organisms that cause diseases, from malaria and thrush to worm and fluke infections. Once again, I don't wish to minimize the very real harms these macroscopic and microscopic conflicts can and have caused. But they don't tell the whole story, either.

The Bible also encourages living at peace with our neighbors, even those of different beliefs and cultures. We already met the Gibeonites from the book of Joshua. In that same book, there is also the story of Rahab, a Canaanite resident of Jericho who is accepted by the nation of Israel and winds up an ancestor of Jesus (Matthew 1:5). More spe-cifically, Rahab is the great-great-grandmother of David, the shepherd boy who would be king.

Rahab's son Boaz marries Ruth, herself an outsider from Midian. How she comes to meet Boaz is told in the book that bears her name. A central feature of the story is Boaz's faithful practice of leaving the gleanings as proscribed in Leviticus 19:9–10. Gleanings are leftovers in a field or vineyard after a first pass of harvesting. Leviticus says to leave them for others who are in need to gather. It is one way of not maximizing one's own asymmetrical possession of resources like we discussed in chapter 6.

Leviticus 19 also says to treat foreigners as native citizens, with love. This is an early acknowledgement that God's people will always live among other active cultures. Those boundaries and edges represent opportunities for friction, but also opportunities for harmony and constructive interaction. And the Bible records examples of both.

In the book of Daniel, the kingdom of Judah is invaded by Babylon. In the midst of exile, the faithfulness of Daniel, Hananiah, Mishael, and Azariah encourages King Nebuchadnezzar to follow their God. As recounted in Jonah, the eponymous prophet reluctantly goes to the Assyrians in Nineveh to share a message from God, which they accept with repentance and gratitude. Naaman, a foreign general, seeks and receives healing from the prophet Elisha (2 Kings 5).

The shortest book of the New Testament, 3 John, is primarily concerned with praising Gaius for welcoming strangers and outsiders, while also criticizing Diotrephes for being unwelcoming and even expelling anyone who did welcome outsiders. Of course, not every relationship in the Bible is amicable. The shortest book of the Old Testament, Obadiah, is a prophecy of coming judgment against Edom for oppressing the people of Israel. Conflict and strife arise, and protective measures are sometimes taken, but these are the extraordinary scenarios rather than the norm.

Ultimately all peoples are invited to be part of the kingdom of God. Overcoming barriers to bring the gospel to Gentiles is a major theme of Acts. Paul describes this with the metaphor of grafting branches onto a vine, where God is the vine (as in Jesus' parable), the nation of Israel are the original branches that are connected by heritage, and the Gentiles are the grafted branches connected by choices (Romans 11). One needn't be born into the kingdom of God to be a citizen.

Thus it is with our microbiome. We acquire new organisms all the time, and in a very real sense they become part of our body. Granted, they don't take on our genome, but they do contribute to what makes us, us. Here the metaphor gets a little muddy, because those who choose to join the body that is the church do take on the Word as well. But that can be a process rather than a single decision, and so we needn't wait until the process is complete to treat people who may not yet be part of the church with the same kindness and love we extend to those who are already a part.

Of course, we cannot ignore the fact that the church has its critics, and interactions between the two are not always collegial. The church and its members are not always innocent in these exchanges; we are capable of instigating hostility. But I maintain that animosity is the exception. We just notice and remember discord disproportionately, in the same way that we remember painful or embarrassing experiences more vividly. We are wired to respond more strongly to negative stimuli, a phenomenon called negativity bias. In fact, it may be related to what we discussed with entropy; there are lots of ways for things to go wrong and so any individual negative circumstance requires more information to describe how exactly things went wrong in that case. Such a bias means we have to consciously make more of an effort to recognize the larger number of ways in which we interact positively with others, since their similarity causes them to blur together.

8.3 Immunity Crisis

I actually think that understanding how our immune system works and deals with the complexity of our bodies can help us deal with negativity bias. I particularly want to focus on T-cells, the parts of our immune system that go around and check up on what all of the other cells are doing. As we discussed earlier, all cells make proteins as part of their regular activity. As they do this, they will take some of these proteins, break them down into small chunks, and put those chunks on the outside of their membrane. There are special membrane proteins that hold these pieces in place on the surface as a signal about what that cell is up to.

When the T-cells come around, they check these protein fragments on the outside of the cell. If those pieces are consistent with your genome, then the T-cell recognizes that as a "business as usual" signal and moves on. If the pieces didn't come from your genome, then the T-cells know that something unusual is going on; possibly a virus has taken over and is using the cell to make virus proteins. The cell making the unexpected protein bits will be identified as needing treatment and will be dealt with accordingly.

How do the T-cells know which protein pieces are consistent with the genome? They are actually trained to do so. Part of the process of becoming a T-cell is spending time in an organ called the thymus (which is what the "T" stands for), interacting with the protein pieces made by the thymus cells. Any T-cells that respond to those pieces are weeded out. Only the T-cells that ignore all the protein pieces are graduated from the thymus and sent out into the rest of the body to keep tabs on possible infection scenarios.

T-cells also coordinate with each other to regulate response. A single T-cell cannot decide by itself to initiate a full immune response; other T-cells must also recognize the problem and concur that a reaction is needed. This is reminiscent of various biblical requirements for at least two witnesses when enforcing discipline. There also needs to be other chemical signals from other cell types, or from the infecting organisms themselves, that make it clear an infection is happening and needs to be dealt with. A whole system of checks and balances keeps your body from being in a constant state of active defensive response, and also de-escalates conditions once an infection has been resolved.

Sometimes the training process or the checks and balances are not completely effective, and the result is what we call autoimmune diseases. Those are diseases where T-cells or other immune components start reacting to the proteins that your body is supposed to make, which as you can imagine is quite problematic. For example, my daughter experienced a condition known as Kawasaki disease. Her blood vessels were inflamed, most likely because her immune system was incorrectly identifying them as foreign or making foreign protein. This may have occurred because she had an infection and then her immune system didn't properly de-escalate.

What are the implications for the church from how the immune system works? For one, it suggests there is a role for the church to keep tabs on itself. We do need to make sure that what we are teaching and how we are acting is consistent with the Bible, and if not, then we need to take the appropriate corrective measures. And no one is exempt from the need for that sort of review. Relatedly, it is also a picture of accountability and transparency. Each cell takes responsibility for making sure that other cells can see what it is doing. I suspect we can all think of actual situations where more oversight, transparency and accountability could have prevented the church from pursuing unhealthy goals.

But what I think is most striking is the kind of check that the T-cells perform. They do not look to see that every cell is making every possible protein that the genome encodes. Among other reasons, that's because no single cell expresses the entirety of the genome and so every cell would fail that test. Instead, they simply look to see that what the cell is doing is consistent with the genome. To me, this is a very practical notion to bear in mind, to make allowances for the fact that no single person can live out every truth in the Bible at any given time. It is also a way to exercise grace with our fellow humans, to assume that if we can see some fruit that is consistent with the Bible then that person is on the right track and should be encouraged to continue.

Galatians 5 describes something along these lines as the fruit of the Spirit. We can recognize who is part of the body by how they live their lives. Titus 1:16 expresses a similar sentiment, distinguishing between those who say they are Christians and those who actually put their belief into action. This all goes back to our concept of faith as an axiom and our behavior as exploring which theorems are consistent with those axioms. Given the infinite nature of the axiom as we discussed, it would be unreasonable to expect every believer to live out every possible theorem. Instead, we should simply consider whether the theorems they do explore actually follow from the axiom.

Considering what the immune system tells us about evaluating our peers can bring us back to the Justice League. We noted that the team core of Batman, Superman and Wonder Woman all have distinct backgrounds, priorities, and motivations. The wider team, including the likes of Aquaman, king of Atlantis, and Martian Manhunter are even more diverse. Yet their shared commitment to justice enables them to distinguish who is League material and who is not.

A healthy Justice League, just like a healthy body and a healthy organization, needs healthy relationships within and without. We examined three different kinds of external relationships: peers from different groups, the wider biological world, and cultural ideas and practices. There is a time and a place to identify individual people, organisms, or ideas that are not beneficial to our group. In most cases, though, a healthy relationship will be a peaceful one of mutual benefit and care.

Internal relationships need to be healthy as well. That requires clear communication, a proper perspective on numbers and growth, and a balance and diversity of functions. A Justice League of just Batmen, or a league where everyone ignored each other, would be no league at all. We can use these principles to keep our churches healthy and thus more welcoming and attractive to those still considering whether to be a part of them. And the same goes for other groups, societies, and organizations; if your group is missing some segment you wish was included, consider the possibility that a lack of group health is telling everyone else to keep their distance.

We've been considering how our bodies work and how they get sick as a way to understand how to work together as a church. This was in part inspired by the biblical metaphor of the church as the body of Christ. We've talked a lot about how it is like a body, but in the next chapter we will look more closely at what it means to specifically be the body of Christ.

CHAPTER 9

Redeemable Ant-Man

The Avengers assembles an impressive assortment of heroes. Each of them could anchor their own film franchise, and several of them have. And yet, in a rare development for a Marvel film, the villain comes very close to stealing the show. It's not hard to see why; Loki is the archetypal schemer, the kind of villain whose cleverness you admire even as you revile their goals. (I'm sure the charisma and good looks of Tom Hiddleston don't hurt either.) Perhaps we also find a little satisfaction in seeing someone who thinks he is better than everyone else taken down a notch.

Early on in the film, Loki obliges us by making his motivations very clear, in an exchange with Samuel Jackson's Nick Fury: he has "glad tidings, of a world made free." When Fury wonders what the world needs to be freed from, Loki replies "Freedom. Freedom is life's great lie. Once you accept that, in your heart . . . you will know peace."

A couple of things stand out to me about Loki's plan. First is the language. "Glad tidings" and accepting something "in your heart" sound specifically Christian to me; we don't usually use the word *tidings* except when we are reading Luke 2 from the King James Bible at Christmas. (If that's not something you do, perhaps you've heard Linus do it in the Charlie Brown Christmas special.) This is at the very least a nice bit of characterization, having Norse god Loki speak in a slightly archaic way to set him apart. Thor's vocabulary and phrasing is similarly Jacobean.

Second, note that Loki's plan is to impose his will on Earthlings in the name of freedom. I don't know if this is meant to be Joss Whedon's interpretation of the God of the Bible, given the textual allusions, but I can't help think there are some who view God in this way, as an authoritarian or totalitarian figure determined to make everyone do things his way for their own good. Under that model, the church is made up of all the people who have been duped into doing what God tells them instead of thinking for themselves. Or, if we suppose there is no God, then those folks have been duped by fellow humans. Either way, it hardly sounds like something anyone would want to be a part of.

Is that what we are actually talking about? If we describe the church as the body of Jesus, aren't we abdicating the right to think for ourselves so someone else can think for us? Are we with those who kneel before Loki at the opera in Germany? Wouldn't we rather be the one German who defiantly remains standing? The film certainly invites us to be like that man, and given all of the dynamics in that scene, it would be hard for me to discourage you from accepting that invitation.

Right before the exchange about freedom, Loki observes that "An ant has no quarrel with a boot." He imagines himself the boot and mankind the ants by way of response to Nick Fury's attempt at conciliation—"We have no quarrel with you." Conveniently enough, that ant metaphor might be useful in unpacking the questions this scene raises for me, so let's take Proverbs advice and "look to the ant." (Thanks for the segue, Joss!)

9.1 Ant Tales to Astonish

Ants are what entomologists call social insects. That doesn't (necessarily) mean that ants are extroverted or gregarious; it's not clear whether they have the capacity to enjoy each other's company in the way that we understand enjoying. Instead, it means that they organize themselves into societies of a certain level of complexity. In other words, they are living out the principles we were trying to get across when we explored the metaphor of the body of Christ, doing far more together than they can do individually. In fact, they might look at our societies and think, "How cute; one day they'll get the hang of living together."

Ants are architects and city planners. Most of us only ever get the tiniest glimpse of what ants build. We think about ants living in ant hills, tiny little mounds of dirt with a single hole in the top for them to come in and out. We've maybe seen an ant farm with its handful of tunnels. Those all seem simple enough; remove some dirt here, pile it up over there, how complicated could it be?

Then one day you get the idea to take some concrete or liquid metal and pour it into an abandoned ant hill. And you keep pouring.

And you keep pouring. And you keep pouring. And just when you think you must have been unlucky enough to be filling a mineshaft instead of an ant colony, it finally tops off and, after time for hardening, you can dig out the colony.

After a lot of digging, what you find really is the proportional equivalent of a city. It's taller than a human, with a complex network of interconnected tunnels and chambers. Those chambers aren't just bigger holes, but a variety of specialized compartments. Some of them are even built in such a way to be climate controlled. And although no one has filled in a colony on this scale, they can go on for miles. Actually, forget proportional—some ant colonies are bigger than our own cities.

Ants are farmers. They cultivate and harvest fungus for food. It is not just that fungus happens to grow in certain ant colonies, or that they build their colonies where the fungus already exists. Scientists have actually catalogued five distinct agricultural systems employed by ants. The ants specifically provide food for their fungus crops, and then harvest the fungus to eat. They build chambers in their colonies specifically for growing fungus in them. Some species of ants have been growing specific species of fungus for so long that the fungus has become domesticated, to the point where that fungus species only grows under the care of the ants; it cannot survive in the wild.

Ants keep livestock. Some ants maintain herds of aphids. Aphids secrete a substance called honeydew that the ants eat. In order to maintain their supply, ants interfere with the wings of the aphids, preventing them from flying away. The ants secrete chemicals that pacify the aphids, increasing the chances that they stay around. Ants will defend these groups of aphids against other predators that might try to eat them. There is some indication that some ants may even eat the aphids directly, instead of or in addition to collecting the honeydew to eat.

Perhaps most intriguingly, ants engage in warfare. Some species actively engage other ant colonies in territorial disputes. They have dedicated soldiers organized in something like a standing army. They show evidence of using tactics and strategy beyond just launching a mass of soldiers directly at the other colonies mass of soldiers. This aggression is generally in service of securing new food sources to feed growing populations.

How are the ants able to achieve all of these complex activities? Part of the answer is specialization. Different ants within the colony fulfill different roles, just like the cells in your body. The exact jobs vary from species to species, although most have some notion of a queen class that is responsible for breeding and making sure there are new generations of ants. Others may have the job of tending the ant eggs. Some dig the tunnels and chambers that make up the colony's nest. For the agriculturally minded species, some ants will have specific roles related to the farming of fungus. All of this suggests a general notion that specialization is related to the ability to undertake more complex tasks.

More to the point, how are all of these complex tasks organized? Where are the blueprints for the colony's nest? Where is the knowledge of farming techniques maintained? It is hard to believe that the individual ants are able to conceive of their activities at that level. They do not seem to have the cognitive facilities required to plan out something like a nest layout from scratch.

Perhaps it is encoded in their genes, but that can only be in the most abstract sense. In that case, does it make sense to perhaps talk about the ant colony as a collective unit having some notion of a will that directs nest building, fungus farming, aphid herding, warfare, and so forth? Is it plausible that such a will could be constructed from the bottom up, out of the individual contributions of the ants? And if that's the case, are the ants free in any sense or do they blindly serve the will of the colony?

As we reflect on those questions, I want to explore one final facet of ant biology. Perhaps you have had the experience of seeing an individual ant or two exploring their environment (perhaps the environment that you prefer to call "my kitchen") in search of food. Once they find a food source, they will return to the colony. Soon more ants will come to that food, take a small piece and carry it back to the colony for the classes of ants, like the queen, that can't go get food for themselves.

Before long, there is a whole brigade of ants moving back and forth between the food and the nest until the food is depleted. This is a routine task for the ants, and I've seen it more times than I can remember; it all seems pretty simple and straightforward. But remember—the ants have no maps, no GPS, and no audible communication that they can use to tell each other where the food is. All of a sudden, maybe it's not that simple.

As you puzzle over ant navigation, you suddenly remember your Hansel and Gretel. When that first ant is out exploring, he leaves a trail of breadcrumbs in the form of chemicals to mark the path he took. Remember, he has no map, so without those chemical crumbs he'd wander forever and never make it back home. Once he finds food, he follows his breadcrumb trail all the way back to the nest.

Along the way home, he puts down a different trail of chemicals; this one is a signal to the other ants that effectively means "if you follow this trail, it will take you to food." There are other kinds of signals indicating other types of destinations, such as "rival ant colony," which allows the ants to deal with overlapping trails; it's not dissimilar to the different color light paths used to navigate Battle School in *Ender's Game*. The other ants at the nest notice there is a food trail, follow it to the food, and on the way back lay down their own "this way to food" trail, which reinforces the signal and thus attracts even more ants to follow it. Once the food runs out, the ants stop leaving the particular chemical that means "this way to food" because there is no food there, and so the signal will eventually fade and ants will stop going to that spot en masse because there is no trail pointing there.

Pretty tidy solution to collective food gathering, no? Just one small problem: that first ant was exploring and so the path that led him to the food probably isn't the most direct route between the nest and the food. If all the other ants follow that trail, they are going to spend a lot of time taking the scenic route. But they have no phone app to tell them which adjustments will make the route more efficient. And yet, if you've ever seen the latter stages of one of these food retrieval operations, the ants are almost always walking a fairly straight line between food and nest. So how do they optimize their route? That comes down to the freedom of the individual ants.

Ants don't follow these chemical trails perfectly. Instead, they exercise some freedom to wander off the path and wander back onto it. These may not be conscious choices in the way that we would recognize consciousness, but I would submit they are free in the sense that the ant has several genuine possible actions and is not externally constrained to only one. And so, in the course of exercising this freedom, an ant will cut a corner on the original path, taking a more direct, shorter route before picking up the original trail again. The next ant will then experience a fork in the chemical road, and is free to choose either direction.

You might imagine all of this deviance and forking would just lead to a tangle of random paths, and it could except for one interesting twist. The ants that take the shorter, more direct routes can get between the food and the nest faster. This means more ants can complete a round trip on these paths, per unit of time, than any other path.

Consequently, the chemical breadcrumb trails on these paths will be stronger, which means that more ants will follow them, which means even more trips will be completed following them, and so on. And thus a short, direct path to the food is established without any top-down organization and because each ant exercises its own freedom.

This doesn't definitively answer the question of whether an ant colony has a will. And perhaps you answer the question of whether the ants are free or not differently. But I think all of this information is suggestive of a scenario where individuals can operate individually, and yet also realize some form of collective will. Or maybe ants are just weird in some way; it is reasonable to wonder whether there are any other examples of such phenomena. Well, what about a person?

9.2 Consciousness, Assemble!

While we think of ourselves as indivisible wholes, after exploring our constituent parts over the past few chapters it's clear we are more complicated than that. I am a confederation of trillions of cells, many but not all of whom share a genome, who have gathered together to be me for a while. Different parts come and go; few were there at the beginning, and some will live on after "I" die. Some organizing principle I identify as myself persists and holds them all together, yet without an obvious hierarchy. There is no "me" cell that can claim superiority or even a first-among-equals status.

Here our body metaphor apparently deviates from the biblical one. Paul equates Jesus with the head that controls the rest of the body. But at the cellular level, there's no top cell. All of the cells are dependent on the others in some way. All cells send signals, and all cells respond to signals sent by other cells. Where do "I" live? We intuit that we reside inside our heads, looking out through our eyes, but something about that picture doesn't fully resonate with modern biology.

One can easily tumble down a rabbit hole reflecting on matters of mind. You start to think about how you think, then you realize you are thinking about thinking, and before long you've got yourself tied up in knots wondering who watches the watcher-watching watchers. Just "who" is doing all this thinking, and is that same person also thinking about my thinking, and so on and so forth. What is the nature of this "I" chap who says "I am hungry" or "I am a nerd" or "I am no one"?

There are the usual suspects. We know neurological activity in the brain correlates with a variety of thought processes, so maybe "I" am my brain. Or maybe "I" am a soul, a nonphysical entity that somehow interacts with my body and can be described as inhabiting it, or at least uniquely associated with it. The Bible makes many references to one's soul, and a similar idea can be found in a variety of other cultural and religious contexts. It is expressly not a scientific concept, since science deals exclusively with the physical, but I don't see that as a reason to dismiss it *a priori*.

Are those the only options? Personally, neither is fully satisfying. How does a nonphysical soul interact with a physical body? What exactly is the point of having it connected to a physical body? I appreciate that philosophers and theologians tackle these questions. Yet because I tend to approach everything through the lens of science, I'd like to see how far quantifiable, mechanistic descriptions can take us.

On the flip side, experience suggests "I" am more than just my brain. A consistent sense of self can survive brain injuries. Because of my interest in the X-Men character Legion, I also wonder about dissociative identity disorder. How exactly does one develop multiple "I"s with just a single brain? Then again, how might multiple souls come to be associated with a single body?

The model of identity that makes the most sense to me is the idea that our mind or consciousness is an emergent level of organization of (at least) our brains. Or, to put it another way, our mind is fully mediated by our brains but not strictly reducible to the brain. The writings of Douglas Hofstadter, particularly his book *I Am A Strange Loop*, express this model in a way I find compelling. The analogy behind that title is that our mind is a form of strange attractor, like we encountered in chapter 3.

Now, I won't pretend that I have a fully developed understanding of how such a mind works. But neither does anyone else; the nature of minds and consciousness is an area of active investigation and discussion. Even when Hofstadter writes about the mind, his reasoning is just as much from analogy as evidence, but I'm hoping by now you have a sense that I'm personally not going to be dissuaded on that basis alone. Of course, that's not to say that there is no empirical support for this idea either. The number of specific brain injuries and neurological deficiencies that correspond to repeatable and distinct mental outcomes, combined with the remarkable plasticity of the mind relative to other kinds of brain injuries, are best explained for me by a mind that is mediated by the brain but not equivalent to it. Similarly, a mediated mind explains how personality and behavior have observed inheritable components, but at the same time are not fully determined by genetics or early childhood development.

Perhaps the biggest issue with this model of the mind is reconciling it with biblical references to spirits and souls. We might be able to identify this mediated mind with one or the other, but many traditions hold that the spirit and soul are separate entities. Yet the properties ascribed to either or both are not definitively enumerated, and attempts to infer those properties from one verse or passage do not always align with all the other passages. There is the further reality that the Hebrew metaphysics of body, soul and spirit appear to be quite different from the Greek metaphysics of the same entities. Thus, to me it makes the most sense to read all of these passages as expressing ideas in the metaphysical categories most familiar to the particular authors and audiences. What they have in common is an acknowledgement that there is an "I" inside each of us who has a responsibility for the actions of our bodies and who maintains a continuity of experience in spite of physical changes, possibly even across a discontinuity in bodily function associated with death.

I would propose that those properties are covered by a mediated mind. The "I" inside of us is the strange attractor that can consider its own cognitive functions. That mind is capable of synthesizing sensory input, reflecting on previous experiences, and perhaps most importantly, imagining a range of possible (and maybe impossible) future scenarios in order to decide how to act. To me, this means that said mind is doing more than automatically, reflexively responding to present conditions; it is freely choosing and can be culpable for the consequences of its decisions. And finally, since the mind is a particular organization of the physical body, it can be reproduced in another physical system without requiring the matter of the original body.

9.3 The Bible on the Mind

I find this emergent model of the mind has some advantages as well when it comes to illuminating my reading of the Bible. For example, it gives additional weight to the idea that the church is to be the body of Jesus. If the mind of Jesus, who as we saw is fully human, is an organizational pattern that comes together from the bottom up, then it is meaningful to talk about that pattern being replicated elsewhere. There wouldn't be the same continuity of experience necessary for identity, and we may not be capable of reproducing that pattern perfectly, but there is at least conceptually a way forward to understand our role as a body. By each freely contributing in our own way to expressing a part of a common genome, a common word, then we can collectively realize the full expression of the Word.

And I find that this bottom-up organization meshes well with the model of servant leadership that the Bible, and Jesus, espouse for the church and other bodies of people as well. Jesus exemplified this approach when he washed the feet of his disciples. He demonstrated that no task was too mean to be below his station, and given his status there is little reason to believe any task is below any of us as well. This model prevents power and influence from concentrating at the top of some hierarchy, where a few individuals are set apart from the rest. Instead, there are no privileged positions among members, and all power and influence belongs to the higher level organization; as another manifestation of entropic love, Jesus allows power to be distributed symmetrically rather than maintaining an asymmetry for his own benefit—whereas with a brain-as-mind model, certain parts of your body are privileged and get to boss the others around. Conversely, with a mind-as-external-nonphysical-entity model, the entire body is secondary.

The Bible also encourages us to transform our minds, a value it shares with most movements for education and communication. An organization pattern can be reorganized. As we explored earlier, organization requires an input of information. Is it any wonder then that meditation on the word would be central to the process of that transformation? In fact, this model of the mind explains quite well why our minds are influenced by the information we feed into them; our minds are wired to organize themselves according to whatever information they receive.

Now, of course this model applies whether one chooses to believe the Bible or not. And so one could argue that believing the Bible is just a self-reinforcing feedback loop. If the Bible is the information feeding into our mind, then our mind organizes around it, inclining us to believe in whatever it says, meaning we read it more, and so on. To which I would say, yep, sure, that is definitely a possibility.

In fact, I'd go even further and say that it is pretty much exactly what I just described. However, the same logic applies to just about any way of looking at the world. Everyone's mind is influenced by the information they take in, regardless of their religious inclinations or disinclinations. That doesn't mean religious beliefs are some kind of trap; everyone's mind can also be changed by new information. No perspective can claim a privileged status as being immune to whatever tendencies exist in the minds of those who share that perspective.

Another interesting dimension of this mental model is the connection to the idea of *imago Dei*, the image of God. The Bible indicates that humans in some capacity reflect the image of God, although it isn't entirely clear what attributes or properties of humanity are covered by that description. Well, one thing that we've established about God is his self-defining nature, his axiomatic status, as suggested by the name he gives himself: "I Am that I Am." And now here we have a model of the mind with a similar self-referential property. The mind exists because it pays attention to itself, where "itself" is a thing that pays attention to itsel . . . hello, rabbit hole. And yet, clearly our minds exist; is it that hard to believe, therefore, in a self-referential God?

This self-referential notion gets me thinking about the concept of sin again. It is possible to understand most or all of the actions the Bible defines as sin as expressions of selfishness. In other words, getting too caught up in one's self-referential loop to the detriment of all else. But didn't I just suggest that the self-referential loop is at least an aspect of the *imago Dei*? Am I now suggesting that it is the very same thing which makes us capable of sin? It does kind of sound that way, doesn't it?

The hypothetical possibility of God being able to sin is not without biblical precedent. First, the Bible says that Jesus has been tempted in every way that we are tempted (Hebrews 4:15). Therefore, it stands to reason that he, and by implication God, has some capacity to sin. If not, would it really have been meaningful temptation? So maybe it isn't so radical to contemplate that God's self-referentialness comes with a theoretical capacity to sin, and thus ours as well.

And second, the very first act that the Bible describes as a sin, eating from the tree of the knowledge of good and evil, is also described as having the consequence of making humans more like God. This has always been paradoxical to me, and so far this model is the best option I've come up with for understanding that paradox. Our self-awareness gives us the ability to understand our choices in a way that makes us culpable for negative consequences, eliminating our state of innocence, bestowing on us a capacity to sin and also a capacity for awareness of sin that we share with God.

Finally, consider that God has modeled for us the exact opposite of self-absorbed sin. For all we know, God could have been content in his self-referential loop all by his lonesome. But instead he chose to create a world to interact with. Even further, he created a world so that he could give of himself to that world. He died himself so that the rest of us could live, and all he asks of us is to do the same. He knows it is possible for us, because it was possible for him. And thus even if his self-referentialness gives him a capacity to sin, the evidence clearly demonstrates that he did not actually commit the sin of becoming focused entirely on himself.

The triune nature of God may also be relevant to this discussion. God is thus profoundly and essentially relational. Such an existence may at least partly explain God's ability to eternally avoid the self-absorption to which we humans are so prone.

Then again, perhaps I have wandered too far afield contemplating the possibility that God could potentially sin. The nerdiness of science, combining what we observe about reality and imagining different possible worlds consistent with the data, necessitates a balancing act. We have to go beyond what we can directly experience to create hypotheses about what we don't yet know. And then we test them against new observations, ensuring that our theories are anchored in this reality. Some of those hypotheses will be found wrong, but that's still valuable information for mapping the landscape of truth.

Bottom-up organization suggests another idea about the image of God that is not mutually exclusive with my self-referential loop suggestion but also doesn't depend on it. It connects the image of God with the body of Christ. If the church collectively is the body of Christ, then to some degree it is also the church that is the image of God. Individual humans may also bear the image of God, just as we can individually be Christlike.

Self-similar patterns at multiple levels of organization are common; we'll see more of them in a later chapter. For now, just think about a brick building. The relatively simple pattern of a rectangle (technically, a rectangular prism) is realized at the level of the individual bricks and the overall building. Thus it's perfectly coherent to say that the image of God may be realized by both a single person and a community of people.

At the individual level, the image of God emerges from the interactions of all the various cells that collaborate to be me. Similarly, at the community level, the image of God emerges from our interactions with each other within that community. Specifically, our love for each other demonstrates that we are the body of Christ. As Jesus told his closest followers, "Everyone will know by this that you are my disciples—if you have love for one another" (John 13:35). This was just hours after Jesus demonstrated bottom-up servant leadership by washing their feet, and just hours before he would demonstrate entropic love by dying for all of us on the cross.

Intriguingly, the church is not the first time we get such an emergent picture of God in the Bible. God manifests physically in the Old Testament several times. The first is when Moses experiences God as a burning bush—an entropy-increasing process, which in this case did not consume the bush because of the presence of God's inexhaustible organization-preserving asymmetry (Exodus 3). By contrast, God's judgment is elsewhere described as a consuming fire, such as in Lamentations 2:3 and 2 Thessalonians 1:8, reminding us of the natural consequence of being apart from God's life-giving presence. Later in Exodus, God would lead the nation of Israel as a pillar of cloud by day and of fire by night (Exodus 13).

What these phenomena have in common is that they are patterns of organization. A single atom cannot be on fire; a single molecule cannot be a cloud. Neither do clouds nor fire impose themselves on atoms and molecules. They emerge from the interactions of atoms and molecules. The cumulative result of many individual oxygen molecules chemically reacting with many individual atoms and molecules of various persuasions is a fire.

Of course, when God became incarnate as Jesus, he was still manifesting as an emergent pattern. His contemporaries may not have fully appreciated it, but Jesus being fully human was also the result of trillions of cells collaborating to be him. The foundations for this picture of humanity were already laid by Greek ideas of atoms and of the distinct reality of forms that can be realized by physical objects. These conceptual tools, obtained through the study of science and which would make it possible to understand the incarnation, preceded Jesus' birth, perhaps as an example of God preparing the soil to receive the germ of an idea.

This image of God is not only emergent, it is also dynamic. God is not inert, he is alive and active. Even within himself, his triune nature implies that he is constantly interacting, relating, and communing. And yet from that constant activity a coherent pattern appears and persists. Indeed, that activity may be necessary for maintaining the pattern. In this way, God's unchanging nature coexists with a vibrant dynamism. God may very well be a state of becoming as much as a state of being.

Perhaps this is one reason why God prohibits the worship of carved images (Exodus 20:4). They may give the wrong image of God, not only because God does not literally look like a calf or an eagle or whatever we might fashion, but also because God is not static, dead, finished. Instead, God is a flame, perpetually becoming itself.

Of course, God doesn't simply interact within himself. God also relates to his creation outside of himself. Thus a full image of God must account not just for the emergence of a pattern but also what that pattern does. How does the body of Christ as a community interact with the rest of the world?

9.4 Giant Size Ant-Man

Let's return to our friends the ants, and to our friend Douglas Hofstadter. In the book *Gödel, Escher, Bach*, Hofstadter imagines having a relationship with an ant colony. Sure, individual ants lack the mental wherewithal to converse with a human, but as we have seen, ant colonies are capable of far more complex behavior than single ants. And so an ant colony might just be a suitable companion.

By way of example, he describes approaching an ant hill. Ants are able to sense vibrations of the ground, such as we make as we walk nearby. These are actually waves that transmit the energy of our footfalls to the ants, and also the information heralding our arrival. Such substantial tremors may be interpreted by individual ants as meaning a possibility for damage to their home and themselves, and so they will act swiftly to shore up their architecture and get themselves to secure shelter.

But we are free to interpret the overall behavior of the colony as a greeting. After all, that's what we call a human response to the arrival of another human. Why can't an ant colony greet us as well? And if the colony can greet us, we can work out other kinds of responses as well. There will be trial and error along the way, just like learning any new language, but it seems plausible in principle. In fact, it's not altogether different from the challenge of Louise Banks figuring out how to communicate with aliens in *Arrival*, or Ender Wiggin coming to an understanding of the Formics in *Ender's Game*.

Or look no further than *Ant-Man* about Hank Pym who communicates with ants and his protégé Scott Lang who shrinks down to ant size. Lang interacts with the ants on their scale and becomes familiar enough with one of them to name him Antony. Pym, however, stays at human scale and interacts with the ants at a more collective level. He designates the ants by number, emphasizing their place within the group rather than acknowledging their individual identities. Lang is the man who becomes like an ant, but for Pym it takes a whole colony of ants to become like a man.

While I personally would be genuinely curious to try to talk to an ant colony, the practicality of that endeavor is not important to our purposes. What we are interested in is imagining how to communicate with a community as opposed to an individual. Because even if you find all this talk of bottom-up organization and emergence and consciousness a bit out there, I do think there is value to reflecting on how our churches collectively communicate to people on the outside. What does it mean for a person to meet Jesus incarnate in the body of our community?

Consider a church with a food bank. When someone is hungry and the food bank provides them a meal or three, they may very well experience the love and kindness and generosity of an individual responsible for distributing the food. But they are also experiencing a collective act of love and generosity of the community that has arranged for the food bank to exist and provided food to stock it and volunteers to make it available. In fact, they can experience that collective love even if the individual who happens to be giving out the food is a little curt or cold or just having an off day themselves. The grace of the overall system can tolerate and redeem missteps by individuals.

A food bank is a simple and positive example, patterned after Jesus' own words and actions. But if it is possible for the church to collectively model Jesus to someone even if the individuals in the church stumble in that regard, then it is also possible for a church to collectively fail to model Jesus even if individuals are following in his pattern accurately. Suppose someone visits a church and is warmly welcomed by multiple members who are not simply polite but also take the time to get to know the visitor, perhaps over multiple weeks and visits. They listen to her story, hear her needs and recognize her strengths and gifts. But over time, it becomes apparent that the church has no programs to meet those needs and no connections to agencies or organizations that can help. Neither does the church have any place for her to exercise her gifts. It has never encountered someone quite like this visitor before; she asks questions for which it has no answers and offers suggestions for which it has no use.

Will that visitor feel like she has met Jesus embodied in that church? Possibly not, despite the best efforts of the individuals to be Christlike to her. In this particular scenario, the body seems to be suffering from poor circulation, to return to our earlier bodily analogies. Any given local church cannot be all things to all people, but it should be sufficiently connected to a larger community to be aware of resources available elsewhere.

Of course, churches are not the only communities of people with the potential for positive or negative traits at the organizational level. Various nerd communities like comic book fandom or Trekkers, and more specifically the crowd at the local comic store or unit of the 501st Legion (a *Star Wars* fan organization), can have structural barriers making it harder for newcomers to join even if the individual members are lovely, well intentioned people. And sometimes self-appointed gatekeepers get in the way of new people becoming a part of a community that is otherwise organized to receive them just fine. If the composition of your nerd community doesn't reflect the full range of people you believe should be included, it might be time to examine whether the values of the group, as expressed in (possibly unspoken) rules or activities or the stories the group tells about itself, actually reflect the values of the individual members.

Another scenario I think about in terms of individual and collective values is voting. For better or worse, and in some cases more accurately than others, the church is associated with particular political positions. On some level, this is the result of our corporate body communicating to outside individuals and also to other communities via the ballot box. We may individually have more diverse positions, and we may be able to express those to our individual friends. But we are also communicating as a group to other groups.

In most voting scenarios, the communication boils down to answering a single either-or question. Recall that answering such a question involves a single bit of information. And so when we vote, we can only send a message of a single bit. We may individually intend a much richer, more nuanced message that in our minds constitutes many bits. But our group-to-group communication channel can only accommodate that one bit, yes or no. And so we may need to reflect on certain issues how to best communicate love as the body of Jesus via just a single bit.

As we do so, we should also consider one final aspect of our ant colony chat. Many of the "internal" (that is, between and amongst the ants) ant-level interactions that collectively represent a colony-level greeting take place out in the open. Thus even if we understand that the colony is saying "Hello!" we are not completely ignorant of how each ant is reacting and how that may represent a fearful instinct rather than a friendly one. Similarly, in our highly networked and perpetually broadcast society, many of our internal deliberations are really happening in public for everyone to see and hear. We might imagine these discussions to be more like our own inward thought process that is genuinely inaudible and inaccessible, and there may have been a time when that was reasonably accurate. But that is not the case now, and so we would be wise to consider how all of our conversations will be perceived by those outside a community such as the church or our favorite fandom. We no longer have the luxury of only considering those audiences when we make what we intend as public pronouncements; the public/private line is blurring. At the same time, we should all extend each other a little grace and recognize that just as we all individually have stray thoughts we would never air, as groups we sometimes need to say things internally so that they can be resolved internally without immediate external judgement.

Thinking back to Loki and the Avengers, failing to appreciate who was listening was part of Loki's downfall. Imprisoned by the team through his own machinations in order to get inside their operation, Loki finds himself visited by team member Black Widow and takes the opportunity to have a chat with her to advance his agenda. He thought he was privately manipulating her, but really he was being publicly manipulated *by* her. Perhaps he believed too strongly in his top-down model of godhood. He thought himself in control, but he underestimated the freedom of agency that others possess.

If our model of the mind is primarily top-down, based on a notion of an external, nonphysical entity, then I can see where the church as the body of Jesus would look very much like serving Loki. But with a bottom-up model of the mind, then the body of Jesus concept needn't carry those connotations. Every member is freely participating. Yes, there is still an element of submission in the sense that we are following the model established by the historical person of Jesus and so some choices and behaviors will be more consistent with his example than others, but such submission is willingly offered rather than demanded or imposed. Power and influence are imbued, not in the members at the top of the hierarchy, but in the entity that arises from the collective will of the members.

Actually, that sounds an awful lot like the Avengers themselves. Notice that no one makes the Avengers a team. Nick Fury provides the conditions for the team to come into existence, but each individual hero makes a choice to participate in something that only exists because they decide to participate in it. Over the course of the final battle, each member serves the others via their own special gifts; no one puts themselves above the rest.

They also serve the people around them, working to protect as many civilians as possible and escort them to safety, even at the cost of increased personal risk. In this, they demonstrate that the purpose of their community is not simply the relationships within the group, but also the collective relationship to the world around them. And just like the church, in the end, they celebrate with a feast. So if you watch the film and think that the freedom from freedom that Loki offers isn't for you, and that you'd much rather assemble with the Avengers, well, maybe being part of the body of Jesus wouldn't be so much at odds with that vision as you might initially think.

PART IV

The Language of Computer Science

CHAPTER 10

Squirrel Interrupted

If you are looking for a comic book that entertains and teaches introductory computer science in the most charming way possible, then *The Unbeatable Squirrel Girl* by Ryan North, Erica Henderson, Rico Renzi, et al. is the book for you. Go to your nearest comic book retailer and negotiate the exchange of fiat currency for all available issues. Read those comics. Repeat monthly until Marvel stops publishing the book, which will be never because you are all reading it faithfully.

The delightful Doreen Green is the eponymous sciurine hero. Where many comic book characters have an angst-ridden origin weighing them down, Doreen has a bushy prehensile tail. She talks to squirrels, especially her sidekick Tippy-Toe, she is strong, and she is agile. And while she can hold her own physically against any foe, she is unbeatable because she applies logic, foresight, and compassion whenever possible.

10.1 Squirrel Computing Power

When she isn't single-handedly saving the world with cleverness and sass, Doreen is an undergraduate computer science student. School is a popular setting for comic books, providing an easy way to establish a diverse array of supporting characters, regular tension between homework and heroing, and an environment familiar to the target audience. Sometimes it is simply a backdrop, but Squirrel Girl takes her studies seriously. She attends lectures on the fundamentals of relational databases, teaches finger binary (which allows counting to 1,023 on your fingers), and illustrates the core features of program flow control. She has a bright future in technology ahead of her no matter how the hero business turns out.

Computer science may seem like an odd fit for a superhero, but in this book it works very well. A main theme of computer science is formalizing how we accomplish tasks—any tasks, from accounting to zoo keeping. Computers can be made to do many of these jobs if we can simply explain to the computer all of the steps in careful detail. And even if we can't (yet) have a computer do a given job, like fighting crime, we can still use the framework of computer science to understand the job and do it more efficiently.

As a means of formalizing how to combat evil, computer science could apply to any superhero book. But it is particularly apt for *The Unbeatable Squirrel Girl* because Doreen's approach to superheroics is more sophisticated and so rewards more detailed analysis. The basic hero process is: (1) find a problem, (2) find the person causing the problem, and (3) punch that person until they stop causing the problem. Once Squirrel Girl has found the person causing the problem, she prefers to listen to that person to understand their underlying concern and then resolve it, or identify how they are causing a problem and circumvent it, or persuade them to pursue a different goal, or sometimes just punch them until they stop. As you can see, her process is more complex, and often provides opportunities for more elaborate planning.

For example, in issue #7 of volume 2, Squirrel Girl confronts the menace that is Swarm, a human consciousness mediated by a swarm of bees, not unlike the ant colony we imagined chatting with last chapter. The story is told in a choose-your-own-adventure format. By engaging us in the decision making, the book highlights the process of problem solving. Since Swarm's body is a looser collaboration than most, we quickly realize that punching will solve nothing and we have to develop a more sophisticated plan. And while the format has been around a long time, the unique features of the comics medium make it easier to see how different choices play out in parallel.

As with most choose-your-own-adventure stories, Squirrel Girl's encounter with Swarm provides opportunities to see how things can go wrong. In a traditional linear narrative, we just see one version of events. If our story is a comedy in the classical sense, which most superhero and action stories in general tend to be regardless of how funny they are, then everything works out by the end. If we didn't know better, we might think someone had planned it that way all along.

10.2 The Programs of Our Lives

Many of us would like our lives to be planned in this way, heading toward some satisfying resolution that will make the challenges and diversions seem worthwhile. Christians generally cast God in that planning role. This creates expectations that God is doing all the heavy lifting on our behalf. It also informs how we tell the stories of events in our lives that already happened; we frame them such that the way things wound up was inevitable and intended all along. And while I certainly understand that perspective, it's not terribly nerdy and so I find myself thinking about alternatives.

Here's an example from my own life. A few years ago, my wife and I decided to move our growing family from our starter house to a brand-new house in a new development. To put a down payment on the new house, we had to close on the sale of our old house. The down payment initiated the construction process, meaning we had sold our current residence for a future one that wouldn't exist for a few months. We were able to rent our old house from the new owner for a few months, but that arrangement was one month too short. To avoid a month of homelessness, we cobbled together a plan involving storage rental, crashing with friends and staying with my in-laws.

Then, about a week and a half before our move out date, we got word that our new house was done ahead of schedule—an entire month early. We were told that never happens, that if anything construction involves delays from weather or lack or supplies or just overly optimistic scheduling. By beating those odds, we could now move directly into our new house! Just one problem: the closing process allegedly took a month.

Taking a chance, I asked anyway whether the closing paperwork could be completed more quickly. I was told they would try, but no commitments were made. So I started making arrangements to move into the house if it worked, but also moved forward with the original plan for a month of nomadic life if needed. We packed, we painted, and we waited.

By midweek, we found out the closing process that was supposed to take a month had been completed in two days! We shifted all of our efforts into the plan to move directly to the new house. The move went swimmingly. All of the different steps that needed to come together did precisely that, generally not a moment sooner than necessary. Sure, it was hectic, and I won't pretend to you that I was poised and graceful for the entire experience. Nevertheless, I was certainly pleased with the results.

I could certainly tell this story in terms of divine Providence in which God arranges all the details so that there is a happy ending. We needed the weather to be clear so that the construction went smoothly; that's something we might ascribe to God. Did God also orchestrate the supply chain so that all the materials were available? When I had to change moving dates at the last minute, had God influenced the schedule so that the movers had availability? What about the painters and closing agents and mortgage brokers and everyone who contributed to bringing the plan together in the final weeks; was God affecting them in some way?

I could ascribe all of those outcomes to God, as they fall within common ideas of what he is capable of. And as a believer, I do feel a certain desire to frame my stories in a way that makes God look good. At the same time, I want to be careful how I do so, in order to honestly represent God and not inadvertently make him look bad. I want to consider how it looks to claim God went to all that trouble just to spare a middle class family some inconvenience in their move to a nice house in the suburbs. That claim feels self-serving when so many other greater needs are apparently going unmet.

I am also aware that the story could be framed differently. Plenty of people were involved in making our move a success. I don't know what kind of effort it took to get a closing together in two days, but as best as I can tell several folks had to go above and beyond their normal process on our behalf. My wife and I had to do a lot of planning and juggling over a couple of weeks to account for two parallel moving scenarios, like the parallel stories in the Squirrel Girl story. Not to mention that the whole scenario could possibly have been avoided if our real estate agent had communicated more clearly during the negotiations for selling our old house and the full rental period we had requested had been secured. Any number of choices were involved, and I also wish to both affirm the freedom of those choices and acknowledge and appreciate the efforts of the people involved, not to mention that we were relatively fortunate to even be in this kind of situation in the first place.

These framings needn't be mutually exclusive either. We already discussed how God's plans may be compatible with our free choices. Since enough of the players involved opted to show my family grace, kindness and love, they collectively demonstrated God's care for us as well. If they had chosen differently, God wouldn't have loved me or my wife or anyone any less, but that particular channel of communication may have not been available.

I also wonder about the versions of our moving story where things didn't work out so conveniently. Would we still tell the story after the fact if it didn't have a neat ending? "Family experiences a normal amount of inconvenience during move" isn't much of a hook; our story is mildly interesting because it is relatively rare. Yet normal amounts of inconvenience during moves happen every day, which is what makes them normal. How is our perspective on divine Providence influenced by this selection filter on which stories get told?

One of the intriguing aspects of the Bible is the number of stories it tells where events don't seem to work out. Yes, there is an overall arc of God's will being realized, but the harmonious reconciliation at the end is in the future. The events, which are a matter of history, paint a far more ambiguous picture. There are individual setbacks, such as the defeat of Israel at Ai in Joshua 7 or the execution of Paul (which prevents further missionary journeys). On a larger scale, the nation of Israel undergoes a permanent schism after the reign of Solomon (1 Kings 12 and 2 Chronicles 10) and the northern kingdom subsequently falls to the Assyrians and is never fully restored. If you expect the Bible to be a pæan to God's glorious triumphs, it is curious to discover so many scenarios that wind up pear-shaped.

Compare the Bible with our stories of great planners and schemers. The joys of a heist movie like *Ocean's 11* (or *12* or *13*) come from seeing a plan click along like clockwork and admiring how every countermeasure was anticipated and neutralized. Sometimes it's the villain with the plan, like Zemo in *Captain America: Civil War*, who so successfully manipulates the heroes that by the end of the film you're left wondering if he won even though he's in a prison cell. *Batman v Superman: Dawn of Justice* similarly ends with a jailed Lex Luthor seemingly right where wants to be, and *The Dark Knight*'s Joker explicitly intends to get caught on his way to goading Batman into using criminal methods to fight crime. *The A-Team*'s Hannibal isn't the only one who loves it when a plan comes together.

We also have a soft spot for heroes who can successfully wing it; there's something to be said for spontaneity. Han Solo's lovable rogue mystique is built around his ability to come out on top when he's flying by the seat of his pants. Dr. Richard Kimble never meant to be a fugitive, but when an opportunity arose he improvised an escape and a murder investigation. Indiana Jones comes right out and admits that he's just making it up as he goes along. (Anything you'd like to tell us, Harrison?)

Real life is generally a mixture of careful symphonic orchestration and jazzy riffs. And I think computer science can help us find a balance with an idea called just-in-time compiling. My moving story illustrates some of the flavor of the concept, which is another reason I brought it up. To me, telling the story in a way that glorifies God means exploring the truth about him beyond asking whether a nice thing that happened to me is proof that God loves me.

10.3 Computing Bit by Bit

To understand just-in-time compilation, we need to go into some of the details of how a computer works. Ultimately, computers are very good at doing arithmetic, sums and products. In fact, we used to give the title of computer to human beings who computed sums by hand as a full time job. Human computers put mankind into orbit, as dramatized in *Hidden Figures*, and helped to break German codes in World War II, as dramatized in *The Imitation Game*—although I prefer Neal Stephenson's account in *Cryptonomicon*. Wartime codebreaking and the associated mathematics informed the development of digital computers, which work on the bits of information theory.

As we've seen, there are a lot of ways to represent a bit of information. However, it would be tough to make a computer that could fit in your pocket if it relied on lamps in church steeples or shooting arrows in the woods. Instead, digital computers use electrical currents. Current flowing through a circuit represents a "yes," while no current represents a "no."

Of course, they don't literally have to mean "yes" and "no" since meaning is extrinsic. They simply have to represent opposites. A more convenient interpretation is "true" and "false;" then we can make circuits representing logic operations like AND and OR. In the first case, the circuit has two inputs, and if both have current flowing into them then current will flow out of the AND circuit, and in all other cases no current flows out. In the second case, there are also two inputs but it only takes current in one of them to get current to flow out.

We can also interpret flowing current as 1 and no current as 0, which is why power switches are marked with 1 and 0 (sometimes mistaken for an abstract line and circle) and power buttons with a 1 inside of a 0. Now we are doing math. Just 1 and 0 by themselves don't give us much, but a long string of 1s and 0s can represent any number you want using binary notation. We are more used to using ten different digits, 0 through 9, but that choice is arbitrary. Instead of a ones place, a tens place, a hundreds place, and so on, binary has a ones place, a twos place, a fours place, an eights place, etc. We count 0, 1, 10, 11, 100, 101, 110, 111, 1000, 1001, 1010, *ad infinitum.*

This is the basis for the counting scheme Squirrel Girl teaches. Instead of using each finger for a distinct number, each finger represents a place. Let a thumb be the ones place, the adjacent index finger the twos place, and so on. Thumbs up is one; pointing is two; thumb and pointer are three. Thumb (1), pointer (2) and pinky (16) up, like Spider-Man shooting a web or someone signing "I love you," is 19 (1+2+16). Just be careful with 4, 128, and 132.

Now we can use combinations of ANDs and ORs circuits to add small numbers, and then you can combine more to add bigger numbers, multiply them, negate them, and do everything we need for arithmetic. Everything a computer does comes down to positive integers, creating a strong and deep connection between number theory and computing. We just assign different meanings to those numbers depending on context, allowing a device that only knows how to do math with 0s and 1s to make it easier for us to edit photos, write text, produce music, draw animations, and fling birds at pigs in oh-so-satisfying parabolic arcs. All we have to do is figure out an encoding scheme and a detailed procedure—or algorithm—for accomplishing a task using only the steps a computer knows how to do.

Now we see how computer programming is about a precise and careful understanding of how we get stuff done. Breaking a task down for a computer is a little like teaching a toddler. Toddlers have a fairly limited repertoire of skills, due to their inexperience and their still-developing motor skills. Like computers, they are also very literal and will do only and exactly what you tell them, which can be both maddening and enlightening. Suddenly you realize all the steps you take for granted, like closing a drawer after you take something out of it or putting your socks on before your shoes.

Reducing every task all the way down to a combination of logical operations on 1s and 0s could get quite tedious quite quickly. So computer chips are built with specific combinations of these circuits in large quantities. Those combinations are referred to as instructions. An instruction might be something like "add 1 to this number" or "multiply these two numbers" or "tell me which of these two numbers is bigger." Adding in binary is based on an exclusive OR operation: 0+1=1+0=1 while 0+0=0 and 1+1=10. If one OR the other input is a 1, the result is a 1; if both are 0s or both are 1s, the result in the ones place is a 0. Checking which of two numbers is bigger is just a matter of comparing digits from most significant to least until one of the numbers has a 1 and the other a 0.

The most rudimentary computer programs are sequences of these instructions applied to numbers stored in binary in the computer's memory. Remember that those numbers could mean anything; they could encode text like the words of this book by assigning different numbers to different characters, or an HD video you recorded on your phone, or the actual numbers of a bank's account balances. The numbers can even represent computer programs by assigning a unique number to each instruction, which means we can write computer programs that manipulate other computer programs or even their own code. Whatever our program is doing, we don't have to worry about how to accomplish it with logic circuits, we just have to use the instructions provided by the chip designer and let them worry about the circuit details. This is the first layer of abstraction from the actual workings of the machine.

Let's look at a specific example to see how programming breaks a task down into the simple steps a computer makes available via its instruction set. A frequent task in computing is sorting numbers so that they are in order. Sorting puts words in alphabetical order, allows us to pick what direction to go in when we are searching for the peak of a function we are optimizing, and shows us which of our favorite songs we've listened to the most. To make the problem a little more visual, imagine that you are sorting a group of children by height, tallest to shortest. This will be equivalent to asking a computer to arrange numbers representing those kids' height in memory so that the numbers go from biggest to smallest.

With real kids, you might be able to just tell them to sort them-selves. Writing a computer program implementing that same approach is possible but complicated and not a natural fit for the available in-structions. The instructions allow us to compare kids two at a time and to move them one at a time. So, assuming the kids are lined up in random order, start with the first two kids and compare their heights. If kid #1 is taller, do nothing; if kid #2 is taller, pull her out of line, move kid #1 to position #2, then move kid #2 to position #1. (In the computer, pulling a kid out of line might actually involve copying their height to a free space in memory, but we can't copy kids as easily.) In either case, now move on to compare kids #2 and #3.

When you've gotten all the way to the end of the line, you stop, but have you completely sorted the kids? In computer programming, you might answer this question by imagining the worst case scenario: what if the kids started out shortest to tallest? In that scenario, the first kid would be the shortest one and at each comparison we'd swap her so that she'd wind up the last kid in line. But now the first kid is still just the second shortest rather than the tallest, who is in the pen-ultimate spot. You can probably see that in this scenario we'd have to pass over the entire line once per kid to finally wind up with a tallest to shortest line.

You might be tempted to say that if the kids start shortest to tallest, you can just flip the line around and be done. But that's not an instruc-tion. The program cannot see the whole line at once and it can't flip the whole line at once. You would have to compare children two at a time to see if they were always shorter-then-taller and if they were, rear-range them one at a time. You can write that program and it would be faster than the other method, but only for one specific scenario.

There are general purpose sorting algorithms faster than the one I've described, but they are not as simple to express in terms of ma-chine instructions. And for a while, stringing together those kinds of instructions was exactly how computer programmers programmed. It's easier to do than wiring the circuits directly, but it can still get to be quite tedious. The resulting programs can be quite lengthy, and the individual steps can be so far removed from how human program-mers think about the activity they want to program that mistakes are easy to make and hard to identify. Early computers also had very little memory, so to make programs as small as possible the instructions were represented by a minimal number of bits represented as three- to six-letter codes rather than a full name summarizing what the instruction does, moving programming even further away from how humans normally think.

So the next innovation in computer science was more verbose programming languages. The programmer types out the details of what she wants to accomplish in language that more closely resembles how she would describe the task to another human, and the computer will figure out what processor instructions are required to actually carry out the task in steps the computer can actually do. Basically, it's a translation problem; the underlying concepts are the same, but the most natural way for the human and the computer to express or represent them are different. In practice, these programming languages probably wouldn't look all that natural to the uninitiated, but they are a significant improvement. The terminology is at least full English words instead of cryptic abbreviations, even if the vocabulary is limited and the syntax is different from sentences.

10.4 Words Go In. Bytes Come Out.

The reason it isn't quite natural language is a compromise between the goal of human fluency and the fact that a computer program has to automatically translate that language into a sequence of processor instructions. As we learned in chapter 1, the English language is rich enough in its expressive capability that ambiguity is inevitable. But in computer programming, we don't want ambiguity. We want the computer to do the same thing every time, given the same conditions and the same request. There can't be any ambiguity in the way that a computer interprets a program, and so we have to use a language somewhat less expressive than English. Still, we can formally prove these languages can express exactly the same range of concepts as the processor instructions.

The program that translates from the human-friendly language to the processor instructions is called a compiler. The text written by the programmer is compiled one time, directly to a sequence of instructions. The resulting program can then be run as many times as one wishes on any computer—as long as that computer's processor has the same set of instructions. Unfortunately, not all processors use the exact same instructions. Sometimes the differences are subtle; other times they are quite pronounced.

Originally, this was the key difference between Apple-manufactured computers, including Macs, and most other desktop computers, which were lumped together generically as IBM compatible, IBM clones, IBM PC compatible, or ultimately just PCs. Apple used a processor with one set of instructions in their computers, while IBM used another processor with different instructions in theirs. IBM compatible machines were made by anyone and everyone, and were compatible because their processors had the same instruction set as IBMs. The same program would have to be compiled twice, once for Macs and once for PCs.

Interestingly, by the time the famous "I'm a Mac. And I'm a PC." ads rolled out, Apple had switched to the same processors as all the other PCs. At the lowest level, Macs and PCs could now theoretically run the same programs without even having to recompile. Yet those ads touted the substantial differences in software available for the different kinds of computers. What was stopping everyone from just running all the cool Apple software on their Windows PC?

Compiling a program a couple of times for different processors is not itself a big deal. Macs and PCs also differ in the software libraries available for them. Computer programs need to do a lot of the same things over and over again, like sorting. Once you've figured out how to sort numbers, you don't want to write that same program over and over again. You might make mistakes, and if you figured out a faster way you'd have to go back and rewrite every program with a sort. So programmers write a sorting program once, compile it into processor instructions, and reuse the compiled version. A collection of compiled algorithms is a library, because anybody can go to it and check out the sorting program that is already there instead of inventing their own.

Ideally, everyone would compile their libraries for Macs and PCs and everything would be the same. But we all know ideals are hard to live up to. Sometimes a program relies heavily on a specific instruction unique to one of the processors. Sometimes a programmer only has a Mac and so they can't check and make sure their program works the same on a PC. And so sometimes libraries just get compiled for only one kind.

The first example is of course the libraries that comprise the Mac operating system and the Windows operating system of PCs themselves. Those libraries provide different, unique algorithms, so programs that use what the Windows libraries provide might not find an equivalent algorithm in the Mac libraries. Incidentally, this is what distinguishes Linux systems; Linux is another operating system that is compatible with PC instruction sets but provides yet a third set of unique libraries. Additional software libraries are built on top of the unique features of operating system libraries, and further software libraries are built on *those*, and so on. Over time, the available libraries are widely divergent between the two environments. Consequently, if you did want to write a program for Macs and PCs, you'd likely have to write separate versions using the available library ecosystems, even though nowadays both versions would ultimately compile to the same instruction sets.

Recall that we started down this path to separate ecosystems because we wanted to translate what a human writes into what a computer can understand, and we chose to do that once in advance. What if we did that translation when we want to run the program instead? That's certainly possible, and it does solve the problem of processor differences, which are still an issue today, only now the difference is between your desktop processor and the processor in your phone or tablet. The main drawback is that translating takes computer resources that could otherwise be used to play your videos, or sort your music library, or do whatever you actually care about accomplishing. If it's a program you use frequently, then your computer winds up translating the same code over and over and over again, which is pretty inefficient.

This is the solution used by website programs like Facebook or Gmail. The code is sent to your computer in the language written by a human (with a couple of clicks, you can see it yourself). Your browser interprets the code into processor instructions, which allows the same website program to work on any computer, phone, or other device. As a result, the website programs cannot use the libraries provided by the operating system; instead, the browser provides some of the same kinds of algorithms like sorting. This arrangement simplifies programming for the human and makes the computers do more work.

Then we come to just-in-time compiling, which cuts down on the computer work while keeping the human programming simplified. The basic principle is versatile enough that it has even caught on outside of computing, in areas like retail sales, making it easier to picture. Retail stores need inventory—let's say cell phones—so that when you want to buy one, they have one to sell. Having lots of phones in a store guarantees they'll always have one, but incurs a cost of storage and makes it harder for the store to adjust when a new phone model comes along. Calling a warehouse and having a phone sent over every time a customer wants to buy one is inefficient and wastes customer time; building the phone on-demand would take even longer. Increasingly, retail chains try to use statistics and just-in-time principles to keep just enough phones in each store to minimize overall cost of storage and shipping.

Applying just-in-time to compiling means the computer translates the code into processor instructions as it goes, only it holds onto the translation results so it can reuse them instead of retranslating. It also keeps track of what parts of the program are currently being used and what parts will be used next and manages the compiling process so that the translated results are ready when they are needed, without wasting time translating parts that are never going to be used. This turns out to be a very effective balance between compiling once ahead of time and compiling every single time you run the program. Browsers use just-in-time compiling to avoid translating the code for Facebook every time you visit that site, for example.

To my mind, Squirrel Girl's superheroing has a just-in-time flavor. Doreen is not Batman, who famously has contingency plans for every scenario he can imagine, leaving him vulnerable when those plans are discovered and countered. Neither is she Gromit in *The Wrong Trousers* who, via cartoon logic, finds himself riding a model train on an unfinished display, frantically laying track one section at a time just in front of the locomotive he occupies. She studies the kinds of villains she's likely to face, works out plans to deal with their schemes, and then adjusts to the circumstances of each situation. The story of her encounter with Swarm, with its branching and backtracking narrative, illustrates this beautifully, but it is evident in all of her adventures. And like a good computer scientist, when she finds an algorithm that works, she reuses it when appropriate rather than reinventing her plans every time.

10.5 A Just-in-Time God

Just-in-time shows up frequently because at its core, it's a pretty simple idea. Implementing it as a solution can be complex, and in programming requires both of the other versions of translating, which is one reason why it wasn't the first translation approach computer scientists employed. But once the pieces are in place, the concept itself is straightforward. And I also think it happens to be a useful way of understanding how God works as described in the Bible.

There are several places in the Bible that discourage getting too far ahead of yourself. For example, when the Israelite people were traveling between Egypt and Canaan, they did not have access to a reliable food source. We are told in Exodus 16 that a bread-like substance called manna was provided every morning for their sustenance. There was always sufficient for everyone, but they were told not to collect more than they personally needed for the day. Any manna that was saved from one day to the next would spoil. (Exception was made for the Sabbath, when they could collect food the day before.) Partly this was a trust-building exercise, and trust is one reason to not try to plan too rigidly, too far in advance. Perhaps it was also a way of reminding the people not to be too self-absorbed; by collecting extra for themselves for subsequent days, they may have been depriving someone else of food for today.

In 1 Kings 17, there is the story of the prophet Elijah, who encounters a widow running low on food because of a drought. Rather than keeping it to herself and her son, she gives what she has to Elijah. She then finds that the little oil and flour she has left manages to make far more bread than she had expected, enabling her to feed herself and her son until the drought ends. This would seem to be another example of provision coming no sooner than it is needed, and also of someone who had a choice between looking out for themselves and trusting their own needs would be taken care of if they provided for someone else's.

Then there is Jesus' teaching. He told his disciples, "Therefore I tell you, do not worry about your life, what you will eat or drink, or about your body, what you will wear. Isn't there more to life than food and more to the body than clothing?" (Matthew 6:25). He then reminds them that birds do not engage in agriculture, relying instead on what they can gather, and they are taken care of. If God cares about the birds, won't he also care about his followers?

But then we remember the ants. The book of Proverbs encourages us to consider the ant as an example of planning ahead. So which is it? Are we supposed to plan ahead or not?

That's where I think the just-in-time notion is helpful. We can't completely avoid the need to plan ahead; in the extreme, that would mean our actions at any given moment would be completely independent of our actions at any other moment. Imagine doing something simple like trying to getting dressed without first going to your closet to get a clean shirt, and instead waiting for a shirt to appear. And then of course you couldn't take off whatever you were currently wearing to prepare to put on the clean shirt either, and so on.

What we are discouraged from doing is not planning, but rather worrying about our future needs. And I think a main reason for that is because worrying is indicative of becoming too absorbed in yourself. You are only thinking of your own concerns and focusing on how you yourself are going to resolve them. As we saw in the last chapter, becoming self-absorbed is symptomatic of sin. Prudent planning doesn't have to be motivated by worry, or a source of worry.

Just to verify that the ant reference isn't a fluke, let's look at some other positive examples of forethought. In Genesis, we get the account of Noah building the ark. Going by the chronology reported there, a period of 120 years elapsed between Noah first receiving the idea to construct the ark, and its completion prior to the arrival of the flood. That's looking ahead quite a bit.

But in Noah's case, just-in-time meant starting preparations that far in advance. He didn't have a huge crew to work with, and he was building a fairly large structure; that was going to take a while. We don't know exactly how much of those 120 years were actually spent building, but we do see that the ark is finished just before the flood started. Without that lead time, the project wouldn't have been finished, and you try getting an extension on an end-of-the-world deadline.

Later in Genesis we get the story of Joseph, the dreamer with the colorful coat. He found himself in a position of power in the kingdom of Egypt. He had a dream warning of a seven-year famine in seven years. So he made arrangements to spend those first seven years putting food aside so that when the famine came, the Egyptians would still be able to eat. And indeed, they had so much food put away that they were able to serve people from surrounding countries who were also starving. Obviously if they had waited until the famine started to store food, it would be too late. That seven year lead time was important for setting aside adequate food.

The first few chapters of 2 Corinthians describe Paul's thought process regarding a change in his plans. Having visited the church in Corinth once previously, Paul had intended to visit them again and had told them as much. However, when it came time to make the trip, it was clear to Paul that his presence would further exacerbate some internal conflict at that church, so he opted to stay away for a time and take advantage of a different travel opportunity that had arisen. He makes it clear that he was planning ahead (1:17) and not just operating completely on a whim. Nor was he trying to say "Yes" and "No" at the same time, contrary to the admonitions for clarity and straightforward dealing we discussed in chapter 6. He was simply updating his plans based on new information.

And then there is Nehemiah, one of the most logistically minded of all biblical figures. In the book named for him, he undertakes the rebuilding of the wall around Jerusalem. It had been destroyed by Babylonians generations earlier and many of the Jews who lived there were forcibly relocated. By Nehemiah's time, the Persians (you may remember them from *300*) have taken over for the Babylonians, and they are more open-minded about Jewish autonomy. So they let a contingent return to the city to restore it.

Nehemiah organizes that effort, which requires no small amount of forethought with regards to potential challenges. He distributes the work evenly around the wall, schedules shifts, and makes sure that the people are also prepared to defend the city should their enemies decide to take advantage of their unfortified position before they were done. It may not have been as long-term of a plan as our other examples, but no one could accuse Nehemiah of winging it either.

That doesn't mean Nehemiah was inflexible. While the wall-building is under way, some defensive challenges arise. Nehemiah recognizes that his original plan is no longer adequate and makes adjustments to the work details and guard duties to improve their readiness. Even though a decent amount of thought went into the original plan, he didn't insist on sticking with it just because he had put effort into it. Nor did he hold up the original project start while he thought through every last possible variation. He just planned as much as he reasonably could, and made adjustments as necessary in response to developing circumstances.

10.6 Squirreling Away Options for the Future

Flexibility brings to mind the notion from computer programming of premature optimization. When you are writing software, there are generally three considerations with respect to how efficiently your program will work: how many instructions the processor has to execute (CPU), how much data storage is needed (memory), and how much data has to be moved around (I/O, for input/output). You want to minimize each as much as possible, but there are usually tradeoffs between them to consider. Cutting down on memory usage, for example, might require sifting through the data and eliminating what you don't need any more, but figuring out what you don't need uses CPU. In some cases, you might have plenty of memory and so it's not worth using CPU to prune it down; in other cases memory is tight and keeping only what data you absolutely need is very important. At the beginning of a project, you don't always know which situation you will be in, and so general programming practice advises against choosing one option over the other. Instead you are encouraged to focus on getting the program to do what it needs to do correctly, and from there you can optimize what needs to be optimized.

What stands out to me is the connection between information, premature optimization, and just-in-time compilation. The problem of premature optimization is one of making a decision in advance of having the information needed to make that decision. By contrast, just-in-time compilation makes decisions based on available information, and gathers information in order to make decisions that need to be made. I think that fits well with our earlier notion of making God our source of order and information. Waiting on God's timing is then just another expression of trusting him to be the source of information.

The life of Saul provides some interesting examples of a breakdown in using just-in-time planning. You may remember Saul as the first king of Israel, father of Jonathan and rival of David from our account of information and arrows. In 1 Samuel 13, Saul is preparing for a battle. He wants to make some offerings in advance of the battle, but he knows that the prophet Samuel is the one who is supposed to handle offerings. However, he does not know when Samuel will arrive.

Eventually, Saul gets tired of waiting for Samuel and performs the offerings himself. Samuel arrives immediately afterward (just in time!) and chastises Saul for his disobedience, informing him that it will cost Saul a dynasty on the throne of Israel. Later, in chapter 28, Samuel dies and Saul gets anxious about where he will get information. To his credit, he seeks it from God first, but when it doesn't come soon enough to suit him he seeks out a medium to have a séance with

Samuel. Saul knows this is not optimal, having just gotten rid of the mediums from the kingdom, but since he has trouble with just-in-time scheduling, he does it anyway. In a metaphysically interesting development, the spirit (or perhaps coherent, emergent pattern) of Samuel himself shows up, immediately chides Saul for doing what he knows he shouldn't, and reminds Saul that he already lost his legacy for a similar display of impatience.

Raiders of the Lost Ark offers perhaps another illustration of this dynamic of information and patience. Remember that everyone wanted the staff and headpiece that revealed the location of the ark. The Nazis, in their haste, try to get that information by force and only wind up with partial data, although they don't know it because they don't take the time to verify that they have the whole picture. Dr. Jones takes the time necessary to get all the details, and naturally the piece the Nazis are missing changes the search location entirely. "Indy, they are digging in the wrong place!" Just-in-time becomes just-in-space as well.

This also reminds us that just-in-time needn't be hectic. It is the Nazis who are acting hastily, not Indy and his allies. Another one of my favorite examples of just-in-time is Thor and his mystical flying hammer Mjolnir, as depicted in the Marvel films. At least once a movie, there is a moment where Thor needs Mjolnir but it is elsewhere. When summoned, it can fly to him, but the timing of the situation requires Thor to begin acting before Mjolnir is in his hand. Then, in a carefully choreographed confluence, Thor, hammer, and "nail" all come together in time and space. In *The Avengers,* the "nail" is the chin of a rampaging Hulk. We learn a lot about Thor as we watch the gamma-powered Goliath bear down on him while he serenely crouches, arm outstretched in anticipation of Mjolnir's arrival; it never occurs to him to worry that it will be late, and his faith is rewarded in glorious slow motion.

Improvisational performance can be energetic, but not necessarily hectic. It seems to me that it could be described as just-in-time composition, in the case of improvised music, or just-in-time writing, in the case of improv comedy. Both require a lot of trust in one's fellow performers. Both also require the patience to wait until one has the necessary information from those partners to know how to proceed with one's own contribution. And note that such performances are not necessarily "anything goes," or something anyone can just show up and do. There is preparation involved, and it takes practice and discipline to accomplish such just-in-time performances. Waiting in this way is not passive or inert, but instead acting in accordance with whatever information we do have available.

Comic book creating has a just-in-time aspect as well. Many comics are published as periodicals on a monthly or even more frequent basis. For economic reasons similar to just-in-time retail stocking, they are produced as close to publication as possible. Because of the collaborative nature of most comics, editors and publishers therefore need to maintain a choreographed flow between writers, pencilers, inkers, colorists and letterers so that everyone is kept busy and pages are moved from one contributor to another just-in-time. This gives comics an immediacy not found in most other fiction, allowing them to comment on current events and respond to reader reactions in a timely way that enhances the sense that the characters are people you live alongside rather than strangers you meet in passing.

Flexibility and responsiveness to newly available information allow just-in-time approaches to strike a balance between long-term commitments and shortsightedness. We know we need to expect the unexpected, but that doesn't mean we can ignore the expected either. A just-in-time perspective allows for both, whether we're undertaking a major infrastructure project or performing art in the moment.

Beyond the idea of just-in-time, the concept of compiling generally illustrates the need for words to be translated into action. We saw the same thing with respect to the genome and the cell, where the words of the genome don't actually manifest until they are translated into proteins. This is also a core theme of the book of James: our declarations of faith are of little value until they are translated into action. "If a brother or sister is poorly clothed and lacks daily food, and one of you says to them, 'Go in peace, keep warm and eat well,' but you do not give them what the body needs, what good is it? So also faith, if it does not have works, is dead being by itself. But someone will say, 'You have faith and I have works.' Show me your faith without works and I will show you faith by my works" (James 2:15–18).

We can even go back to the way data is represented via electric circuits as an illustration of words being physically incarnate. Words themselves seem nonphysical in a way, but when we write them down or type them into a computer they take on a physical form. Or rather, they provide an organizing form or pattern to physical matter. Note that these words are mediated by the circuits, but are not fully reducible to them; current in a circuit now may be part of the word *yes* and later part of the word *no*. Yet it is not until the words of a computer program are thus mediated that the works they describe can be realized physically. Likewise, the Word mediated by flesh accomplished great works as the person of Jesus and as the church.

Feeding and clothing those in need is pretty simple as works go. There's no denying, however, that the practices of various Christian communities have grown diverse and complex. Some of the variation can be explained by a similar process to what happened with Macs and PCs. Small differences in separate communities led to small changes in practice, and further traditions were built on those separate practices, and so on. Eventually we reached a point where the formal and ornate rituals of the Catholic or Orthodox churches seem completely incompatible with the everyday casualness of a suburban evangelical congregation. Is it even plausible they all share a common instruction set underneath, and if so, what could it possibly be? Those are questions we'll take up in the next chapter.

CHAPTER 11

BASIC Actions Simulate Infinite Complexity

For every widely appreciated expression of nerdhood—your *Star Wars*, your *Star Trek*s, your star charts—there is a more niche domain of nerdiness. Case in point: martial arts films. While baseball is probably the sport most associated with number crunching, that's external analysis that can be applied to any activity. I assert that martial arts actually embody the iterative, unfolding nature of mathematics that also explains how the simplicity of the gospel can adapt to the complexity of modern life.

11.1 Dueling In Martial Mathematics

A particular school of martial arts starts with a set of assumptions about the kinds of combat situations one will encounter, the weapons that will be available, the way your opponent or opponents will react, and so forth. Some techniques are primarily for formal sports settings, with rules about allowable attacks and equipment and overseen by referees. Others were developed in the context of battlefield encounters, for trained groups confronting other groups as a unit. And some assume you will be in a back alley trying to defend yourself from multiple, potentially larger assailants. All of these assumptions inform what is or isn't allowable or possible within the context of a given style, just as assumptions define what is and isn't expressible in a given field of mathematics.

A contest between practitioners of different arts, then, can become a sort of referendum on which assumptions are the most useful, relevant, or powerful in terms of their expressiveness. Some encounters are decided based on execution; one combatant may be more skilled, or more disciplined in their training, or purer of motive. But the films I find most fascinating are the ones structured so that the core philosophies of the arts are on display. In those films, it is common to see those philosophies pitted against each other in a way that doesn't revolve around fisticuffs. In *The Magnificent Butcher,* two masters face off in a calligraphy battle. In *The Grandmaster* one master challenges another to break a cookie in his hand. *Hero* features the most esoteric contest of all, a battle entirely within the minds of the combatants; they both know each other's styles so well that the outcome is inevitable given the starting assumptions.

Or, if you prefer movies you don't have to read, consider the Matrices. Yes, all three of them; I told you I appreciated them all. The dynamic between Keanu Reeves' Neo and Hugo Weaving's Agent Smith in their three fights drive the central plot. In the first film, Neo defeats Agent Smith because his humanity affords him greater flexibility and creativity within the Matrix, while Agent Smith can't exceed his original programming—notice how all the agents spawn in the same initial conditions, for example. On the other hand, defeating Agent Smith doesn't actually get Neo any closer to his goal of freeing humans from the Matrix. Since his gifts are only relevant in the Matrix, he keeps entering it to look for the means to their freedom at the risk of continuing to encounter Agent Smith. In the second film, they fight again. Smith clones himself to get a numerical advantage, which Neo can't overcome directly, but he can fly away whenever he wants; it's a stalemate. In the third film, Agent Smith can now match Neo's power set, but Neo has learned that being defeated by Smith is actually the means to achieving his goal.

To give a more practical example, let's talk about judo. Judo is a Japanese art, primarily intended as a sport, making it suitable as an Olympic event. Therefore judo assumes you will face a single opponent dressed in a regulation uniform. Most of judo's techniques are throws and pins, and these are largely initiated by grabbing the opponent's uniform in a particular way. The uniform top is basically a loose fitting jacket, and the grabs often focus on the lapel or sleeve of that jacket.

That's all fine for organized competitions, but not always applicable in unstructured fights. In the movie *Flashpoint*, Donnie Yen and Collin Chou face off in a climactic final battle. They both employ a variety of grappling techniques from judo or arts related to judo. Neither is wearing an actual judo uniform, but both are wearing jackets. And so at one point Donnie Yen very purposefully removes his jacket, effectively denying Collin Chou of the ability to initiate those judo techniques.

So what do you do when your fighting technique's assumptions no longer hold? One approach is to add more and more assumptions and more and more techniques. Often that involves studying multiple arts, combining the moves they teach and employing them conditionally in the different scenarios to which they apply. Actual martial arts develop this way. For example, Korean Hapkido combines kicking and striking techniques from one set of disciplines with the grappling and throwing moves of others.

Combining styles is also a common feature of movie plots. The protagonist gets defeated in the first act, then spends the second act learning a new art that specifically counters the style by which he was defeated so that he can be triumphant in the third act. Jackie Chan's *Drunken Master* is a typical example. Jackie is beaten by Hwang Jang-Lee because Jackie can't get out of the way of his powerful arsenal of kicks. So he learns Drunken Boxing, which emphasizes flexibility and unpredictability.

In short, one approach to deal with increasing complexity is an ever-more complex fighting technique. That unfortunately has a scalability problem. You can't possibly enumerate in advance all of the scenarios you will encounter, let alone devise the appropriate counter. Even if you could, the number of people that could learn your system is probably vanishingly small, and that's before you consider the amount of practice time to learn those systems. Fortunately, there is another approach to deal with complexity.

I mentioned *The Grandmaster,* a meditation on what it means to be a kung fu master. The Chinese concept of kung fu goes beyond martial arts to passion for and mastery of any specific field that requires dedication and discipline, making it not entirely unlike being a nerd. Toward that end, it features a number of martial arts masters putting their philosophies to the test against each other. The Hung Gar practitioner Master Yong exemplifies this "gotta catch 'em all" approach, boasting of his large repertoire of techniques. He faces off against Ip Man, who teaches Wing Chun; Ip Man notes that he only has three arm strikes in his style, but they are all he needs. And, true to his word, he is able to utilize those three strikes expertly to counter all of Master Yong's varied attacks.

The Grandmaster is fictionalized, but Ip Man was a real man who did teach Wing Chun. His most famous student was Bruce Lee. Bruce Lee continued to develop this philosophy of handling complexity with simplicity and flexibility. The ultimate expression of his thinking was the martial art he developed called Jeet Kune Do. Lee sometimes described it as a style without style, or in *Enter the Dragon*, "fighting without fighting." It is basically an attempt to identify minimal movements that achieve particular goals, and then combine those movements as needed for a given situation. To put it another way, it tries to break down fighting techniques to more atomic building blocks and focus training at that level. The Jeet Kune Do practitioner then applies them as a given situation requires rather than relying on prescribed sequences of techniques.

Bruce Lee's unfinished film *Game of Death* was intended to be a showcase of this style without style. The climax is a series of battles against widely differing foes, including the Filipino martial artist Dan Inosanto, who uses eskrima sticks and nunchaku, the Korean Hapkido master Ji Han Jae, and Kareem Abdul-Jabbar, a 7′2″ NBA star and real-life student of Bruce Lee. Each opponent presents a unique challenge, but instead of having the opportunity to train specifically for each one, Bruce Lee's character faces them in order as he climbs to the top of a tower. Consequently, he must be fully aware and present in each confrontation in order to understand what each opponent's strengths and weaknesses are and react accordingly.

Of course, these scenarios were still entirely scripted and choreographed in advance to illustrate the philosophy Bruce wanted to communicate to the world. It's easy to make simplicity look effective when both sides agree in advance to the outcome. Thus we might ask whether this notion of applying simplicity to complex situations can be established more rigorously.

Martial arts are popular for motion pictures because they are visual and dynamic. They provide an excellent medium for externalizing and visualizing internal, philosophical differences. Their dynamic physicality is one way to make a film visually compelling; computer graphics are another. I'm fascinated by their ability to show us versions of the world that cannot currently exist.

11.2 Artistic Simulations of Cinematic Illusions & Images

The movie *Doctor Strange* demonstrates the value of both of these cinematic tools quite effectively. The film is structured like a martial arts film. In the first act, Stephen Strange suffers defeat because of a deficiency in his training; he hasn't learned humility and succumbs to his own hubris. He studies under a wise old monk and trains hard to learn the skills he lacks, including a surprising amount of actual martial arts for someone studying sorcery. In the climactic final confrontation, he combines his original training as a surgeon and healer with his newfound perspective on his self-importance to resolve a global crisis in a fairly unique way for a superhero, i.e., without punching his problems.

Along the way, Stephen and we the audience are treated to a symphony of kaleidoscopic visuals that are only possible thanks to computer graphics. Blurring the lines of magic and science, the sorcerers in the movie can manipulate the geometry of space and time, implying a control over physics even more fundamental than we currently manage in reality rather than the circumvention of physics more typically associated with magic. Cities fold back on themselves and repeat as if reflected in a hall of mirrors, perhaps an homage to the finale of Bruce Lee's *Enter the Dragon*. Wormholes connect otherwise distant points of time and space. And we visit fantastical dimensions where psychedelic imagination is made manifest.

All of these complex visuals are made possible by computers. And, it should be added, the hard work and long hours of programmers, animators, painters, compositors, and other digital artists who employ those computers to realize their art. I am focusing here on their computational tools simply because I am interested in metaphors from beyond typical human experience. How computers generate graphics illustrates how we can get complexity from simplicity.

Before we get to the full complexity of modern movie visuals, let's talk about computer graphics in general. As we discussed last chapter, computers work with numbers, words and data. The computers themselves can do all of their work via their internal representation of 1s and 0s as electrical currents. But their human operators find it helpful to see what's going on, just like movie audiences sometimes like to see the external results of ideas rather than just watch characters think and talk about them.

The simplest and most obvious visualization of what the computer is doing is via text. Computers were originally designed via analogy to typewriters with a comparable keyboard for input and a screen that can reproduce the experience of type appearing on paper. Yet the connection is merely metaphorical, and does not capture everything a computer is capable of. In reality, a computer screen is a grid of tiny dots, or pixels, which can each display millions of colors independently of what every other pixel is doing. Computers have complete control over those pixels, allowing arbitrary visuals of incredible richness. But still, someone or some algorithm needs to decide what to draw.

For reference, high definition video involves images 1,920 pixels wide by 1,080 pixels tall, for a total of 2,073,600 pixels. To look good on a big screen, movie graphics might be rendered with four or eight times as many pixels, if not more. By my estimate, a two hour movie at 24 frames per second would involve 59,719,680,000 (nearly 60 billion) pixels. Deciding on a color for each pixel one by one would get tedious quickly. Besides, we don't think of the world that way anyway, as individual, unrelated dots of color; we think in terms of shapes and objects.

We start with the simplest of shapes: squares and rectangles. We just need to specify the location of the upper right and lower left corners, which can be done with four numbers, a horizontal coordinate and a vertical coordinate for each of those two corners. That's much simpler than keeping track of every pixel inside the rectangle. An arbitrary quadrilateral is a little trickier because you need to specify all four corners, meaning eight numbers are required. And then pentagons, hexagons, heptagons, and so forth each add an extra two numbers as the number of corners increases by one.

With some math, we can actually prove that any arbitrary polygon can be represented as triangles. This simplifies matters in one respect, since each triangle only needs three points. But interesting graphics involve complex polygons, so there are still lots of triangles to keep track of. And we are still just keeping track of a list, albeit a list of triangle coordinates.

We got rid of the need to list all pixels by coming up with a procedure for coloring a group of pixels, namely filling in all the pixels inside a polygon with a color. Then we just needed the procedure and its parameters, the coordinates of the polygons. We might thus imagine having a procedure to generate polygons, further simplifying what we have to keep track of. And in fractals we have one such procedure.

Fractals are shapes that are self-similar. This means that fractals have patterns at the largest scales that are also discernible as one zooms in on portions of the fractal. Generating such a pattern can involve iteratively applying the same procedure over and over again such that the output of one iteration is the input for the next iteration. We've actually already seen this technique in chapter 3 with the logistic and Hénon maps. Those were defined with equations that were applied iteratively, so numbers calculated from one step are the input numbers for the next step. And in the case of the Hénon map, the resulting strange attractor is a fractal.

Not all fractals have to be expressed as a mathematical equation. One of the most basic fractals, the Koch curve, is generated by the pattern of a line segment with a notch in the middle. Draw a line segment, then erase the middle third and replace it with a notch, which is just the two sides of the equilateral triangle that would be completed by the erased portion. Now we have four line segments, so we can erase the middle third of each of those and replace them with notches defined the same way. And look! The resulting shape is made of sixteen line segments, each of which has an erasable and replaceable middle third. And so on. Figure 11.1 illustrates the first few iterations.

We can also draw this same fractal using a slightly different procedure that is recursive. A recursive procedure uses itself to complete its activity. By way of illustration, the title of this chapter is crudely recursive. Using each letter to start a new word, BASIC can be expanded into BASIC Actions Simulate Infinite Complexity. And the BASIC in that phrase can be expanded in the same way, and so on.

So a recursive version of our fractal procedure would have a line-segment-drawing algorithm that goes something like this. When drawing a line segment from point a to point b, first find points c and d that divide the segment into thirds. Then find point e equidistant from c and d and at 60 degree angles from the line between a and b. Now draw line segments ac, ce, ed, and db using our line-segment-drawing algorithm.

A fun feature of this procedure is that, as currently defined, it will consume an infinite amount of computational resources and never actually draw anything. Can you see why? To avoid this infinite regress, we need a branch in the flow that actually draws something instead of just subdividing and delegating. If we are drawing pixels on a screen, we might first check whether points a and b are so close that they occupy a single pixel and if so draw that pixel and be done without calling the line-segment-drawing algorithm again. Then we will only repeat the process a finite number of times and actually render a drawing on the screen.

Figure 11.1: The first few iterations drawing the Koch curve.

Whether truly recursive or just iterative, applying the same procedure over and over to the output of the previous round is a powerful and versatile technique. Some of the *Doctor Strange* visuals were created this way. Most obvious is the fractal hand, where Strange's fingers each sprout a hand from their tip, and then each finger on each of those hands sprouts a hand, etc. But in fractal fashion, the more you look, the more self-similar patterns there are in Strange's cross-dimensional journey.

This technique is also how martial artists train. As shown in *Doctor Strange*, *Drunken Master*, and any number of other martial arts films, training is built on repetition of simple movements and exercises. In that case, the output of each iteration is the trainee, and it is that same trainee who is the input for the next iteration. Through repeated practice of the basics, muscles are built and sophisticated fighting styles are mastered.

Another means for achieving complexity from simplicity is combinatorics, all the ways to combine elements of groups. For example, the sorcerers in *Doctor Strange* have the ability to reshape cities, folding them back in on themselves. Obviously the movie crew didn't film actual cities being folded, spindled, and mutilated. Digital cities were created to be manipulated by computer algorithms and digital artists.

Some films will painstakingly reproduce actual cityscapes building for building. Other films generate cities procedurally. Libraries of windows, doors, roofs, sidings, and other features make it easy to mix and match elements to create a wide variety of realistic buildings. Even modest numbers of each feature provide substantial numbers of unique buildings when combined. Thus a simple collection of simple pieces has the potential for a diverse and complex set of interactions.

We've already seen another example of this approach in developmental biology. Our bodies don't have unique signal molecules for every step and every facet of our development process. Instead, a comparatively small set of signals are combined in different ways at different times. Those combinations create a wide range of contexts that foster all of the cell types and tissues and organs and muscles and bones that make up you.

Even more powerful is using combinatorics to create different contexts or starting parameters, and then employing an iterative or recursive process on each of those different initial inputs. This is how the Mandelbrot set—that most famous of fractals, immortalized in coffee table books, mall kiosk prints, and even a song—is generated. The equation of the Mandelbrot set couldn't be simpler:

$$z_{n+1} = z_n^2 + c$$

Yet a cursory glance at an image of the set (Figure 11.2) reveals a wealth of detail. Even more remarkably, we can zoom in and find the same level of detail, with the same shapes repeated in various locations. And unlike Google Maps, there is no limit to the zoom. We have every reason to believe that you could zoom in on the Mandelbrot set forever and never find an image with less detail. Not just a really long time. Not just until the universe reaches maximum entropy, making it impossible to find an entropy gradient to use to make electrons flow to power your computer to draw the pictures (although it wouldn't matter because both you and your computer would not exist). But for an infinite amount of time.

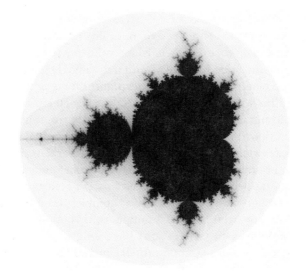

Figure 11.2: Black points are in the set; the gray scale indicates how quickly a point diverges from inclusion criteria.

How do we draw the pictures from that one simple equation? Each dot in the picture represents a point c in the two-dimensional plane known as the complex plane. For a given value of c we start by setting z_0 equal to 0. Then we apply the equation over and over again. Then we use z_0 to calculate z_1 using the equation, use z_1 to calculate z_2, and so on.

If that sequence of numbers z_n stays close to 0 and never gets further away than a fixed distance, then that particular point c is in the Mandelbrot set and we draw it black. If those numbers keep getting bigger, then the number is not in the Mandelbrot set. The simplest representations render those points white; here we have used a gray scale indicating how quickly the sequence grows. The glossy color images use a color coding scheme based on the same idea.

How do we know which values of c will generate a sequence that stays close to 0? We can see certain sequences grow very quickly without ever getting any smaller at any step; for many of these, we can prove that they will continue to grow and thus are not in the Mandelbrot set. For other values of c we can prove they will stay bounded. For example, the sequence generated by -1 just alternates between 0 and -1 forever and so -1 is provably part of the Mandelbrot set.

However, there are many values of c that generate a sequence of numbers that doesn't repeat or cycle, but nevertheless stays bounded . . . as far as anyone has calculated. In theory, when drawing a picture of the Mandelbrot set, we could spend an infinite amount of time trying to decide whether just one of these points is part of the set. Obviously, that would make it hard to ever finish the whole picture. And so practically what we do is check for so many iterations, and if the sequence stays within particular bounds we've chosen ahead of time, then it gets drawn black; otherwise it gets colored as described earlier. Mathematically, there is no ambiguity about whether a particular value of c is in the Mandelbrot set. It is perfectly valid to define membership in the set based on the behavior of an infinite sequence. But practically, there are limits to how well we can determine the absolute truth of whether a point is in or out.

Finally, how can a sequence can stay bounded indefinitely? The example starting from -1 seems like maybe a special case, and it basically is. Numbers on the x-axis that are between 0 and 1 are also easy to understand because when you square them, they actually get smaller. From that, you might expect the Mandelbrot set to look more like a circle. And if the coordinates were regular numbers, that would be the case.

But we are working with the complex plane, which means dealing with the square root of negative one. Most values of c will have a multiple of that square root as a component. As a result, when we square them they tend to have both positive and negative parts. In some cases, these parts will always balance each other out so that the sequence of squares stays close to 0; others times they won't. Surprisingly, the pattern of which numbers generate sufficiently balanced sequences to stay bounded, and thus the shape of the Mandelbrot set, is infinitely complex. There are points in and out of the set next to each other everywhere we look, no matter how closely we zoom in.

The Mandelbrot set is an abstract example of a fractal and procedurally generated imagery. Combinatorics and iterative processes can also be used to produce trees, mountains, and other natural imagery, because the actual objects are themselves fractally self-similar. The branching pattern of trees is fractal. Certain spiral shells are fractal. Romanesco broccoli is fractal. Mountains are fractal. Rivers are fractal. And so it is possible to use simple fractal definitions to draw very complex, naturalistic terrain and foliage without having to store a lot of detail.

11.3 Keep It Simple, *Sensei*

We've been talking about film graphics, but this principle of simple rules generating complex patterns has other applications. In fact, we've already encountered an example. (Don't say ants.) That's right—ants! They use simple rules to decide how to navigate, and yet they are able to coordinate to find food. Other simple rules govern the building of their nests, and we've already discussed how complex they can be. You can kind of see how this has to be the case, because ants just don't have the brain power for anything but simple rules.

Bird flocking is another example. Think about how fighter planes fly together. There is a clear hierarchy: there are predetermined positions in the flight pattern, and each pilot is expected to fly their plane in their designated location and follow directions from further up the hierarchy. But bird flocks have none of those things. They don't have assigned spots or practice drills. They are able to maintain a flock apparently by following some simple rules, most likely involving flying near other birds, but also not too close. We can't exactly ask them for the rulebook directly, but we can observe how flocks form, and we can also simulate agents that have a few rules and see which rules lead to flocking behavior.

And then there are our brains. Apart from the normal cell activities of making proteins, digesting sugars, and so forth, nerve cells know how to do one thing. When one particular nerve cell's neighboring cells send it chemical signals, that cell accepts those signals and decides whether to send its own signal or not. They are a little more sophisticated than the electrical circuits we saw earlier that are only either on or off. Nerve cells can send signals of varying intensity, and they can send a couple of different chemicals. But that's about it.

Yet that simple behavior of individual neurons combines to do, well, whatever it is that brains do. I made a case for the brain mediating consciousness, and maybe you found that convincing and maybe you didn't. But even if you didn't, chances are you would still be comfortable with the idea that the brain is where our consciousness, whatever it is, interacts with our physical bodies, given how many observations there are of brain activity correlating with different mental activities, and given that the nerve signals that keep our hearts beating and that also initiate voluntary motions like typing a book all originate in the brain.

This problem of complexity also turns up in the question of how we are to live our lives. We have to make a variety of decisions every day, in a range of contexts and involving a host of details. And judging by the numbers of different categories and types of "stuff" that exist in our present society, the complexity of those decisions is only increasing. Whether any of us individually is getting smarter is a separate question, but I don't think it would be very controversial to assert that the transition from hunter-gatherer tribes to the metropolises or megalopolises of today is accompanied by an increase in the set of objects one can make decisions about. Does this mean that we need an ever-increasingly complex set of rules to guide our decisions?

This appears to have been the rabbinical solution during the time of Jesus. Many of us think of the Bible as a rulebook, and while that is overly reductive, it does contain a variety of rules. The books of Leviticus and Deuteronomy are largely enumerations of laws on very detailed topics, like fabrics ("You must not wear clothing made with wool and linen meshed together" [Deuteronomy 22:11]) or mildew in Leviticus 13. These represent the totality of the law that was given to Moses on Mount Sinai; most of us are only familiar with the Ten Commandments recorded in Exodus (and those ten by themselves are hard enough for any of us to keep up with).

Despite the breadth and volume of Mosaic law, there are a number of topics they don't deal with explicitly. Some of those were scenarios that didn't even exist at the time, such as whether activating an electrical circuit constitutes doing work and thus is prohibited on the Sabbath. So the approach to these situations was and is for the religious leaders to consider them as they arise, make a decision, and introduce an extension of the law. This is really not that different to how our current governments deal with the same problem. The framers of the constitution could scarcely imagine computers, for example, and so all of the laws we have about computer technology couldn't have been written until they were actually invented. And so we write new laws to handle new situations, and we also have courts to interpret those laws wherever the laws themselves weren't specific enough to cover every permutation. Those court decisions form precedents that are a form of law themselves. These decisions of the religious leaders would have occupied the same roles of laws and precedents.

As you might imagine, in the roughly fourteen hundred years between Moses and Jesus, there were plenty of opportunities to expand the law. According to the Gospels, by the time of Jesus it had become a source of pride among religious leaders just to know the extent of the law, and then also to be seen as following all of it. The Gospels record a number of instances where one or another group of religious leaders would try to corner Jesus, posing to him a binary question where either way he would be breaking a law or running afoul of some power or another. On one such occasion, Jesus encountered a man with a paralytic hand on the Sabbath. The leaders asked Jesus whether it would be lawful to heal his hand, knowing that Jesus regularly performed healing miracles. They also knew that working on the Sabbath was contraindicated by the law, specifically the Ten Commandments. Healing could be considered work. Jesus opts to heal the man, citing the precedent that helping an animal in distress was permissible. Surely showing compassion to a fellow human was at least as worthwhile as showing compassion on an animal.

But is Jesus just creating more rules? My sense is no. Instead, I think Jesus is proposing an alternative, scalable approach to dealing with complexity. It's the same approach we've already seen: establish a few simple rules and apply them in any given situation. We've already demonstrated that it is feasible for simple rules to cover an infinite array of possibilities with nuance; why not for life decisions as well? Jesus even provides us those simple rules explicitly. When asked for the most important commandments, he offered this reply from Matthew 22:37–40.

> " 'Love the Lord your God with all your heart, with all your soul, and with all your mind.' This is the first and greatest commandment. The second is like it: 'Love your neighbor as yourself.' All the law and the prophets depend on these two commandments."

Conveniently enough, we already have an operational definition for what it means to love: to increase the asymmetry of another, possibly at the cost of taking on greater symmetry for ourselves. The application to this particular scenario is straightforward enough; a diseased and dysfunctional limb is in a state of symmetry relative to a healthy, functional one, so healing it would bring greater asymmetry to the man's life. The cost to Jesus isn't as clear, but it's also not strictly necessary. In the long run, these confrontations with the religious leaders would lead to Jesus' death, so at the very least the cost was an escalation of the tension between the two.

While Jesus was the greatest advocate for the centrality of love as a guiding principle, it was not without precedent. In 1 Samuel 21, David and some of his soldiers arrive at the temple in need of food. The only food available is the bread set aside to be eaten by the priests serving there; it was against the law for anyone else to eat it. Nevertheless, the priest gave it to David and David accepted and ate it. In that original account, no indication is given that this was the wrong choice, despite being contrary to the law. Jesus would later refer to this event, and not only does he fail to censure David, he commends the decision making as correct. This may not be immediately obvious as an act of love, but recall that food is our body's source of asymmetry, organized structure that can be transformed in a useful way.

The book of Hosea is the story of a prophet who is called to marry a prostitute. Further, he is told that his wife will continue to practice her chosen profession, which will ultimately lead to her having children that are not Hosea's. Nevertheless, he is called to raise them as his own. This arrangement would probably raise eyebrows even today, so you can imagine that it was not an obvious life choice at the time. And yet it was order-giving in several ways. First, Hosea would be giving love to his wife and her children when no other obvious candidate was available. There likely weren't any social structures or formal institutions to provide for the well-being of those children in particular, so having an adoptive father would have been a very welcome ordering for them. And second, Hosea was providing an illustration for the nation of Israel of what the love of God actually looked like. This kind of information-spreading is also tied to our definition of love.

In Acts, we read of the apostle Peter being faced with an opportunity to interact with Gentiles, or anybody who isn't a Jew. The law had more than a few things to say about associations between Jews and Gentiles. Pragmatically, Gentiles couldn't be completely avoided, but the general sentiment from the Bible is that being in the company of Gentiles was in an "only when absolutely necessary" category. But as we've seen earlier, even the Old Testament laws made allowances for Gentiles being brought into the fold, and Jesus had said that his message was for the whole world. So getting the word to the Gentiles was going to have to happen at some point. Peter was introduced to this idea by seeing a vision of foods that Jews were forbidden to eat, and being invited to partake. He rejects the idea at first, thinking it a test, but ultimately realizes that he is meant to eat and that the invitation is symbolic of a call to step beyond customs about Jewish/Gentile relations. Once again, Peter is making the choice in the direction of love, by favoring the option that shares information with others, even at the potential cost to himself of being ostracized by his own people.

All of this emphasis on love, however, does not always mean making the choice that flaunts the rules. Rules represent their own form of asymmetry, separating what is permissible from what is not. For parents, it is particularly important for them to understand that there are times when making rules and enforcing rules is the loving choice, because it provides structure and order for our children when they are incapable of providing those things for themselves. This might explain, for example, why the Bible has so many rules in the first place, particularly in the early going.

Love also doesn't mean making the choice with the most warm fuzzies. One story that stands out here is that of Abraham and Isaac. Abraham is the father of the nation of Israel, and yet for most of his life he was childless. He and his wife eventually had a son, Isaac, but when Isaac was a young boy we are told that God asked Abraham to sacrifice Isaac. Killing Isaac would surely seem to violate the principle of love, but note that loving God is given precedence over loving our neighbors. And so Abraham starts to follow through, only for God to provide an alternative sacrifice just-in-time. This may have been God's intention all along, and the purpose of the exercise may have been to solidify Abraham's faith, demonstrate how God was different from the other gods worshipped by Abraham's contemporaries (child sacrifice was not unheard of in the worship of those deities), and provide an illustration of substitutionary sacrifice (dying so that others might live) that would have its ultimate expression in the death of Jesus.

Finally, all of this nuance and contextualization doesn't mean that anything goes, or that everything is a moral gray area where relativism reigns supreme. Recall that the Mandelbrot set has no end of nuance. And yet, for every single point there is a definite answer as to whether it is part of the Mandelbrot set or not. It is just not always possible to discern that answer perfectly with finite resources. This notion makes a lot more sense to me than the popular concept of gray areas. We can affirm that there are right and wrong choices. But we can also acknowledge that our fellow man, and even we, will not always be able to perfectly discern which is which. That is where a notion of grace is handy, to make allowances for the finite limitations with which we must deal. Fortunately, we have an operational definition of that one as well.

Simplifying the commandments in this way is itself also an act of ordering and information-sharing. Learning all of the laws extant in Jesus' time would have been a fairly daunting task, which would mean that the set of people who could consider undertaking it would get narrower and narrower over time. It would likely require a certain level of literacy, not to mention extensive study of the law itself. Those options would not be available to everyone. By providing a simple framework at the foundation of the law, Jesus greatly increased the number of people who had access to the information in the law, and thus we're able to benefit from the asymmetry that these rules could provide their lives.

The trade-off is that one needs to be more engaged with the circumstances one finds oneself in, in order to determine how to apply the simple rules. We saw this with the martial arts application; systems like Wing Chun and Jeet Kune Do simplify what needs to be learned in advance, but require more awareness during a confrontation. In the case of the Mandelbrot set and other fractals, the calculations need to be done for each point or location, rather than figured out in advance or copying results from elsewhere to the present situation. And Jesus modeled this level of engagement with his teaching. He avoided making pronouncements of how others should act from a distance. Instead, he preferred to meet people where they were, understand the questions that they were specifically asking, and speak into those specific circumstances.

This specific engagement and contextual awareness will mean that the expression of the underlying principles will look different. This brings me back to my final martial arts story. *Game of Death*, to the extent that it was filmed, was made decades ago, and so it has had time to influence subsequent films. The narrative structure of a sequence of battles with no breaks has been repeated a number of times.

One of my favorite homages was in *Ong Bak*, a Thai martial arts film that served as the international debut of Tony Jaa. We are introduced to his skills in one of these sequences, this time presented as a last-man-standing underground tournament. Tony Jaa's character is reluctantly (that's how you know he's the hero) pulled into the tournament, and after dispatching his first opponent with a single kick, he is matched against a Chinese martial artist. At first glance, you might assume that this is a fellow who has studied his Bruce Lee (which he has). Besides the ethnic similarity, he dresses like Bruce Lee, has the shifting stance and sophisticated footwork of Bruce Lee, and uses kicks and strikes patterned after Bruce Lee's most famous cinematic moves. Tony Jaa on the other hand looks nothing like Bruce Lee, and his character's style is grounded in Muay Thai, the traditional martial art of Thailand. And yet his economy of movement, simple repertoire of techniques, and adaptive style more closely emulate the core of Jeet Kune Do than having the right outfit.

In *Ong Bak 2*, Jaa takes these concepts one step further. He designs a fight sequence where he actually uses two different styles to take on two different opponents simultaneously. When facing one opponent, he adopts one stance and employs a Chinese Hung Gar style. Then, in the same shot, he will turn and face the other opponent in a different stance using a Muay Thai style. These adjustments are contextual awareness at its finest.

Perhaps we can think of Christians in a similar fashion. We are all trying to follow Jesus and the example he set for our behavior. But the end result of those attempts can vary widely. Without endorsing every single act done in Jesus' name, I think a good deal of this variety can be explained through the application of simple principles in different contexts. The combinatorics of different cultural elements and personal experiences provide unique inputs for how we apply the commandments to love.

Further diversity is achieved through the iterative processes that are commonly referred to as spiritual disciplines. Prayer, reading the Bible, worship, fasting, and other religious practices all involve consistent repetition. Even the discipline of regular work is considered worthwhile and transformative, as suggested in 2 Thessalonians 3. The processes are essentially the same; the Bible is the same text, and prayer, worship, and fasting have repeatable patterns. The input each time is the person who was the output of the previous iteration. Through that repetition, behaviors and minds and lives are transformed.

An essential element in those transformations is memory. We change because we remember what has happened in the past, which informs our choices in the future. In short, we learn. Our next chapter will explore further how learning transforms.

CHAPTER 12

Mutatis Mutandis

Do you ever feel you are the exception while the rest of the world is the rule? I assert that the X-Men feel this way. Try as they might, they can't catch a break when it comes to public perception. The world either fears them or hates them. Finally, they reach a point of embracing the fear in the hope it will lead to respect.

The X-Men are the main mutant superhero team in the Marvel Universe, from which the previously discussed X-Factor is an offshoot. Reading X-Men is where I got my start as a comics fan thanks to my friend Ronnie, and they remain my favorite. As a nerdy, socially awkward near-teenager, I was just the right age for a story about misunderstood outsiders. Unlike most Marvel superheroes who come by their special abilities through deliberate, designed acts of creation (their own or someone else's), the happenstance of genetics bequeaths mutants their powers. The uncertainty inherent in their origin makes people suspicious of them.

12.1 Protecting a World That Is Biased toward Them

In a story called "Everything is Sinister!" by Kieron Gillen, Carlos Pacheco, Rodney Buchemi, et al. at the beginning of *Uncanny X-Men* volume 2, team leader Cyclops is fed up with the way mutants are treated by the wider society of the Marvel Universe. Superheroes like Captain America, Iron Man, the Fantastic Four, and even Spider-Man (despite the best efforts of sensationalist newsman J. Jonah Jameson) are respected and adored by the public for their world-saving exploits. The X-Men have saved the world and even the universe their fair share of times, but public opinion never shifts. So Cyclops assembles a team of their heaviest hitters to apply a little shock and awe with their hero-ics, so at the very least the world will be reminded not to mess with mutants the next time it is saved.

No sooner is the team together than one of their main adversar-ies, Mr. Sinister, obliges them with a crisis to resolve. Sinister believes himself to be superior to the X-Men, the pinnacle of human potential, and yet they thwart him at every turn. Habitual defeat is a common challenge among super villains; they are characters in fictional worlds where the heroes always have to win in the end, where stories are pub-lished on a monthly basis for fifty years, and where fans want to see their favorite villains again and again. Consequently, they can never win, but they are doomed to keep trying. Mr. Sinister doesn't know any of this, of course, but he is aware of his history and his record of failure begins to weigh on his self-confidence.

Fortunately, Mr. Sinister has a plan to confront this pattern of incompetence directly. He obsesses over cloning and he can transfer a consciousness from one body to another, so he combines these in-terests to clone himself and transplant his consciousness to the new body whenever things are looking bad for his present incarnation. This is a handy trick for someone who is narratively obliged to lose a lot and keep coming back for more. His latest plan is to clone a version of himself that knows nothing about the X-Men except the most basic initial details, and then have that version predict their actions based on those few facts. Since Mr. Sinister Prime knows what the actual X-Men did, he can compare the predictions of his clone with reality. If a clone gets something wrong, Mr. Sinister Prime starts over with a new clone, using the old one as a basis but making a few changes. Eventually, a clone gets the entire X-Men history right, suggesting that he should be able to predict what they do next.

Armed with that foreknowledge, Mr. Sinister Prime will be able to anticipate the X-Men's actions and plan accordingly. He expects that this will allow him to succeed where he has failed in the past, because now he will be prepared with the right counter for their every attack even before they've struck. Initially his predictions pan out; he's in just the right place at just the right time to challenge Cyclops' new team. He announces his intention to remake the world in his image. The X-Men naturally object, but his countermeasures are always one step ahead of them. The situation looks dire for our heroes, until one of them does something they had never done before. That innovation catches Mr. Sinister unprepared, and leads to his undoing.

I'm very fond of this story, and one reason is because Mr. Sinister is thwarted by underfitting. Underfitting comes from machine learning, a discipline of computer science concerned with drawing inferences, or learning, from data. A common task in machine learning is training or constructing a model of the system you want to study—say, the X-Men—based on some observations, and then verifying how well your model describes the system by seeing how it performs predicting another set of observations. Mr. Sinister built a mental model of how and why the X-Men behaved as they did using their past behavior as his data set. But his model failed to represent their full potential, and thus was underfit.

Underfitting is related to a central tension in machine learning called the bias-variance tradeoff. In order to make inferences from data, we have to start with some idea about the shape of the answers we will infer. This is called the bias of the model, and we can think of it as essentially a set of axioms that define what answers are possible and what answers are not. Basically, in the full world of ideas there are an infinite number of possible inferences or models we might reach and only a finite number of data points to inform our choice. In order to make any progress at all, we have to restrict ourselves to a finite subset of inferences so that the data can actually prefer one over the others. As an extreme example, Mr. Sinister probably ruled out all models where the behavior of the X-Men was explained entirely by external physical forces like gravity rather than their own conscious muscle movement; that's bias in the machine learning sense, and in this case we can probably agree an eminently reasonable presupposition.

Sometimes our chosen bias is too strong or too narrow, meaning that our guess in advance over what possibilities to include and what inferences to exclude was incorrect and we left out answers that include important features of the system we're modeling. This is underfitting, and it's what happened to Sinister because his concept of what the X-Men were and were not capable of was too narrow. Their new shock and awe paradigm was not even a possibility in his mind. Testing models on new observations not involved in training is important because it can reveal underfitting.

That testing can also reveal the flip side of the bias-variance tradeoff, which, as you might imagine, is overfitting. In this scenario, our inferred model captures many facets of our training data, including the little idiosyncrasies that are peculiar to those observations but not actually essential features of the system overall. Instead of being too beholden to our initial guess, we are now too beholden to the variability of our observations. And would you believe there is an X-Men story about overfitting too?

While mutants are born with the X-gene that will give them X-traordinary powers, those powers emerge at adolescence. So the X-Men operate a school where adult mutants help teens cope with the changes their bodies are going through—growing hair in new places, becoming faster and stronger, and shooting force blasts from their eyeballs. Y'know, puberty. This barely-a-metaphor is another reason the X-Men appeal strongly to real life teens and preteens like I was.

In *Wolverine and the X-Men* by Jason Aaron, Chris Bachalo, Nick Bradshaw, et al., a rival school is opened by villains. More precisely, the school is run by a group of nonmutant children with aspirations of villainy. These immature headmasters also focus on X-Men history. They hire from the X-Men rogues gallery to work at their school, they assume the name and distinctive attire of the Hellfire Club because it is a classic X-Men foil, and they even conspire to recapitulate specific events from the most famous X-Men stories. But unlike Mr. Sinister, they have no concept of what the X-Men are really about and so are reduced to fixating on minutiae. This is the essence of overfitting.

By contrast, the actual X-Men school is properly grounded by the presence of adults who root the education in core values like equality, tolerance, and protection of the weak. At the same time, the students infuse fresh experiences and perspectives where those values can be realized. In this way, a balance between bias and variance is reached, preventing both overfitting and underfitting. Narratively, this balance is illustrated through flashforwards that reveal the present-day students as adult teachers and leaders in the future. The conspicuous absence of the junior Hellfire Club from these vignettes makes it clear that their overfit approach won't pass the test of new scenarios.

I initially read the story as a critique of those comic book fans who are always looking backwards to old stories and wishing the current stories reproduced their trappings rather than their themes. When I realized the overfitting parable of *Wolverine and the X-Men* was a companion to the roughly contemporaneous underfitting tale in *Uncanny X-Men*, I saw an opportunity to describe how the specific knowledge communicated via the Bible interacts with the knowledge communicated more widely via creation. Like bias in machine learning or axioms in logic, the Bible provides a fixed starting point for our exploration of how the world works and why. Yes, as such it introduces certain constraints, but the kind of useful constraints that facilitate learning by giving shape to our inferences and keeping us from overfitting to diverse details of life. On the other hand, ongoing new observations of creation and new ideas from science keep us from underfitting to overly narrow ideas of what the Bible and God are about.

12.2 The Twelve (Preliminary Evolution Concepts)

And so we are reminded of the purpose of the entire book: to read the Bible and science together in a way that enriches both. The bias-variance tradeoff offers a useful way of articulating the value of each, providing a common starting point and new data for fresh perspective. There is another reason I want to talk about machine learning and the X-Men, specifically the particular machine learning algorithm employed in the story, which has further metaphorical potential.

The Mr. Sinister story in *Uncanny X-Men* is a rare X-Men adventure that actually gets evolution right. Evolution is a natural topic for X-Men comics given the centrality of mutation to their origin, and so it is mentioned regularly. Characters debate whether mutants represent a new species, *Homo superior*, just a new subspecies, *Homo sapiens superior*, or something else altogether. Nearly all of them agree these mutants are the next step in evolution. But mainly the villains emphasize these topics, using them to justify ruling, enslaving, or flat-out eliminating "ordinary" humans in the name of survival of the fittest. They believe if they don't strike first, humans will wipe out mutants—which suggests to me that they have a pretty backwards notion of what "fittest" actually means. What both *Uncanny X-Men* and *Wolverine and the X-Men* understand is that evolution is not about individual superiority; evolution is about group learning.

Thus I am talking about evolution in the context of computer science and machine learning rather than biology. Whether or not evolution is the mechanism by which present biological diversity came to exist—a question I suspect you know is hotly debated in some religious communities and on which you likely have some thoughts—the set of mechanisms studied together under the heading of evolution has been shown to be a useful learning tool in computer science. Curiously, despite studying biology for nine years as an undergraduate and graduate student at leading secular universities, I had no occasion to actually study evolutionary principles in any detail until I was doing a postdoc with a computer scientist. Having seen evolutionary biology applied via metaphor to computer science problems, I realized the ideas of evolutionary biology and evolutionary computer science are also conceptually quite relevant to understanding the Bible.

When I first conceived of this book, evolution was not included. Creationism, intelligent design, and evolution have been discussed *ad nauseum* in a variety of books, videos, podcasts, debates, freshman dorms and sarcastic memes. I felt like there was plenty new to say about science and the Bible beyond the first three (or eleven, since Noah's flood often gets dragged in as well) chapters of Genesis. And evolution is so challenging for many Christians that the word itself can shut down a conversation effectively enough to warrant its own corollary to Godwin's Law.

By the same token, though, it is *the* topic; neglecting it altogether would be like *Star Trek* without time travel, a Marvel movie without a credits scene, a version of Sherlock Holmes without any mention of *the* woman, Irene Adler. If we are going to develop the church body as a place where the science literate and the science enthusiastic are welcome, then we need to deal with evolution credibly and not just hold it at arm's length. We also need to respect the reality of the Christian community and appreciate that this elephant cannot be swallowed all at once.

My solution is to explore evolution the same way we tackled every other topic: as a model, a parable, a useful idea independent of its accuracy as a description of reality. I hope by this point I have established my credibility to discuss evolution's metaphorical potential in a way that is biblically sound and scientifically rigorous. And because we've reached the last chapter of the book, I've at least had the chance to first share some of my other ideas. If you check out now, I hope you at least found something worthwhile in what came before, even if it was just a clearer picture of what you do not believe.

If you are still here, thanks for practicing grace by giving me a chance, and for remembering that you are equally welcome to see this last chapter through and decide you don't agree with any of it. I appreciate that grace, because I'm going to need a little more of it. I've got one more surprise. It turns out, and I was just as surprised as you when I realized it, this *entire* book has actually been about evolution.

First, several of the illustrations we've already seen actually demonstrate one or more mechanisms of evolution. Proposing theorems and proving them true or false? That's variation and selection. So is testing different points for inclusion in the Mandelbrot set. T-cell training is another form of selection. The divergence of Mac and PC software? That's speciation. The many meanings of "love?" That's functional expansion by duplication. Once you start seeing this stuff, it's everywhere.

Second, many of the concepts that we've discussed previously come into play in evolution and could be derived from evolution. Exploring those concepts in other contexts first makes it easier to understand evolution, which is admittedly counterintuitive. We also got the benefit of seeing a range of scientific concepts, and of not spending the entire book on a potentially contentious topic. Instead, we get to ease into it.

Like fractal algorithms, evolution is an iterative process involving simple mechanisms. A combination of variation, inheritance, and selection produces new generations as output that are the input of the next round of evolution. By introducing cooperation, the power of combinatorics can be employed to generate even greater variety of inputs and thus greater diversity of outputs. There were several major cooperative milestones that expanded evolutionary potential significantly. These include the combination of individually replicating genes into chromosomes, the combination of individual cells into multicellular organisms, and in social organisms the combination of multiple organisms into colonies, hives, and communities. Iteration and combinatorics make it plausible for the simplicity of evolution to generate such astounding diversity.

Like compilers, evolution employs just-in-time adaptation to keep up with a changing environment. Information about the future is scarce to nonexistent. Planning ahead therefore has limits. There is still work to be done, however, because we can anticipate that change of some form will come. Waiting until the environmental changes results in adaptations that are too late. These were the conditions we saw were most well-suited to a just-in-time approach.

Like ant colonies and possibly consciousness, evolution starts from the bottom-up. It can be fruitful without a defined end goal or a central planner. It can start with the simplest organisms, expanding diversity and complexity incrementally and adaptively. Social elements emerge only when there are sufficient individuals to take advantage of them. These social elements create new levels of organization and new structures that are mediated by the lower levels but not strictly reducible to them.

Like our bodies, evolution is a balance of cooperation and defection. As with infectious diseases, there will always be the possibility for conflict, imbalance, and the few to exploit the efforts of the many. We notice the rapid flow of resources and asymmetry accumulation associated with predation because it is sudden, striking, and negative, just like we notice the sudden flow of electricity in a bolt of lightning. What we overlook is the slow, steady flow of resources associated with cooperation, just as we don't notice the constant flow of electricity that makes the occasional strike of lightning possible. Only symbiosis is constructive in the long term. Only solutions that care for the presently disadvantaged ensure that they will be around when their variations turn out to be essential. Only structures that create new niches to be occupied expand diversity and guarantee that the widest number of variations are currently viable and present for the future.

Like a developing body, evolution relies on varying contexts to provide shades of meaning and interpretation that facilitate diversity. If proteins could only ever have one canonical function, evolution would likely not be as fruitful and possible not even occur at all. Mutations would only ever break existing function. But since new contexts provide opportunities for new interpretation, yesterday's useless mutation becomes today's invaluable adaptation.

As a process of chemistry and life, evolution is a balance of information entropy and information storage. Mutations increase the variability of genomes, and so if we consider life in the abstract as a message source and individual genomes as individual messages, then mutation increases the entropy of the source. Selection on the other hand decreases information entropy by removing variations. In this way, it acts as an information storing mechanism, by creating and maintaining low entropy sources. The information being stored is a record of the various environmental circumstances encountered by a lineage, and also a record of the lineage itself. For example, T-cells graduated from the thymus store information about which proteins are not part of the host body.

Like momentum and velocity, evolution is relative and depends on the specific features of the biological space in which it operates. Fitness is not an absolute scale but is always assessed in relationship to the present environment, and always in relationship to other variations. And while we talk about fitness as a landscape, by way of the hill-climbing metaphor of optimization, fitness changes are not always smooth and gradual like rolling hills. Genetic mutations occur in a space with many dimensions, making our usual spatial metaphors and visualizations of limited value. Fitness changes that might seem significantly different and thus widely separated may be readily connected by one or a few mutations. We inhibit our intuition of evolutionary biology if we only picture organisms trying to get from one fitness hill to another across a vast valley instead of also considering genetic geometry.

Like photons, evolution challenges our existing categories. Wondering how species change into one another is the wrong question. Species do not change biologically; a species is a label for particular characteristics. Individual organisms change, and not all organisms across all of time fall neatly into the existing categories. Species designations are helpful for organizing and for clarity of communication, but we must ultimately let organisms tell us about themselves rather than requiring them to fit into predefined categories.

Like chaotic dynamics, evolution involves freedom and grace. The nature of the genetic code for translating DNA into proteins is such that it allows for some deviations in genetic sequence without change in protein sequence. This is a first level of grace, where multiple variations can lead to the same end result. Similar graciousness exists at the level of protein function and metabolism. There are even multiple ways to achieve high-level functions like vision and flight.

Like an optimization search, evolution is subject to multiple constraints and there are consequences for choosing different paths. The most basic notion of fitness is a measure of how many children one has, but there are many constraints that influence reproduction and thus fitness. Therefore, the results of evolution are not guaranteed to be optimal by any single criteria because of the other constraints involved. And individual choices will lead to different fitness outcomes, some of which are better than others. Fortunately, it is possible to repent and mutate back onto a more fruitful path.

Like proving theorems from axioms, evolution is an exploration of a space defined by starting assumptions. Before we even get to living organisms, the laws of physics and the properties of chemicals put constraints on life. Just like some theorems are true and some are false relative to particular axioms, some organisms are viable and some are not. Evolution is the process of putting into works those starting assumptions. The specifics of the first organisms add further constraints on the particular details of how the variation, inheritance and selection necessary for evolution will play out.

Like languages, evolution involves groups that can no longer interact fruitfully because they have been apart for too long. New species arise when populations are separated for an extended period of time, preventing the variations that arise in one from being shared with the other. Eventually, the variations that accumulate make the two groups incompatible with one another should they come back into contact. Their universal genetic code means that on some level they are speaking the same language, but the vocabularies are different and the interpretations of shared words may have changed.

12.3 Evolutionary's Song

The preceding discussion should have given us a flavor for how evolution as an algorithm and as a biological process connects conceptually to what we have already discussed. We could develop any or all of those ideas further and explore their biblical connections, but to a large extent we have already done so in the earlier chapters. We are now ready to go into more detail on the unique features of evolution so that we can later discuss their associations with ideas from the Bible. By building on what has come before, hopefully the discussion of evolution will seem like a reasonable extension of what we've already talked about rather than a complete departure.

Evolutionary algorithms have been employed for a variety of problems in computer science. I've used them for specifying regression models (more complicated versions of the line fitting problem we saw in chapter 2); solving a given regression problem involves a smooth surface, as we saw, but actually choosing what variables to include does not, making the optimization more challenging and an evolutionary algorithm a useful alternative. Evolutionary algorithms can produce music that is aesthetically pleasing to humans, a criterion that is impossible to quantify mathematically for more traditional optimization. They can even be employed to solve computational problems from biology that are not related to evolutionary biology, such as RNA structure prediction.

Evolution is an algorithm for sampling a space of all possible solutions to find good ones. Unlike certain optimization techniques as applied to certain problems, an evolutionary algorithm is not guaranteed to find the best solution. But an evolutionary algorithm can be very useful in scenarios where no algorithm is guaranteed to find the absolute best solution but a pretty good solution is still useful. For example, if we are trying to maximize a function but we can't calculate which next step will take us uphill or downhill, an evolutionary algorithm might be useful. Or if we are dealing with a problem whose conditions can change, we can employ an evolutionary algorithm.

At the core of evolutionary algorithms are a few simple processes. We need a process to manufacture change or generate variations. Then we need a process to amplify some of those variations more than others. Typically this involves reproduction or inheritance, a way of copying variations, and selection, so that not all variations are copied equally.

Variation, inheritance, and selection can all be accomplished in computer programs to solve the problems we discussed. There are also clear biological examples of variation, inheritance, and selection at work that are not controversial. My personal favorite involves the immune system and how it responds to infections. Antibodies are proteins made by special blood cells called B-cells that specifically recognize one particular infectious agent and bind tightly to it. Antibody binding can then serve as a flag to other immune cells that an intruder needs to be dealt with, or it can directly interfere with the infection process. The specificity of antibody binding is achieved via variation, inheritance, and selection.

To understand those component processes of evolution in more detail, let's see how they are realized both for antibody creation and for making music. Since we are talking about machine learning, we might ask what is being learned in each case. For music, the algorithm is learning what kind of music is aesthetically pleasing to humans. To be clear, this is not learning in the sense that when we are done, the algorithm will be able to discuss music in terms of harmonic theory or melody construction or anything like that. Instead, the algorithm is learning how to create aesthetically pleasing music, like an artisan learning a skill rather than a student learning lessons.

The biological example is similar; your body is learning how to create antibodies that match the current infection. For every viral, bacterial, fungal, or parasitic strain that might infect you, there needs to be a corresponding antibody that complements it precisely. Having separate genes for every single potentially needed antibody would be a huge burden on our genome. And new viruses and bacteria emerge periodically, requiring the constant addition of new genes. Clearly, an enumeration solution isn't practical. Instead, our bodies evolve antibodies on demand, thereby learning what is required rather than relying on pre-existing solutions.

The learning starts with variation. In an evolutionary music algorithm, we're not talking about formal music theory variations. Instead, individual notes might be moved up or down the scale, or bars from different melodies might be recombined. Other algorithms use looped music or sounds as building blocks whose tempo or sequence can be varied.

Antibody variation involves several steps. Through a fairly unique genetic arrangement, there are a number of antibody genes available via a combinatorial solution that mixes and matches modular units. The resulting array of antibodies gives our bodies a starting place for handling infections. B-cells choose one of the several hundred different initial combinations and make that antibody and stick it on the outside of their membrane, waiting to encounter a matching infection. Then, once a virus (for example) comes along, whichever B-cell makes the antibody that mostly closely matches will bind to that virus. At that point, further variation is introduced by mutations, changes to the DNA sequence of the antibody gene.

Once we've made variations, we need to amplify them through copying or inheritance. For our computer music, copying is straightforward. Computers are very good at taking a sequence of 1s and 0s, which is ultimately how our music is represented, and reproducing the same sequence elsewhere. I imagine you've copied a computer file to or from external storage, or by sending it via e-mail, or by downloading it.

DNA sequences can also be copied. When a B-cell finds the infection it recognizes, T-cells will recognize that a match has been found, and will send chemical signals to the B-cell to start dividing. The activated B-cell creates progeny cells with copies of its antibody gene.

Technically, the variations are actually introduced at this stage by a copying process that is not 100 percent accurate, unlike computer file copying. Normal DNA mutations will provide some variation, but rather slowly and all over the genome rather than just in the antibody gene. To speed things up, there is a mechanism for specifically making more changes than normal just to the antibody gene, in order to explore the space of possible antibodies more thoroughly.

Finally, we need a way to selectively amplify certain variations. For antibodies, this is achieved by having the strength of the signal to divide be proportional to how closely the antibody matches its target. B-cells whose mutated antibody gene matches the virus even more closely will get even more signals encouraging division, and so their progeny cells will proliferate. B-cells whose mutated antibody gene does not match the virus as well will not get division signals. This is the selection component, and over time most of the B-cells in your blood will be descended from one whose antibody matched the virus very, very closely.

In just a few hours or a couple of days, this process can improve the strength of binding between an antibody and its target by several orders of magnitude. As a result, our bodies can get rid of those unwanted viruses and bacteria, even if their particular strain did not exist when we were born. Even better, once the infection is resolved, some of the B-cells with the matching antibody are kept around so that in the future we can respond even more quickly if an infection with the same virus occurs again. Via an evolutionary mechanism, the diversity of our antibody repertoire increases, maintaining all of the ones we started with and adding ones for every infection we have encountered, even if we did not know we were sick. Our body has learned how to respond to that particular infection when it did not have that skill previously.

For evolutionary music algorithms, selection typically involves humans playing the role that the T-cells do for antibodies. Humans listen to the resulting music and vote on the variations they like the best. Variations with the most votes are copied and further varied more than variations with few votes. Arguably, the same process occurs with music in general. Musicians make new music, audiences listen to it and vote with their time and dollars, and over time musicians learn to make more of the music audiences like. Similar dynamics occur all over the Internet, as we "like" and "favorite" photos, memes, news stories, and everything else on various social media platforms.

And that's it. Variation, inheritance, and selection are all we need for evolution to occur, whether we're talking about a computer program or a biological system. The simplicity of the processes, however, shouldn't mask the genuine concerns they raise for some as mechanisms of creation. For example, variation and mutation are often described as random. Randomness turns many people off to the idea of evolution. Aesthetically, a roll of the dice feels like the opposite of creation, purposeless and without intent. At the same time, it represents freedom and an opportunity for the created to collaborate in its own creation.

We can think of the randomness this way. Let's say we have complete control over our genome and can choose the specific variations we will produce; in a computer program, this is a perfectly plausible scenario. What changes should we make? Well, that depends on the details of exactly what we are trying to learn. But we don't have that information, which is why we are trying to learn it, so we cannot make an informed decision.

Still, we can know that some kind of change in external circumstances is likely, since the past is full of change. Musical tastes change; new viruses and bacteria come and go. Keeping everything exactly the same doesn't make sense. From that perspective, making some small changes at random is fairly rational. The risk of a catastrophic change is small since the changes are small, and there is at least some possibility of making the relevant changes, whereas by keeping everything the same there is no such possibility. And if you are one individual in a population where everyone makes different changes, the possibility of everyone making the wrong choice is less likely and the possibility of someone making the right choice is more likely. So variations are not so much random changes as rational changes in the absence of information.

There is even biblical precedent for God using mechanisms that we describe as random because we cannot predict their outcome. The laws that Moses received on Mt. Sinai made allowance for certain questions to be answered via chance. That law proscribes the use of Urim and Thummim, a set of either-or objects used by priests to divine bits of information from God in particular situations. Other decisions, such as who to blame for a storm in Jonah or who to choose as an apostle in Acts, are based on the casting of lots. Nowadays, we flip coins, like Two-Face. I'm not necessarily advocating coin flips when seeking God's will, simply observing that the Bible allows for apparently random input in the face of incomplete information.

Like uninformed or random variation, selection can get a poor reputation based on misconceptions. X-Men villains certainly have some goofy ideas about selection. Natural selection is sometimes linked with the idea of nature "red in tooth and claw," which conjures images of animals viciously slaughtering each other, the sick and the weak being eliminated so that the strong can survive. We've all seen the nature videos; there is no denying that predators exist, nor that eating other animals is a viable lifestyle in the animal kingdom.

Selection has no requirements for such bloodthirstiness and is actually focused on life and reproduction rather than death. In fact, selection can work just fine without death at all. As long as a change results in a particular variation being amplified more than others, that new version will become more widespread in the population than the original. And a change that reduces amplification will not spread as widely. Predation and death may contribute to selection when they exist, but they are not necessary elements of evolution. In our evolutionary music algorithm, nothing has to die, not even in some figurative, digital sense.

Selection also needn't mean that life is every man for himself. Cooperation can be just as viable or useful an approach to increase reproduction as competition. Social relationships and social structures can be the outcome of evolutionary processes. Those social elements just need to be flexible enough to allow variations, to be reproducible or copyable in some fashion, and to introduce changes that can influence selection.

The social groups do not have to be genetically determined, although that is one option. Social elements can be taught behaviorally, or communicated symbolically, as a means to reproduce. Individuals may perform behaviors in slightly different ways, introducing variation. Symbolic communication can be interpreted variably, or remembered imperfectly.

Social elements require cooperation, and cooperation is an effective way to solve "tragedy of the commons"-style problems. Tragedy of the commons scenarios arise when some shared resource is limited such that it can be used up over time by individual acts of consumption that each appear negligible. The marginal cost of adding one more car to the roads is negligible, but keep adding them and there will be maintenance costs and the need to increase capacity. One person tossing some bread crumbs to a goose is not big deal, but when everyone does it parks become overwhelmed with geese and what geese leave behind, not to mention the disruption of geese migration. Landfills, fossil fuel sources, our collective attention—these are all resources that are used in very small amounts at any given time but that can be used up without careful management.

Being able to solve those problems can make the group using those solutions more well suited to certain circumstances than asocial individuals would be. Still, the tragedy of the commons is that it will always be possible for noncontributors to also get the benefits, but such defection is not viable in the long run because the resources of the social group will be depleted. Cooperation is the best way we've found to build groups to solve those problems, but cooperation will always be susceptible to selfish exploitation.

Or, to frame cooperation and defection another way, a large resource like fossil fuels represents a significant asymmetry that can be used fruitfully. Eventually, consumption will distribute it symmetrically through the system. Maximizing the benefit requires a network through which the asymmetry flows slowly and widely toward symmetry, which we would recognize as cooperation. There will always be the possibility for a few individuals to use up lots of asymmetry all at once for their own benefit. But in the long run that large benefit to themselves just means they've created a different asymmetry that eventually will flow away from them.

Selection does not have to be ruthless, allowing for cooperation as well as predation. It also does not operate on some absolute scale of fitness that places a single individual or species at the pinnacle. We cannot take every organism alive and order them from least fit to most fit. Which organisms and which traits will be selected for or against is highly contextual. Further, at any given time there are many different contexts or niches to occupy. Asking whether humans or bacteria are more fit is nonsensical as their niches are completely different.

Or to put it in musical terms, it is not meaningful to ask which music is more fit: Beethoven's *Ninth Symphony* or The Beatles' *Revolver*? Both are popular and have been widely heard and sold in various formats. Even if we could theoretically agree on a single measurement, like total revenue generated, and accurately add it up in a way that allowed for direct comparison, would that tell us anything about the relative musical merits or the likelihood that one or the other will still be around in one hundred years' time? There is no need to declare a single winner, as both have plenty of appeal among overlapping but distinct groups of enthusiasts.

A more interesting question is whether those groups are becoming more divergent or if they still share enough of a common language and experience for meaningful conversation. If you recall, that's where we came in, only with science and the Christian church. The science community has grown increasingly distinct from everyone else, Christians or otherwise, because they are observing an increasingly separate world thanks to ever more powerful telescopes and microscopes. Even when we share English as a common language, we often have no idea what each other is saying. Arguably, something similar has happened with Christian communities, as the Christian subculture becomes more isolated, often quite deliberately. The end result might as well be separate species, unable to fruitfully communicate.

As a result, a lot of modern science is counterintuitive for intuitions shaped by human-scale experiences. Evolutionary biology is often described this way. But this is precisely the value of science, to help us understand those features of the world that are not readily apparent. If we could intuit how the world works, we would have little need for science. And these counterintuitive concepts are the most useful as metaphors, because they help us understand ideas that would not occur to us otherwise.

12.4 The Mutant Metaphor

Having seen how evolution works as an algorithm and addressed some of the common concerns about its mechanisms, we are prepared to see how its concepts can enrich our discussions of the Bible. Let's start with the counterintuitive nature of evolution that I mentioned, and how that makes it valuable for transforming our minds. I find a similar sentiment in the book of Job. Job loses his family, his wealth, and his health in a series of calamities. Afterwards, he engages in a series of dialogues with his friends about why he is suffering in this way. His friends suggest that perhaps Job did something to deserve this pain (the text makes it clear Job did not).

Believing our personal suffering to be punishment for our actions is a common intuition, but it is overly focused on ourselves. In the end, Job has a conversation with God, who surprisingly does not just provide Job with direct answers. Instead, he raises a lot of questions about whether Job understands how the world works. To me, this feels like an invitation to explore those phenomena in order to appreciate the mechanisms involved that have nothing to do with us.

Looking at another facet of evolution, the asymmetry of cooperation and defection reminds me of the asymmetry in the concept cleanliness and uncleanliness. A ceremonial concept of cleanliness is a significant part of Israelite law, with detailed descriptions of what can make someone unclean and how to restore cleanliness. As Haggai reminds us, uncleanliness spreads easily by contact from an unclean object to a clean one, while cleanliness does not spread in the opposite direction (Haggai 2:10–19). Instead, cleanliness takes concerted effort to establish and maintain.

Selection is a useful metaphor for how we are to cultivate righteousness. We are called to "put to death whatever in your nature belongs to the earth" (Colossians 3:5), that is, whatever is sinful; this is a process of negative selection. Or recall the similar sentiment expressed in 1 Thessalonians: "Examine all things; hold fast to what is good" (5:21). Becoming righteous is a process of preferentially amplifying those habits and behaviors that are fruitful.

Evolution also provides us with a new way of thinking about creativity. Finished products do not emerge all at once, but are arrived at via a process of exploration. The Bible describes God as a potter, and sculpting clay is by no means an instantaneous event (Isaiah 64:8). A potter gets his hands dirty and sculpts over time, gradually transforming the clay from what it was to what it can become.

Even better, the creative, transformative process can be studied, allowing it to be replicated. God says we are made in his image, which presumably includes building and creating. Being able to study how God creates is therefore a great blessing. So too is the opportunity to co-create with him, as evolution allows us to do.

Evolution also combines creativity with learning. Each generation builds on what came before. This is a powerful reminder to be mindful of those who have gone before us and to make use of the wisdom they have already earned. At the same time, we should also look to give future generations something useful to build from.

With that learning process comes a record of what has happened in the past. If we believe that God is creating through the process of evolution, then our genomes are a record of God's creative work. That record may not be as detailed as we might like, but it does contain information from which we can infer the broad strokes of creation. Of course, it only goes as far back as the beginning of life on Earth, but fortunately star light from distant galaxies brings us information going back even further. Through a combination of astronomical, genetic, and biblical records, we have an account of God's work stretching nearly from the beginning of time to the present.

As we discussed, creating such a record is a mix of variation and selection. Thus variety and novelty are an important part of learning more about God. We needn't be afraid of new ideas, although we also must be willing to accept that some of them will be shown wrong. That's how science works; negative results still contribute to how we learn through science. Our theology needn't be any different.

And if God requires infinite bits to describe, as I theorized, then the finite understanding we have so far is incomplete. We may thus have an obligation to continue putting our faith into practice and living out new theorems to learn more of those bits. This resonates for me with the command in Genesis 1 to be fruitful and multiply. Multiplying leads to greater variation, and more opportunities to learn.

Indeed, over the whole scope of the biblical story we can see the people of God learning more about the kingdom of God by asking, "Does it include them too?" It starts with Adam and Eve. To begin with, there is only Adam; his solitariness inherently limits what he can accomplish. Then Eve comes along—via duplication with variation. Eve is made, not *de novo* as Adam, but from Adam's rib. And she is not another man, but a woman, different, new: a change. Yet the kingdom of God is for her as well.

Abraham meets Melchizedek and learns that the kingdom of God includes him. The Israelite spies learn that the kingdom of God includes the Canaanite Rahab and her family. Joshua learns that the Gibeonites can be a part of it, Naomi sees that Ruth is included, and Daniel welcomes Nebuchadnezzar. The book Song of Songs celebrates the unique qualities of the husband and wife in a multiethnic marriage. Jonah is reluctant to invite the Ninevites, but invited they are. Jesus' disciples aren't so sure about the Samaritan woman, but Jesus is. Peter has his doubts about the Gentiles, but thankfully he realizes we are all welcome in the kingdom of God as well. As Paul tells us, God "wants all people to be saved and to come to a knowledge of the truth" (1 Timothy 2:4).

The essence of the kingdom is not found by reducing it down to some lowest common denominator, some singular perfect example of the person God wants. The essence of the kingdom is found in diversity, in telling the gospel story in new contexts. Diversity brings multiplicity; multiplicity brings combinations and social organization. And so we see a process that will result in a sufficiently emergent, transcendent level of organization that can be considered a worthy bride for the son of God himself. The church is the present stage in the development of that bride; who knows what she will look like in maturity?

As a creative process, evolution is also ongoing and unending. Evolution is about building on the past to live into the future. It is oriented forward, but can never forget where it came from. It forges a legacy, then hands it on. It is always the story of a new creation, just like the Bible.

You know who loves to build the future? Nerds. And that's why I love 'em and want to spend as much of that future with them as possible. The story of the Bible is so exciting to me because it opens up the possibility of an infinite future, which is what it will take for me to get to know all you awesome nerds. But that will only work if you are in that infinite future with me.

12.5 Days of Future Past

A nerdy future brings us all the way back to where we came in with Douglas Adams and *The Restaurant at the End of the Universe*. I shared my personal interest in the Bible, in science, and in science fiction and I proposed doing the empirical work to see if we could harmonize my passions. I laid out a few questions to guide our exploration. Let's revisit them and see how we did.

Can we define abstract ideas like faith and sin and grace in terms that make sense to nerdy, funny scientists? Using the language of mathematics and the paradox of "no one," I proposed a definition of faith as a choice of axioms, and the works that flow from that faith as an unpacking of what those axioms imply. I described sin in terms of mathematical optimization and a choice of objective function to maximize. And I used chaotic dynamics to give us a working definition of grace as a system that tends back to an intended outcome, like a strange attractor. Whether those definitions make sense to you is another matter, but at the very least I think we demonstrated some relevance of mathematical concepts to the big, abstract ideas of theology.

Can a life lived two thousand years ago shed light on our modern situation? The life I had in mind was that of Jesus of Nazareth, the self-styled "light of the world." And so we used the physics of light, including special relativity, quantum wave-particle dualism, and solar entropy to discuss the role that Jesus plays in the Christian tradition. Light has proved to be a fruitful model system for experimenting on a wide range of interesting physical phenomenon, not least because our senses are highly attuned to light and so we can directly perceive the results of those experiments. Likewise, Jesus modeled the nature of God for us in a way that was accessible to the senses of our fellow human beings. Even though Jesus the man no longer walks with us in that tangible way, hopefully we learned some things about him and God that are still relevant today.

Can we develop a community that incorporates a diverse assemblage of people? The Bible already introduced the metaphor of the body to illustrate the group dynamics of the church; we extended that metaphor with modern biological understanding. The principles for maintaining a healthy group dynamic are also applicable to just about any community. The challenges of living together with people unlike us haven't changed all that much in a few thousand years, and so on this topic in particular I think the Bible remains highly practical even if the more philosophical or theological elements seem old-fashioned.

Can simple principles from the past encompass the complexity of the present? Here we employed the language of computer science, which deals explicitly with rules and procedures and formalizing how we make decisions in life and carry out tasks. Although the Bible is not exclusively or even primarily a rule book for how to live, it does provide some norms and lays some claims to how we should live if we choose to believe its message. We looked at how computers translate words into actions, and saw how just-in-time principles arise in computers and in the Bible. We saw how simple rules and procedures can generate complex outcomes such as infinitely detailed computer graphics, making it more plausible to believe that a couple of simple commandments about love can actually cover the full range of modern human experience. And we examined evolution as an algorithm for learning and creativity, which has some conceptual connections with how the Bible approaches those topics.

Now, we shouldn't be surprised that I think I was successful on the terms I set out; books don't tend to get published on failed premises. The question is whether you think I was successful, and if so what does that mean? I suppose it could simply be a testament to my own skill as a writer to score some rhetorical points. But I think the fruitfulness of using science to discuss the Bible speaks to a common author of the two. The Christian tradition has always testified to that common authorship, so these results are consistent with that tradition.

Christian tradition also tells us that the world as it is is not as the world could be. I postulated that idea is at the core of nerdiness, whether we are fantasizing about what the world might be like or using science to test which of various alternate worlds is the one we live in. I connected that with the German concept of *Weltschmerz* or "world pain," a sense that the world has deviated for the worse, and suggested that God experiences *Weltschmerz*.

One feature of the world that pains me and I believe pains God is the fact that so many feel they need to choose between science and belief in the God of the Bible. The Bible itself does not require this choice, and many scientists are either religious believers themselves or content to tolerate the beliefs of others. Still, many report feeling torn between the two. Certainly in my own experience, many in the nerdy communities of science fiction and comic book fandom take it as given that religious beliefs are out-of-date and superseded by science. Meanwhile, I've felt like an outsider in various churches because of my nerdy passions and my scientific approach to various questions. And so if I could modify the world to relieve some *Weltschmerz*, I would like to see churches become more welcoming to the scientifically literate, and my fellow nerds more comfortable giving the Bible and Jesus a chance.

If we're talking about change, it makes sense to talk about chemistry. Chemical reactions transform molecules from one type to another. Some molecules transform rapidly; white phosphorus will rapidly oxidize in the presence of air at room temperature, which is why it is used to ignite matches. Other molecules like plastics resist transformation, which is why plastic lingers in the environment.

A key difference between reactions is the activation energy of the reaction. Even if a transformation results in a net release of energy, the input molecule(s) needs extra energy to enter an intermediate configuration on the way to the output molecule(s). The more unstable or strained the intermediate state, the more energy it takes to get up

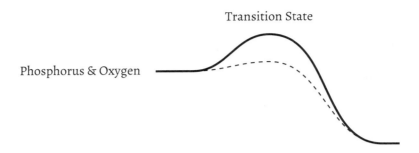

Figure 12.1: Energy diagram of a chemical reaction with (dashed) and without (solid) a catalyst to lower the activation energy

and over that hump of instability. A catalyst can reduce that barrier by recognizing the intermediate state and making it more stable. They do not provide any energy; they just lower the hump to make it easier to get over, as illustrated in Figure 12.1.

My desire is to be the catalyst that makes the transformation easier for those that choose to participate. There's actually an equivalent idea in the Bible. Isaiah talks about removing "all the obstacles out of the way of my people" (Isaiah 57:14) and Romans includes an exhortation to "determine never to place an obstacle or a trap before a brother or sister" (Romans 14:13). The image in both places is of a stumbling block, which does exactly what it says on the tin. We are called not to deliberately make following God any harder than it needs to be.

The tricky thing about chemical reactions is that they are all two-way streets. Plastics have to be assembled from simpler molecules; carbon is oxidized to carbon dioxide by animals, and then reduced back to carbon with the oxygen separated by plants. Going in either direction requires clearing the activation barrier. Keeping the energy barrier high, or even making it higher, is the way to keep things as they are.

The chemistry of activation barriers makes me wonder if sometimes we Christians make transformation more difficult so that the faithful are less likely to stray. Maybe we don't do it deliberately, or even knowingly, but I can see where it might feel better to not try to be a catalyst so that things stay as they are. Let the scientists have their science, and the Christians have their Bible. Maybe that seems preferable to some, but I think it's worth the risk to make the message of the Bible as accessible as possible.

And really, from my perspective, it's not that much of a risk. I think the Bible has a lot to offer anyone who is willing to give it serious consideration. Such consideration is all that I would ask of anyone. I can appreciate being turned off by the Christian church; its history is certainly replete with deeply regrettable choices. I can sympathize with finding individual Christians hard to deal with—even if that individual Christian is me. I won't promise you will find church to be fully satisfying, nor all Christians delightful to be around. But I am confident you will find something in the Bible worth your time.

I am similarly confident that learning more science will be worth your time, regardless of your current level of knowledge. Given the numerous practical benefits of science, various advocacy campaigns for science education, and the general scientific orientation of the modern world, such encouragement is perhaps less necessary. So consider this a plug specifically for the more abstract or less intuitive areas of scientific exploration. These include evolutionary biology, climate science, and other topics where some religious communities have been more reluctant to engage. If God is the source of truth, then all avenues that reveal truth will help us know him better.

We started at the end. The Bible finishes with a wedding in Revelation 19, a vision of the future that is inclusive and integrative. And yet I can sympathize with the sentiment among nerds that such a party isn't for them. Who would want to attend a party where everyone is different from you, and the things you value aren't appreciated?

No one will care if I am missing. No one like me will be there. There will be no one there to talk to about science. No one will want to chat about X-Men comics or kung-fu movies. No one will appreciate hearing my model for reconciling the geometry of quantum electrodynamics with the geometry of general relativity. If that is how you feel, that no one wants you in the new creation the Bible describes, well, let me assure you: Yes, I do.

Further Reading

When I was in the seventh grade, my friend Ronnie (later the "Who" to my "No one") told me about a new comic book coming soon that he thought I would like. Boy, did I ever. The book was *X-Factor*, technically an existing series but with a new creative team, a new line-up, and a new direction that was just what I wanted from a comic book, even though I didn't know I wanted anything from comic books. That was my first introduction to monthly superhero comics, to X-Men, and to the character who would become my favorite, Jamie Madrox the Multiple Man.

I have since read essentially every X-Men comic book ever published (certainly the main continuity books; I may have missed a Pizza Hut promotional comic here or there), so it is hard to imagine my life without them. At the same time, if someone hadn't said to me "Here is a comic I think you will like because I know your taste, and if you have questions because you are coming in on the middle of a story, I will answer them," I don't know if I would have ever started reading them. And so I hope that in some small way, this book does the same for you, whether for comics or science or the Bible. Toward that end, here are a few notes on how to get started, and where to find more information on the topics I've discussed.

Note on Reading the Bible

The Bible is really an anthology of sixty-six separate books of assorted lengths and genres, written over centuries by many authors. Some traditions include additional books, but I am not aware of any Christian tradition that uses fewer than sixty-six, so I've stuck to those. These books are typically divided into the Old Testament (thirty-nine books) and the New Testament (twenty-seven books). The Old Testament books are about the nation of Israel, and consequently most are significant to the Jewish traditions as well. The New Testament books are about Jesus and his followers.

Because people refer to bits of the Bible a lot, there is a convention for indicating specific parts. First is the name of the book (e.g., Ecclesiastes), then the chapter number (e.g., 12), and verse number (e.g., 12). These coordinates didn't appear in the original writings, but they are convenient for reference and most Bibles will have them if you want to follow along.

One useful resource is the online Bible at lumina.bible.org. In addition to the full text of the Bible in multiple languages, the site provides a number of study tools. There are translation notes and manuscript notes, providing transparency to the challenging and nondeterministic process of reconciling multiple manuscripts of the original Hebrew, Aramaic, and Greek texts and translating from those languages into English. There are also original language texts with dictionaries and search tools so that you can see where that same word from the original language is used throughout the text.

If you are looking for a place to start, try the book of Mark. It is the second book of the New Testament and the shortest of the four books about the life of Jesus. If you think you might be willing to consider following Jesus, you might as well start by learning more about him. From there, you might try another book about Jesus such as John, or perhaps Romans, a letter by Paul to Christians in Rome that takes some of the narrative threads from throughout the Bible and weaves them into a coherent and comprehensive picture of who God is and how we can relate to him.

If you're not sure about Jesus and want to try something different, perhaps Ecclesiastes might be to your liking. As I mentioned in the beginning of the book, Ecclesiastes tackles some of the big questions like the purpose of life and does so in a way that feels relevant to modern conversations. Ecclesiastes is in the middle of the Old Testament, in a section sometimes called "wisdom literature." Right before it is Proverbs, a collection of pragmatic teaching that is applicable regardless of how you feel about the rest of the Bible.

What I would not recommend for someone coming to the Bible fresh is starting with the first page and trying to read straight through. Even many long-time Christians find that challenging; innumerable well-intentioned plans to read the whole Bible have stalled out in Leviticus, or even the genealogies in Genesis. If none of my suggestions above appealed to you, then read a little bit about what is in different books and pick one that is appealing. There are exciting narratives in books like Judges and Esther; Ruth is a sweet love story; a wide range of poetry is collected in the book of Psalms. The end of the New Testament has several short letters; the book of 1 John will probably take you less than an hour to read and then you can say you've read an entire book of the Bible.

Finally, consider finding someone to read the Bible with you. Maybe you already know someone who is more familiar with it who would be willing to join you. If not, I bet there is a pastor or priest or church leader nearby who would be thrilled to hear that you want to try reading the Bible. And if that's intimidating, I'll bet you will find it worthwhile to read with another fellow newbie, even if you have no intention of believing it and just want to know what it says for academic purposes. If the Bible has held the interest of humans of all descriptions for two thousand years, there's a good chance you'll find something interesting in it as well.

Additional Natural Theology Reading

At some point, you'll probably want to supplement your Bible reading with other books about the Bible or theological topics. Here I will focus mainly on books related to science, but obviously there are lots of other theological subjects worthy of your time.

If you are interested in personal experiences of believers in the sciences, *The Language of God* by Francis Collins is a good place to start. Collins led the Human Genome project before taking up the top position at the National Institutes of Health. His personal testimony and his thoughts on reconciling modern science with the Bible have been encouraging to many. For those intimidated by Collins' credentials, *Finding God in the Waves* by Mike McHargue or *How I Changed My Mind About Evolution* edited by Kathryn Applegate and J. B. Stump may provide more accessible personal narratives.

For a more comprehensive approach to natural theology, I'd recommend the work of John Polkinghorne, a physicist who took up a second career as a theologian. *The Faith of a Physicist* is a good place to start. Polkinghorne works through the individual statements of the Nicene Creed, a traditional summary of the core Christian teachings, and explains how he understands and affirms them in light of his scientific training and outlook. The question and answer format of *Questions of Truth* (with Nicholas Beale) may be helpful to some. *Belief in God in an Age of Science* is another popular one. *Quantum Physics and Theology* is much more accessible than the title suggests, focusing on how the process of science and the process of theology share common approaches while avoiding the challenging particulars of quantum physics.

Like Polkinghorne, Alister McGrath started out as a scientist before becoming a prolific theologian. He has a more academic focus than Polkinghorne, having written several theology textbooks, but he has written for wider audiences as well. *The Big Question* and *Surprised by Meaning* are two of his more recent books dealing specifically with science and faith questions. I personally found *The Open Secret* to be encouraging as it lays out a philosophical and theological foundation for natural theology consistent with my own approach; it may be a little technical for some.

Not every scientist can be a theologian, and not every theologian a scientist. So the collaboration of biblical scholar Scot McKnight and biologist Dennis Venema on *Adam and the Genome* is an interesting model. The book deals more narrowly with questions about Adam and Eve and how they fit into population genetics estimates of a human population no smaller than ten thousand individuals at any time. I'd like to see more collaborations and conversations of this sort.

Another theologian who is open to contemporary science though not a scientist himself is Thomas Jay Oord; I've found his perspective thought-provoking and helpful. *God in an Open Universe* deals with some of the usual science and faith questions. *The Uncontrolling Love of God* deals exclusively and extensively with the problem of evil, how a creation where pain and suffering exist is compatible with a loving Creator. Oord's answers may not be for everyone, but I appreciate his commitment to taking on such a difficult question and doing so in a way that takes evolutionary biology seriously.

If you are especially interested in Genesis and understanding what the original audience would have understood from the text, the recent work of John Walton may be helpful. He has several "lost world" books (including *The Lost World of Genesis One*, *The Lost World of Adam and Eve*, and *The Lost World of the Israelite Conquest*) that deal with the historical and cultural context of Genesis. Walton really explores the idea that interpreting the Bible is more than just translating the individual Hebrew words and also requires communicating the conceptual framework of the original authors and audiences.

N. T. Wright is another theologian whose interests lie in helping modern readers appreciate the conceptual world of the Bible. His books span a wider range of biblical texts and authors, with a particular emphasis on the New Testament writer Paul. *Simply Christian* or *Simply Jesus* might be good places to start. *Surprised by Hope* is popular, as are his books on Paul, including most recently a biography simply titled *Paul*.

Note on Reading Science Books

Not long after I was introduced to X-Men comics, I discovered the world of popular science books. I did some babysitting for a few of my neighbors, the kind of babysitting that mainly involved reading and watching TV while the children slept and their parents got out of the house alone for a couple of hours. One of those neighbors had a copy of *Hyperspace* by physicist Michio Kaku that I stumbled on. In those pages was a fantastic world of warped time and space, wormholes, and hypercubes, the stuff of science fiction. And yet that world was not simply the product of Kaku's imagination; it was the world I lived in.

Reading *Hyperspace* was another of those life-changing moments. I realized just how much more science there was than I had learned in school. At the same time, I realized I could learn about topics like general relativity and quantum physics, previously known to me only as unattainable ideas, without having to take years of classes. Not that I was or am opposed to higher education; on the contrary, I was already planning on pursuing a degree in biology and so I didn't think I could also fit in a course of study in physics. Suddenly I was no longer obliged to narrow my scientific studies to one discipline. Granted, I wouldn't attain the mastery that comes with prolonged and focused attention, but I could begin to appreciate the big concepts.

Over the next couple of years, I read nearly every popular science book on cosmology and particle physics at my local library. Then I started branching out into math, computer science, and even biology topics that my courses weren't covering fast enough. The Internet opened up further opportunities, as the web started to become reality toward the end of my high school career. Those books were revealing to me the ideas that would eventually form the basis for this book. The following are some of the highlights.

Books on Language

Douglas Hofstadter is a big influence on me and this book. I read *Surfaces and Essences: Analogies as the Fuel and Fire of Thinking*, which he wrote with Emmanuel Sander, late in the process of writing this book, but their exploration of the power of analogy and the way it influences our thinking provided a helpful framework to hang my thoughts on. Some of their ideas about cognition may be somewhat speculative, but there are plenty of interesting observations here about language and how it works, or perhaps how we work with it.

Steven Pinker has several helpful books on language as well. *The Stuff of Thought: Language as a Window into Human Nature* similarly gives language an important role in cognition. *The Sense of Style: The Thinking Person's Guide to Writing in the 21st Century* is a writing style guide, but one informed by research on how our minds process language. It's a worthwhile read even if you don't imagine yourself a writer at the moment. I tried to keep Pinker's advice in mind while writing this book; my apologies to him and to you for any failures to absorb certain lessons or to implement them consistently.

Creating Language: Integrating Evolution, Acquisition, and Processing by Morten H. Christiansen and Nick Chater is a little more academic than the other books, but even as a nonlinguist I found it a fascinating read. As the title suggests, Christiansen and Chater tie together how languages change over time to adapt to our minds, how we learn languages as children, and how we process language into a single theory. There are some interesting points about information processing and learning here as well.

Books on Mathematics

Douglas Hofstadter's classic *Gödel, Escher, Bach: An Eternal Golden Braid* is a good place to read more about incompleteness theorems, which were the work of Kurt Gödel. The book also covers some introductory computer science topics, and the art of Escher is relevant to the geometry of relativity. James Gleick's *The Information: A History, A Theory, A Flood* and Charles Seife's *Decoding the Universe: How the New Science of Information Is Explaining Everything in the Cosmos, from Our Brains to Black Holes* are good sources on information theory; the former deals with everyday applications, while the latter explores the role of information in the big questions of science. *Meta Math!: The Quest for Omega* connects information theory and incompleteness. It is by Gregory Chaitin, the man who formalized that connection.

James Gleick also has a book on chaos mathematics, *Chaos: Making a New Science*, with some history and more details on the math. Fractals are also covered. *A New Kind of Science* by Stephen Wolfram is a little challenging to recommend, as it is formidably long and a bit grandiose. Still, I think it provides another helpful perspective for how mathematical systems can be robust or gracious in disorganized contexts.

There are two more math books that aren't directly related to the topics I discussed but I believe are still worth your consideration. *Love and Math: The Heart of Hidden Reality* by Edward Frenkel is a beautiful examination of how math can enrich our lives and our thinking; Frenkel also believes in the analogic power of math. *How to Bake Pi: An Edible Exploration of the Mathematics of Mathematics* by Eugenia Cheng specifically draws analogies between math and baking in order to make mathematics more relatable.

Books on Physics

Roger Penrose is science writer whose work has made a strong impression on me. In particular, I appreciate Penrose's enthusiastic and optimistic belief that lay audiences have an appetite not just for the ideas of modern physics but also the mathematics. His most ambitious work in that regard is *The Road to Reality: A Complete Guide to the Laws of the Universe*, which contains a fair amount of mathematics in order to present relativity, cosmology and quantum physics in rigorous mathematical terms. I'll admit I've not read the entire thing, but have found it a helpful reference and an aspirational goal. More recent and less comprehensive is *Fashion, Faith, and Fantasy in the New Physics of the Universe*, which also covers relativity and quantum physics while making some insightful observations about the philosophy of science.

I already mentioned Kaku's *Hyperspace*. Stephen Hawking's *A Brief History of Time* and Kip Thorne's *Black Holes and Time Warps: Einstein's Outrageous Legacy* are both classics. Tobey Maguire's Peter Parker has a copy of Thorne's book in the *Spider-Man* film, and Thorne also consulted on the movie *Interstellar*, which led to a research paper and the book *The Science of Interstellar*. All are particularly good sources for relativity.

Symmetry and the Beautiful Universe by Leon M. Lederman and Christopher T. Hill is a more recent volume that ties several physics topics including relativity and quantum physics together via the theme of symmetry. I found it quite a refreshing perspective. The book also doubles as a profile of Emmy Noether, a mathematician whose contributions to modern physics deserve to be more widely known.

The Seife book on information *Decoding the Universe* is also a good place to read more about entropy and its connection to information theory. Penrose's *Cycles of Time: An Extraordinary New View of the Universe* also discusses entropy, particularly on the grandest scales of the universe.

Although mentioned only briefly, the Higgs boson is a relatively recent discovery that may be of further interest. Lisa Randall's *Higgs Discovery: The Power of Empty Space* has a helpful account. Lederman and Hill also have a book on the topic, *Beyond the God Particle*. Note that while the nickname "The God Particle" has taken off in the popular press, the Higgs boson has no more theological or philosophical significance than any other subatomic particle and most scientists, including the coiner of the name, regret the moniker.

Books on Biology

A good deal of popular science books on biology feature evolutionary biology to some degree. I believe they are worth your time regardless of what you currently think of that science. And contrary to what you might expect, plenty of them are not opposed to religion. For example, in *The Making of the Fittest: DNA and the Ultimate Forensic Record of Evolution*, Sean B. Carroll makes a concerted effort to point out that religious beliefs do not automatically put one at odds with science in general and evolutionary biology in particular, and even explores examples of secular opposition to biological research for balance. Carroll's *Endless Forms Most Beautiful: The New Science of Evo Devo* is an excellent source for more on developmental biology.

Martin Nowak, who wrote *SuperCooperators: Altruism, Evolution, and Why We Need Each Other to Succeed* with Roger Highfield, is an Austrian Catholic who deserves to be more widely known in the United States conversation on science and religion. The book discusses his research on evolution from the perspective of his Christian faith, focusing on how evolution can reinforce cooperation and social behavior rather than just cutthroat competition and individualism; there's some material on ants along the way. *The Major Transitions in Evolution* by John Maynard Smith and Eörs Szathmáry explores a related theme, demonstrating how major innovations in evolutionary natural history all involved a move from individualism to collaboration or collective activity. Complexity apparently goes hand in hand with the kind of specialization that comes through dependency and trust. Nick Lane covers some of these transitions in greater detail in *The Vital Question: Energy, Evolution, and the Origins of Complex Life*, including the chemical precursors of biology.

The Triple Helix: Gene, Organism, and Environment by Richard Lewontin has some interesting insights on biology, particularly the extent to which biology is not fully determined by genetics and DNA. Andreas Wagner's *Arrival of the Fittest: Solving Evolution's Greatest Puzzle* looks at the space that biology explores via evolution, highlighting the unique geometry of DNA mutations and their biological implications. *Design in Nature: How the Constructal Law Governs Evolution in Biology, Physics, Technology, and Social Organizations* by Adrian Bejan and J. Peder Zane offers yet another perspective on biology and life, emphasizing flow as an organizing principle.

For diseases, especially infectious diseases, there are plenty of books with sensational titles like *The Hot Zone: The Terrifying True Story of the Origins of the Ebola Virus* and *The Demon in the Freezer: A True Story* (both by Richard Preston) that warn of the dangers of specific infections while also highlighting the public health efforts to identify and contain these diseases. I don't have any problem with these books; in fact, *The Coming Plague: Newly Emerging Diseases in a World Out of Balance* by Laurie Garrett was an inspiring and influential book for me when I was getting ready to start my education in biology and public health. But they only represent part of the microbial story. *I Contain Multitudes: The Microbes Within Us and a Grander View of Life* by Ed Yong provides a more comprehensive look at the cosmos of the microscopic.

As I mentioned in the text, Douglas Hofstadter's *I Am a Strange Loop* influenced my perspective on the mind, and built on some themes in the earlier *Gödel, Escher, Bach*. Roger Penrose has also written on the topic in *The Emperor's New Mind: Concerning Computers, Minds, and the Laws of Physics*; I gather his perspective has fallen out of fashion, but it's still an interesting take. If you want even more about ants mixed into the topic, try Edward O. Wilson's *The Social Conquest of Earth*. Stuart A. Kauffman is another intellectual I admire, and he offers some thoughts on the mind in *Reinventing the Sacred: A New View of Science, Reason, and Religion*, which also explores the nonreducibility of biology and offers a fairly positive view of religion even if Kauffman himself explicitly rejects a personal God. *Phi: A Voyage from the Brain to the Soul* by Giulio Tononi tackles the topic with a heavier emphasis on consciousness as information processing and particularly information integration.

Books on Computer Science

Computer science topics are covered in several of the books we've already mentioned, including the Gleick and Seife books on information and *Gödel, Escher, Bach*. *A New Kind of Science* and *Chaos: Making a New Science* cover fractals and the complexity achievable from simple rules. Howard Bloom's *The God Problem: How a Godless Cosmos Creates* is not exclusively a computer science book, but does highlight the creative potential of iterative and recursive processes. It's a wide-ranging book touching on mathematics and physics as well in a somewhat idiosyncratic fashion. (Bloom was originally a publicist for musicians.) It is also probably the most explicitly antagonistic to theism of my recommendations, although the strongest statements are largely confined to the first few pages, after which Bloom basically takes for granted that if he can explain mechanistically how the world came to exist in its present form then the need for God is eliminated.

Neal Stephenson's *In the Beginning . . . Was the Command Line* has more details on the practical history of computers, Microsoft and

Apple, and so on. I might also suggest his novel *Cryptonomicon*, a historical fiction about the life of Alan Turing that contains some excellent passages on computing. Separating the fact and the fiction is a little tricky, but I think it's worth the effort.

For an explicit look at the connection between mathematics, computation, and evolutionary biology, take a look at Gregory Chaitin's *Proving Darwin. Complexity and the Arrow of Time* (edited by Charles H. Lineweaver, Paul C. W. Davies, and Michael Ruse) deals with a number of topics related to complexity, especially the challenge of defining and quantifying it. The essay by David Krakauer deals with evolution as a learning process. Stuart A. Kauffman also contributes a paper, as does Christian philosopher Philip Clayton.

Note on Reading Comics

Many people associate comic books with superheroes, and superheroes with the comics publishers Marvel and DC. Yet relatively few people read those comics. Marvel and DC have been continuously publishing stories about their most well known characters for fifty and seventy-five years, respectively, making it challenging to know where to start. Unfortunately, the publishers don't always make it easier.

Take *X-Factor* for example. The story I referenced in chapter 3 started in 2006 with issue #1, helpfully enough, and runs continuously through issue #50. The next issue of the story is *X-Factor* #200. That's because that issue #1 was actually the first issue of volume 3.

Volume 1 of *X-Factor* also started with an issue #1 in 1986 and was about the original X-Men characters as adults operating on their own as a separate team. Issue #71 of volume 1, from 1991, started the new direction my friend told me about, with Peter David as writer and Wolfesbane and Multiple Man as characters. That volume ended in 1998 with issue #149, having changed creative teams and rosters several times along the way. Volume 2 was a four-issue miniseries that is largely unrelated.

Peter David, Wolfesbane, and Multiple Man returned to *X-Factor* with the start of volume 3, as I mentioned. Issue #50 resolved a number of story threads in that volume while not fully ending the story, not unlike the season finale of a TV show. In order to highlight the narrative break, and to take advantage of some convenient numbering,

Marvel decided to add the 50 issues of volume 3 to the 149 issues of volume 1 to get 199, which is why issue #50 of volume 3 is followed by issue #200 (technically of volume 1). The same narrative would continue through issue #262. And so if you want to read the whole saga of Wolfesbane, Multiple Man, Layla Miller and friends, you want the 2006–2013 issues of *X-Factor* from volume 3 (#1–50) and then volume 1 (#200–262). Got it?

The most convenient way to read all those issues is to subscribe to Marvel Unlimited, a service that provides access to nearly the entire back catalog of Marvel Comics, including all the Marvel stories I referenced: *Journey into Mystery, Ms. Marvel, Thor: God of Thunder, The Unbeatable Squirrel Girl, Uncanny X-Men, Wolverine and the X-Men, X-Factor,* and *X-Men: Legacy.* Your local book store, comic book shop, or library might also have paperback collections that bind roughly a half dozen issues together. Comic book stores will also have individual back issues. But in the case of both those trades and individual issues, selection will vary and no single location will likely have a complete collection of a longer story like all of *X-Factor,* although a library system with multiple branches might have them all across their different locations or could get them through interlibrary loan. Your library may also have comics in their digital collection or available through a service like Hoopla.

The comics referenced in the text are all personal favorites that I thought illustrated my points, but they are by no means my only comics recommendations. If you like *Ms. Marvel* or *The Unbeatable Squirrel Girl,* Marvel has published several other titles with younger heroes including *Moon Girl and Devil Dinosaur* by Amy Reeder, Brandon Montclare, Natacha Bustos, et al. and *The Unstoppable Wasp* by Jeremy Whitley, Elsa Charretier, Megan Wilson, et al., both featuring scientifically minded heroes and the latter highlighting real-world scientists at the end of each issue. There is also a younger Spider-Man, Miles Morales, whose story can be followed through *Ultimate Comics Spider-Man* volume 2, then *Miles Morales: Ultimate Spider-Man,* then *Spider-Man* volume 2, by Brian Michael Bendis, Sara Pichelli, David Marquez, et al. DC has *Batgirl* volume 4, starting from #35, by Brenden Fletcher, Cameron Stewart, Babs Tarr, et al., and *Supergirl* volume 7 by Steve Orlando, Brian Ching, Michael Atiyeh, et al. All of these titles also come with the recommendation of my preteen children.

If you like the metafictional aspects of *Journey into Mystery*, perhaps try *Six-Gun Gorilla* by Simon Spurrier, Jeff Stokely, Andre May, and Steve Wands, published by BOOM! Studios and available in a single collected volume. A longer metafictional tale is *The Unwritten* by Mike Carey, Peter Gross, Chris Chuckry, et al. from Vertigo, in which a father writes a series of *Harry Potter*-esque novels with his son as the main character as a way to bring the magic of fiction into the real world. *The Unwritten* is for more mature readers; Marvel's *The Unbelievable Gwenpool* by Christopher Hastings, Gurihiru, Danilo Beyruth, et al. is metafiction for a preteen audience.

Pantheons like Norse gods in *Thor: God of Thunder* are popular in comics. They help bring the mythical subtext of superheroes into the text, and they also represent well-known characters in the public domain. DC's *Wonder Woman* volume 4 by Brian Azzarello, Cliff Chiang, Tony Akins, et al. has an interesting take on the dynamics of the Greek pantheon. *The Wicked + The Divine* from Image by Kieron Gillen, Jamie McKelvie, Matt Wilson, et al. explores music idols instead of superheroes as literal manifestations of a variety of deities. Also from Marvel, *Incredible Hercules* (which helpfully starts with #112, as Hercules was taking over the book formally titled *Incredible Hulk*) by Greg Pak, Fred van Lente, Rodney Buchemi, et al. tells a story of myths and monsters being replaced by science, with some curious commentary on the rationality of religious beliefs in a world where magic and gods are empirical realities.

Finally, if you want more X-Men (and you do), there's plenty. *Astonishing X-Men* volume 3 #1–24 by Joss Whedon, John Cassaday, Laura Martin, and Chris Eliopoulos features some of the most well known X-Men characters in a relatively continuity-light set of adventures. *X-Club* by Simon Spurrier, Paul Davidson, Rachelle Rosenberg, and Cory Petit features a team of scientists doing super-science; Spurrier writing Dr. Nemesis is not to be missed. Previous stories of David Haller, central character of *X-Men: Legacy* volume 2, include *New Mutants* volume 3 #1–24 by Zeb Wells, Leonard Kirk, Diogenes Neves, et al. and *X-Men: Legacy* volume 1 #245–253 by Mike Carey, Khoi Pham, Clay Mann, et al. And for help with X-Men history and themes, try the X-cellent podcast *Jay and Miles X-Plain the X-Men*.

Comic books are an intensely collaborative medium, typically involving a scripter and one or more artists who might divide the work of sketching, inking, coloring and lettering the art. Even when individual contributions can be summarized as "she wrote the words" or "he colored in the white spaces," everyone contributes to telling the story. Identifying a single author is generally misleading and reductive, but listing them all can be impractical when many artists are involved. I have tried to identify primary creators in the main text and adopt the academic convention of indicating that others contributed with the oh-so-unsatisfying et al. To all those thus abbreviated, you have my apologies and the sympathies of grad students, post-docs and faculty everywhere. For completeness, I have included full credits here for the stories referenced in the main text.

Journey into Mystery volume 1 #622–645 was written by Kieron Gillen, with Dan Abnett, Andy Lanning, and Matt Fraction contributing to individual issues. Pencils were by Richard Elson, Douglas Braithwaite, Carmine Di Giandomenico, Whilce Portacio, Stephanie Hans, and Mitch Breitweiser. Inks were by Richard Elson, Carmine Di Giandomenico, Roy Allan Martinez, Stephanie Hans, Mitch Breitweiser, and Jeff Huet. Colors were by Ulises Arreola, Jessica Kholinne, Chris Sotomayor, Ifansyah Noor, IFS, Arif Prianto, John Rauch, Andy Troy, Stephanie Hans, Rachelle Rosenberg, and Bettie Breitweiser. Lettering was by Clayton Cowles.

Ms. Marvel volumes 3 and 4 were written by G. Willow Wilson. Pencils were by Adrian Alphona, Takeshi Miyazawa, Marco Failla, Nico Leon, Mirka Andolfo, Jake Wyatt, Francesco Gaston, Elmo Bondoc, and Diego Olortegui. Inks were by Adrian Alphona, Takeshi Miyazawa, Nico Leon, Marco Failla, Mirka Andolfo, Jake Wyatt, Francesco Gaston, and Elmo Bondoc. Colors were by Ian Herring and Irma Kniivila. Lettering was by Joe Caramagna and Travis Lanham.

Thor: God of Thunder volume 1 was written by Jason Aaron. Pencils were by Esad Ribic, Ron Garney, Emanuela Lupacchino, Simon Bisley, RM Guera, Nic Klein, Jackson Guice, Das Pastoras, and Agustin Alessio. Inks were by Esad Ribic, Ron Garney, Emanuela Lupacchino, Tom Palmer, Simon Bisley, RM Guera, Nic Klein, Das Pastoras, and Agustin Alessio. Colors were by Ive Svorcina, Simon Bisley, Nic Klein, Lee Loughridge, Giulia Brusco, Dean White, Das Pastoras, and Agustin Alessio. Lettering was by Joe Sabino and Chris Eliopoulos.

The Unbeatable Squirrel Girl volumes 1 and 2 were written by Ryan North, with Will Murray and Chip Zdarsky contributing to individual issues. Pencils were by Erica Henderson, Chris Giarrusso, Steve Ditko, Kyle Starks, Joe Quinones, Chip Zdarsky, and Andy Hirsch. Inks were by Erica Henderson, Tom Fowler, Chris Giarrusso, Steve Ditko, Kyle Starks, Joe Quinones, Jacob Chabot, Chip Zdarsky, and Andy Hirsch. Colors were by Rico Renzi and Erica Henderson. Lettering was by Travis Lanham and Clayton Cowles.

Uncanny X-Men volume 2 #1–3 was written by Kieron Gillen. Pencils were by Carlos Pacheco, Rodney Buchemi, Paco Diaz, and Jorge Molina. Inks were by Cam Smith, Walden Wong, Roger Bonet, Paco Diaz, and Jorge Molina. Colors were by Jim Charalampidis, Frank D'Armata, Rex Lokus, Rachelle Rosenberg, Jorge Molina, and Dommo Sanchez Amara. Lettering was by Joe Caramagna.

Wolverine and the X-Men volume 1 was written by Jason Aaron. Pencils were by Nick Bradshaw, Chris Bachalo, Ramon Perez, Pepe Larraz, Steven Sanders, Jorge Molina, Giuseppe Camuncoli, Todd Nauck, Shawn Crystal, Salvador Espin, Pasqual Ferry, Nuno Alves, Michael D. Allred, Matteo Scalera, Duncan Rouleau, and David Lopez. Inks were by Walden Wong, Tim Townsend, Norman Lee, Nick Bradshaw, Jaime Mendoza, Ramon Perez, Al Vey, Pepe Larraz, Victor Olazaba, Steven Sanders, Craig Yeung, Cam Smith, Andrew Currie, Todd Nauck, Shawn Crystal, Pasqual Ferry, Nuno Alves, Michael D. Allred, Matteo Scalera, Mark Irwin, Jay Leisten, Duncan Rouleau, Chris Bachalo, and Alvaro Lopez. Colors were by Laura Martin, Matt Milla, Chris Bachalo, Justin Ponsor, Morry Hollowell, James Campbell, Guru-eFX, Thomas Mason, Rachelle Rosenberg, Peter Pantazis, Matthew Wilson, Lee Loughridge, Laura Allred, Jason Keith, Israel Silva, Frank D'Armata, Edgar Delgado, and Chris Sotomayor. Lettering was by Clayton Cowles, Joe Caramagna, Chris Eliopoulos, and Rob Steen.

X-Factor volume 3 was written by Peter David. Pencils were by Valentine De Landro, Leonard Kirk, Emanuela Lupacchino, Pablo Raimondi, Dennis Calero, Neil Edwards, Marco Santucci, Paul Davidson, Larry Stroman, Ryan Sook, Khoi Pham, Scot Eaton, Roy Allan Martinez, Renato Arlem, Carmen Carnero, Bing Cansino, Sebastian Fiumara, Mark Nelson, Karl Moline, and Ariel Olivetti. Inks were by Pat Davidson, Jay Leisten, Leonard Kirk, Guillermo Ortego, Pablo Raimondi, Dennis Calero, Craig Yeung, Marco Santucci, Andrew Hennessy, Paul Davidson, Jonathan Sibal, Wade von Grawbadger, Sandu Florea, Patrick Piazzelunga, Renato Arlem, John Dell, Valentine De Landro, Roy Allan Martinez, Bing Cansino, Sebastian Fiumara, Rick Magyar, Rick Ketcham, Patrick Piazzalunga, Mark Nelson, Karl Kesel, Edgar Tadeo, Dave Meikis, and Ariel Olivetti. Colors were by Matt

Milla, Jeromy Cox, Brian Reber, Jose Villarrubia, Rachelle Rosenberg, Chris Sotomayor, Frank D'Armata, Rob Schwager, Nathan Fairbairn, Chris Chuckry, and Andy Troy. Lettering was by Cory Petit, Joe Sabino, and Joe Caramagna.

X-Men: Legacy volume 2 was written by Simon Spurrier. Pencils were by Tan Eng Huat, Paul Davidson, Khoi Pham, Jorge Molina, and Jay Leisten. Inks were by Craig Yeung, Paul Davidson, Jay Leisten, Walden Wong, Norman Lee, Khoi Pham, and Jorge Molina. Colors were by Rachelle Rosenberg, José Villarrubia, and Cris Peter. Lettering was by Cory Petit and Chris Eliopoulos.

Acknowledgments

Writing can be a solitary experience, so I started to have an inkling that these ideas might become a book when I realized I'd have enough people to thank for these acknowledgements. We'll work backwards chronologically, which also takes us from the folks who made specific contributions to this book to the folks to whom I am generally indebted.

At Hendrickson, my editor Carl Nellis championed the book from the proposal stage onward, and also saved me from myself many times over with invaluable suggestions for revisions. To the extent that I have communicated what I actually meant to say, you may thank him and the other readers.

Various family, friends, and colleagues have provided feedback on the manuscript at different stages. Jeffrey Paul Wheeler, Barry Luokkala, Susan Cook, and Peter Venable graciously provided their domain expertise in various sciences by reviewing for correctness. Hannah Eagleson helped shape the proposal and sample chapters into a submittable form, and has also provided encouragement and advice on marketing; she was also critical in helping me connect with Hendrickson. Thomas Grosh IV also provided feedback on the proposal and has encouraged my writing for many years. Through the Emerging Scholars Network of InterVarsity, he has provided me with a blogging platform where I got invaluable practice writing about science and faith for a wide audience. Kevin Hutchison read an early chapter and provided some helpful suggestions.

I also had the opportunity to give talks on some of this material before it took shape as a book. Thanks to Hollis Haff, Mark Bolton, Adam Jackley, and New Community Church of Wexford for allowing me to teach two four-week classes. Bellefield Presbyterian Church also permitted me to share some of those lessons with its congregation.

And Kyle and Jessica DeBruyn generously agreed to alpha test those presentations since they could not attend the actual classes.

Naturally, the theology in this book has been influenced by various pastors, Sunday School teachers, small group leaders, Christian school teachers and others over the course of my entire life. Likewise, I have benefitted from numerous science educators at the elementary, high school, collegiate, and graduate levels. Not to mention all the conversations about comic books, movies, science, and theology with friends, especially as a undergraduate and graduate student. Parsing out the individual contributions of all these people is obviously impossible, but collectively they have my gratitude.

He's come up several times already in the book, but special mention to Ronnie Simon, my best friend in junior high and high school. It's hard to imagine what this book would look like if he hadn't introduce me to the world of X-Men and comic books. Unfortunately, he left us just before high school graduation, so I won't get a chance in this life to thank him personally. I hope he doesn't mind me telling a little bit of his story along the way since he no longer can.

My parents were also a big influence on the form this book has taken. They have always encouraged my curiosity and my education wherever it took me, and indulged my nerdy passions with trips to the comic book store, the movies, and so on. They absorbed criticism from other parents when my interests were different from other church kids and Christian school kids, never once discouraging me from reading a particular book or asking a particular question. And they have encouraged every step of the journey to write this book. My dad read and offered feedback on the entire manuscript, in the case of some chapters several times for different iterations.

Finally, my wife Jodi has been a tireless champion of my pursuits since the foggiest ideas first started forming in my head. She has put up with long nights writing, assumed driving duties so I could type on the go, left me to my distracted thoughts as needed, and otherwise picked up my slack so I could devote time to this project. Not to mention countless additional acts of support yet to come as I promote the book and follow wherever it takes me.

For all this and more, I am eternally grateful to everyone mentioned here, and everyone who should be but whom I somehow overlooked.

Index

Page numbers in **boldface** indicate a reference to a figure.